D1498367

Virginia Woolf's Major Novels

Virginia Woolf's Major Novels:
The Fables of Anon

MARIA DiBATTISTA

NEW HAVEN AND LONDON   YALE UNIVERSITY PRESS   1980

Published with assistance from the foundation
established in memory of Philip Hamilton McMillan
of the Class of 1894, Yale College.

Designed by Sally Harris
and set in IBM Baskerville type.
Printed in the United States of America by
Vail-Ballou Press, Binghamton, N.Y.

Published in Great Britain, Europe, Africa, and
Asia (except Japan) by Yale University Press,
Ltd., London. Distributed in Australia and
New Zealand by Book & Film Services, Artarmon,
N.S.W., Australia; and in Japan by Harper & Row,
Publishers, Tokyo Office.

Library of Congress Cataloging in Publication Data

DiBattista, Maria, 1947–
    Virginia Woolf's Major Novels: The Fables of
    Anon.

    Includes index.
    1. Woolf, Virginia Stephen, 1882–1941—Criti-
cism and interpretation. I. Title.
PR6045.072Z615   823'.9'12   79-18422
ISBN 0-300-02402-9

For My Mother and Father
Ch'avete intelletto d'amore

Contents

Preface

Virginia Woolf observes in her diary: "No critic ever gives full weight to the desire of the mind for change. Talk of the many-sided—naturally one must go the other way. Now if I ever had the wits to go into the Shakespeare business I believe one would find the same law there—tragedy comedy and so on." The Woolfian mind is a mind very much "at play," critically and imaginatively discharging its various energies in the Shakespearean "business" of tragedy, comedy, and so on. But Woolf's is also a mind at work, charting a perilous course through life—"that little strip of pavement over an abyss"—towards a more permanent and more authoritative literary domain.[1]

To write about Woolf's narrative art is to address larger questions of literary succession, that complex process of evolution, adaptation, and transformation that informs her novels and identifies Woolf's place in the history of English fiction. Literary change, as Woolf perceives it, is fundamentally genealogical. A family of books competes, contests, and sometimes "succeeds" in pressing claims to ascendancy. Under a general law of genealogical succession are subsumed any number of family romances, sibling rivalries, and wars of epochal pretenders ("Edwardians" versus "Georgians"). The period in which Woolf writes, between the acts of two world wars, may itself be a struggle for succession where Woolf's

1. Virginia Woolf, *A Writer's Diary* (New York: Harcourt Brace Jovanovich, 1954), pp. 188-89, 28.

insistent questions—"Who shall inherit? Who shall succeed?"—
echo through the pages of *Women in Love, Ulysses, Parade's
End, Howards End,* and countless other works of "modern"
generation.

In the chapters that follow, I will give full weight to the
natural and literary laws that define and delimit the compass
of change and succession in Woolf's fiction. I begin with
Mrs. Dalloway, the novel in which, as Woolf phrases it, she
"found out how to begin (at 40) to say something in my own
voice" and continue with discussions of *To the Lighthouse,
Orlando, The Waves,* and *Between the Acts.* I have not provided a separate chapter for *The Years,* which Woolf called
her "Essay-Novel," preferring to consider it briefly in the
introduction because its discursive treatment of mutability
makes it an exemplary model of Woolf's psychic and aesthetic
providences.

In focusing on the problems of narrative authority, narrative voice, and narrative succession in Woolf's major novels,
I have tried to assess carefully (and be mindful in assessing) the
advances and solutions represented by her fiction: her advo-
cacy of the role of literature as "disinterested culture" in a
time of factionalism and totalitarianism; her transvaluation of
the convention of narrative omniscience through the recreation of the many-sided voice of "Anon," the voice of
the one in the many; her critique of those abolutist patriarchal fictions whose "will to power" she opposed in her own
discrimination between authoritative and authoritarian fictions. Throughout, I have also tried to give appropriate weight
to the autobiographical and impersonal impulses, to the
naturalistic and lyric designs that shaped and directed the
often experimental course of her literary life. But it *is* a literary career I am concerned with, and so my method, whatever
its failings or perils, is to read the writer through the imaginative writings, to approach the artist through the structures
of her artifacts. I have referred when I felt it necessary to the

evidence of Woolf's critical and feminist essays in order to suggest the ways her distinct historical life and her particular literary, social, and political views were *consumed* (Woolf's word)—not merely translated—in the literary testament of her fiction, the hallmark of which, finally, is its impressive impersonality and its moving reluctance to inflict a vision upon, or define a reality for, others.

Acknowledgments

Acknowledgments can prove one of the more pleasant accountings in a book providing that, as Woolf herself once expressed it, the list of names to whom one is indebted does not raise expectations that the book can only disappoint. Many colleagues and friends have helped me substantially, and though I have no wish to implicate them in my own critical improvidences, I am grateful for the opportunity both to admit and to repay intellectual and personal debts. I offer thanks in the same spirit with which so many offered assistance. A primary debt is to my husband, Michael Seidel, of Columbia University, who has been and remains a wise, patient, supportive, and often wry counselor and critic. His help, devotion, experience, and professionalism have transformed what could have been the arduous work of composition and revision into a more profitable and less anxious labor.

Professor J. Hillis Miller of Yale University has continuously supported this project and his aid has been of inestimable value. I thank him and I deeply appreciate his many efforts. A former colleague at Yale and a good friend, Edward Mendelson, deserves special mention for encouraging me to undertake a study of Woolf and for taking on the role of adversary when my own personal advocacies threatened to overwhelm my critical judgment. At a crucial time in the writing of this book, Dudley Johnson of Princeton University provided advice of great importance to the course of my work. His suggestions for revision, critical emphasis, and direction have proven both economical and clarifying. My debt to Carolyn Heilbrun of Columbia University, who provided so much constructive criticism, offered so much valuable commentary, and contributed so much of her own literary resources, can never be adequately acknowledged or repaid.

I have also been especially fortunate in benefitting from conversations with friends and colleagues, Carol Kay, Judith Wilt, David Bromwich, David Quint, Alfred Mac Adam, Jim Nohrnberg, Paul Fry, and Brigitte Peucker. All have influenced and enriched my thinking on Woolf and on the larger generic issues I wanted to address in my study of the modern novel and its ancestry. Special thanks are reserved for Princeton colleagues who read my work in progress. Ralph Freedman has been an invaluable resource for me. Jonathan Arac has proven himself exceptionally generous in sharing with me the depth of his erudition and the range of his insights. Joanna Lipking has helped me strengthen my arguments with her readiness to exchange ideas and information. Larry Danson refreshed my vision of the project in its final stages with his detailed and spirited comments. And I am particularly grateful to Walton Litz, whose skills and encouragements proved strategic and beneficial from the beginning to the end of my work.

An earlier version of my *To the Lighthouse* chapter appeared in *Virginia Woolf: Revaluation and Continuity,* ed. Ralph Freedman (Berkeley and Los Angeles: University of California Press, 1979). I thank the University of California Press for permission to reprint. For permission to cite fragments of Virginia Woolf's unpublished essays on "Anon" and "The Reader," I thank Quentin Bell and the Henry W. and Albert A. Berg Collection, The New York Public Library, Astor, Lenox, and Tilden Foundations. I am grateful to the staffs at the libraries in which I worked, especially to those at the Firestone Library of Princeton University and the Berg Collection of The New York Public Library. My thanks also to the Trustees of Princeton University for awarding me a Bicentennial Fellowship, which enabled me to revise this project and initiate another. I conclude with thanks to Marilyn Walden who helped in preparing the manuscript and to Sheila Huddleston who helped edit it. I reserve special thanks for my editor, Ellen Graham, whose expertise and efficiency saved me from countless difficulties. It was a pleasure to work with her. My final thanks repay my most intangible debts, that to my sister, Dina DiBattista, and to my parents, to whom I have dedicated my book as a token of a much greater love.

M.D.B.

Princeton
June 1979

1

Introduction

"Considering how much we talk about writers, how much they talk about themselves, it is odd," Virginia Woolf notes in 1940, "how little we know about them":

> The politician says that a writer is the product of the society in which he lives, as a screw is the product of a screw machine; the artist, that a writer is a heavenly apparition that slides across the sky, grazes the earth, and vanishes. To the psychologists a writer is an oyster; feed him on gritty facts, irritate him with ugliness, and by way of compensation, as they call it, he will produce a pearl. The genealogists say that certain stocks, certain families, breed writers as fig trees breed figs—Dryden, Swift, and Pope they tell us were all cousins. This proves that we are in the dark about writers; anybody can make a theory; the germ of a theory is almost always the wish to prove what the theorist wishes to believe.[1]

From the calculated stance of a common reader "uncorrupted by literary prejudice," Woolf perhaps suspected the theoretical "determinisms" of the later nineteenth and early twentieth century as much as she did the astral phenomenology bequeathed by the Romantics. And although she knew that the judgments of the common reader were often "hasty,

---

1. Virginia Woolf, "The Leaning Tower," *Collected Essays* (New York: Harcourt, Brace and World, 1966), vol. 2, p. 162.

1

inaccurate, superficial,"[2] her trust in common sense and her respect for the tests of time were such that she could dispense with the imperious but myopic totality of theories and hazard a simpler, more supple model of artistic generativity:

> Books descend from books as families descend from families. Some descend from Jane Austen; others from Dickens. They resemble their parents, as human children resemble their parents; yet they differ as children differ, and revolt as children revolt. ["Leaning Tower," p. 163]

Because Woolf talked at length about her own writing, we do not have far to look for what she called certain family likenesses in a heritage of great individual differences. She defined her own beginnings as a novelist, as children often define their identity and select their community, through attitudes of revolt. She was not alone in her rebellion in that her sense of literary identity and community extended beyond the confines of Bloomsbury to embrace the "Georgians." Joyce (despite early reservations), Lawrence, Forster, Strachey, and T. S. Eliot formed for her an extended family, complete, of course, with sibling rivalries. But she closed ranks with them in order to pursue her celebrated quarrel with the Edwardian "materialists," Bennett, Wells, and Galsworthy, themselves the heirs of nineteenth-century positivism, who slavishly abdicated the powers of the imagining mind to the body of material facts:

> It is because they are concerned not with the spirit but with the body that they have disappointed us, and left us with the feeling that the sooner English fiction turns its back upon them, as politely as may be, and marches, if only into the desert, the better for its soul.[3]

The soul, whom she was to christen Mrs. Brown in her essay "Mr. Bennett and Mrs. Brown," had been totally ignored by

---

2. Virginia Woolf, "Preface," *Common Reader* (New York: Harcourt, Brace and World, 1953), p. 1.
3. "Modern Fiction," *Collected Essays,* vol. 2, p. 104.

the Edwardians. They had preferred looking "very powerfully, searchingly, and sympathetically out of the window; at factories, at Utopias, even at the decoration and upholstery of the carriage; but never at . . . life, never at human nature." Woolf's revolt, polite and judicious, is nevertheless absolute: "For us those conventions are ruin, those tools are death."[4]

Woolf's "spasm of rebellion" against the Edwardians she knew to be both natural and inevitable "whenever from hoar old age or callow youth the convention ceases to be a means of communication between writer and reader, and becomes instead an obstacle and an impediment."

> At the present moment we are suffering, not from decay, but from having no code of manners which writers and readers accept as a prelude to the more exciting intercourse of friendship. The literary convention of the time is so artificial . . . that, naturally, the feeble are tempted to outrage, and the strong are led to destroy the very foundations and rules of literary society. ["Mr. Bennett and Mrs. Brown," p. 334]

Woolf was not feeble, and so not tempted to outrage. She was, as Forster rightly judged, "tough, sensitive, but tough."[5] But whether she was tough enough or tempted enough to destroy the foundations and rules of literary society is another question. In "Modern Fiction," the essay that forms the prelude to Woolf's aesthetic, her outrage, revolt, and doubts modulate into a more constructive attempt to redefine the code of manners that must regulate literary society. For Woolf, the communications between writer and reader are transacted in that "moment of importance" which discloses the feeling of "an ordinary mind on an ordinary day":

> The mind receives a myriad impressions—trivial, fantastic, evanescent, or engraved with the sharpness of steel. From

---

4. "Mr. Bennett and Mrs. Brown," *Collected Essays*, vol. 1, p. 330.
5. E. M. Forster, *Two Cheers for Democracy* (New York: Harcourt, Brace and World, 1953), p. 242.

all sides they come, an incessant shower of innumerable atoms; and as they fall, as they shape themselves into the life of Monday or Tuesday, the accent falls differently from of old; the moment of importance came not here but there; so that if a writer were a free man and not a slave, if he could write what he chose, not what he must, if he could base his work upon his own feeling and not upon convention, there would be no plot, no comedy, no tragedy, no love interest or catastrophe in the accepted style, and perhaps not a single button sewn on as the Bond street tailors would have it. ["Modern Fiction," p. 106]

The grammar, indeed the decorum, of novelistic discourse is generated and validated by the spontaneous operations of the mind as it receives, shapes, and assesses the myriad impressions penetrating the mind and altering its internal structure. The mimetic function of fiction resides for Woolf in an extreme psychological naturalism in which, according to Erich Auerbach, consciousness is rendered "in its natural and purposeless freedom," a freedom "which is neither restrained by a purpose nor directed by a specific subject of thought."[6]

Woolf's psychology, indebted as it is to the British school of "sensationalism," necessarily predicates that the form-engendering power of the mind naturally shapes the life of Monday or Tuesday into orders that are not adventitious, but truly expressive of the life apprehended from "within."[7] Yet

6. Erich Auerbach, *Mimesis* (Princeton: Princeton University Press, 1968), p. 538.
7. For a more extended analysis of the philosophical "realism" informing Woolf's fiction, see S. P. Rosenbaum, "The Philosophical Realism of Virginia Woolf," *English Literature and British Philosophy,* ed. S. P. Rosenbaum (Chicago: University of Chicago Press, 1971), pp. 316–56. See also Harvena Richter's excellent treatment of the influence of George Moore and William James in Woolf's image of the "luminous halo" in her *Virginia Woolf, The Inward Voyage* (Princeton: Princeton University Press, 1970), pp. 20–22. Richter also suggests that the source for Woolf's phrase, "the semi-transparent envelope" may be in the C. K. Scott Moncrieff translation of the "Overture" to Proust's *Remembrance of Things Past.* See *The Inward Voyage,* p. 36n.

there is no way to authenticate, much less communicate, the legitimacy of these interior and "natural" orders without appealing to the collective experience encoded in the conventionality of a shared language and the anterior and thus predetermined syntax of literary form—plot, comedy, tragedy, love interest, catastrophe. Woolf may argue that the task of the novelist is "to convey this varying, this unknown and uncircumscribed spirit, whatever aberration or complexity it may display, with as little mixture of the alien and external as possible," but she also implies that the modernist must devise new means to support the imagination of the reader who is called upon to imagine what he can neither touch nor see.[8]

Thus Woolf's essential and often neglected qualification: the conventions are not to be used *in the accepted style.* The task of the novelist is "to contrive means of being free to set down what he chooses."[9] Contrive is the interesting word in this rather flat pronouncement; in context it suggests the need for an "artless" art whose code of manners would appear more natural than the "artificial" conventions observed by those mechanists of fiction, the Edwardian materialists. Woolf's argument in "Modern Fiction" is not to discard the received conventions, but to divest them of their tyrannical power to assign value and determine emphasis.

Woolf turned first to the Russians in her search for a method that would simultaneously express, enclose, and communicate her belief that the point of interest, the "that" rather than "this" of the modern novel, resided in the unknown and still dark places of psychology. In "Modern Fiction" she opposes the Russian novelists, Chekhov, Turgenev, Dostoevski, Tolstoy, novelists of the soul, to the Edwardian materialists: "If we want understanding of the soul and heart where else shall we find it of comparable profundity?"[10] Woolf

8. "Modern Fiction," pp. 106–07.
9. "Modern Fiction," p. 108.
10. "Modern Fiction," p. 109.

appreciated the presence of Russian novels for their salutary
effect on British writers, "sick of our own materialism." But
she also recognized that the soul, "the chief character in
Russian fiction," remains fundamentally bewildering to the
common reader and the native writer of British fiction: "The
'soul' is alien to him. It is even antipathetic. It has little sense
of humour and no sense of comedy. It is formless. It has slight
connection with the intellect."[11] If life, as Woolf insisted, is a
"luminous halo, a semi-transparent envelope surrounding us
from the beginning of consciousness to the end," that halo
bears little resemblance to those worn by the saints of Russian
hagiography, and that envelope bears no foreign address. Even
Woolf's admiration of the Russian school of "spiritual" fiction
is expressed in a "voice of protest," a voice, as she explains,
bred "by the instinct to enjoy and fight rather than to suffer
and understand" that is, in her view, endemic to British fiction: "English fiction from Sterne to Meredith bears witness
to our natural delight in humour and comedy, in the beauty
of earth, in the activities of the intellect, and in the splendour
of the body."[12]
    As the mind receives myriad impressions, it takes its colora-
tions and assumes its shapes according to a "bias taken from
the place of its birth." When the atoms fall and shape themselves into the life of Monday and Tuesday, they fall, willy-
nilly, into Bond Street. The "body of literature" must be
clothed according to manners and idiosyncrasies that define a
national style. Woolf's catalogue of what constitutes the essential spirit and the essential style of the literate body of English
literature—the comedy of manners, the delight in intellect, the
pleasures of reason, the love of the earth, the material as well
as the spiritual forms assumed by the varying spirit of life—
makes all too clear where she located herself in the modern
literary world. Only in the British tradition could she and did

11. "The Russian Point of View," *Collected Essays*, vol. 1, p. 242.
12. "Modern Fiction," pp. 109–11.

she find that "absence of self-consciousness, that ease and
fellowship and sense of common values which make for intimacy, and sanity, and the quick give and take of familiar inter-
course."[13] In her essay on George Meredith, Woolf resurveys
the modern literary scene and suggests a more appropriate
literary line of descent:

> Our prolonged diet upon Russian fiction, rendered neu-
> tral and negative in translation, our absorption in the con-
> volutions of psychological Frenchmen, may have led us
> to forget that the English language is naturally exuberant,
> and the English character full of humours and eccentrici-
> ties. Meredith's flamboyancy has a great ancestry behind
> it; we cannot avoid all memory of Shakespeare.[14]

It is an ancestry fundamentally comic, and it is from the
tradition of Sterne and Meredith, Austen and Dickens, all
continuers of the Shakespearean, typically British mind, that
Woolf's own art descends. In her search for a code of manners
to regulate the literary society and to promote the ease of fellowship with which reader and writer ideally communicate,
Woolf took her cue from Meredith, who urged, in his own
essay on comedy, that cultivated women recognize "that the
comic Muse is one of their best friends":

> They are blind to their interests in swelling the ranks of
> the sentimentalists. Let them look with their clearest
> vision abroad and at home. They will see that, where they
> have no social freedom, comedy is absent; where they are
> household drudges, the form of comedy is primitive;
> where they are tolerably independent, but uncultivated,
> exciting melodrama takes its place, and a sentimental
> version of them. Yet the comic will out, as they would
> know if they listened to some of the private conversa-

13. "The Russian Point of View," p. 238.
14. "The Novels of George Meredith," *Collected Essays,* vol. 1, pp. 231–32.

tions of men whose minds are undirected by the comic
Muse; as the sentimental man, to his astonishment, would
know likewise, if he in similar fashion could receive a les-
son. But where women are on the road to an equal foot-
ing with men, in attainments and in liberty—in what they
have won for themselves, and what has been granted
them by a fair civilization—there, and only waiting to be
transplanted from life to the stage, or the novel, or the
poem, pure comedy flourishes, and is, as it would help
them to be, the sweetest of diversions, the wisest of de-
lightful companions.[15]

The renovation of the literary tradition depends, as Meredith suggests and as Woolf's polemical writings advocate, on
the reexamination and transformation of those common values
that form the basis of civilization and of civilized discourse in
the novel. Woolf's feminist priorities—that women secure their
economic and social independence and acquire the habits of
freedom and courage to write exactly what they think—were
coincident with society's interests, allowing as they did both
women and men to come into fruitful contact with "the common life which is the real life."[16] Woolf's social vision, like
Meredith's, advocated the law of equal association and the relations such equality creates, the relations of "pure" comedy.
Woolf's Muse is what Meredith calls "the first-born of common
sense, the vigilant Comic, which is the genius of thoughtful
laughter."[17]

To ignore or minimize the course, occasion, and subject of
Woolf's thoughtful laughter is, finally, to misrepresent the
intelligence—what Meredith calls the humor of the mind—
embodied in her fictions. Louise Bogan's criticism of the

15. George Meredith, "An Essay on Comedy," in *Comedy* (Garden City, New
York: Doubleday Anchor, 1956), p. 32.

16. Virginia Woolf, *A Room of One's Own* (New York: Harcourt, Brace and
World, 1957), p. 117. Hereafter cited as *Room*.

17. Meredith, "Essay on Comedy," p. 32.

Woolfian mind and its expressive styles voices the most serious —and representative—reservations about Woolf's achievement:

> Before the unknowable, the ungraspable, her competence failed; but even here she was partial mistress of the situation. She stopped the investigation at the exact moment it got out of hand. Time and again we come upon the little flourish of style as she avoids the abyss.[18]

For Bogan, as for many critics, the Woolfian "flight toward some 'heightened state of consciousness' is always coming up short against the sudden opacity of her spiritual nihilism, the underlying pessimism of the 'enlightened' woman."[19] Perhaps Bogan is right in identifying the underlying pessimism of Woolf's fiction, but she misjudges the competence of Woolf's intelligence. In a diary entry describing a vision of "violence and unreason," Woolf confronts her own terror: "ourselves small; a tumult outside: something terrifying: unreason."[20] But if the vision is nihilistic, the will remains resolute. This is the great theme of *The Waves:* "Effort, effort, dominates: not the waves: and personality: and defiance" (*WD*, p. 159). The Woolfian imagination represents a force born in opposition to the profound and reasonless law of life—death, impermanence, the perpetual vain fight. The genius of her thoughtful laughter resides in belittling, not acknowledging, the power of death and mutability, a genius that leads Woolf to appreciate and record a remark of Montaigne's about death: "Odd—the silliness one attributes to death—the desire one has to belittle it and be found, as Montaigne said, laughing with girls and good fellows" (*WD*, p. 180).

Confronted with the spectres of violence and unreason, Woolf notes in her diary a still fruitful desire: "Shall I make a book out of this?" The book Woolf refers to was to become

18. Louise Bogan, *The New Republic,* May 29, 1950, pp. 18-19.
19. Ibid., p. 19.
20. Virginia Woolf, *A Writer's Diary* (New York: Harcourt Brace Jovanovich, 1954), p. 176. This edition of the diary hereafter cited as *WD*.

The Years, the novel in which Woolf claims to have discovered
that "you can only get comedy by using the surface layer"
(*WD,* p. 248). The surface of all Woolf's narratives are comic,
their depths tragic, but the writing of *The Years* bears the
stamp of conscious intention. One scene from the novel illus-
trates how Woolf combined the tragic "matter" and the comic
rhythms of her fiction. The time is "Present Day," the moment is one of those representative moments in Woolfian fiction when the meditative mind comes up short, *not* against the
sudden opacity, but against the sudden transparency of its
spiritual nihilism. Peggy Pargiter, an "enlightened" woman of
the modern type, hears the inarticulate, mad grumblings
of unreality:

> The far-away sounds, the suggestion they brought in of
> other worlds, indifferent to this world, of people toiling,
> grinding, in the heart of darkness, in the depths of night,
> made her say over Eleanor's words, Happy in this world,
> happy with living people. But how can one be "happy,"
> she asked herself, in a world bursting with misery? On
> every placard at every street corner was Death; or worse—
> tyranny; brutality; torture; the fall of civilisation; the end
> of freedom.[21]

At the center of Peggy's meditation, abiding in the depths
of all Woolf's mature fiction, resides a pure negativity—Death;
or worse, tyranny; brutality; torture, the fall of civilization,
the end of freedom. While the immediate historical reference is
to the European war, the negativity sounded is metaphysical
and typically modern—the Conradian heart of darkness, the
reasonless source of life itself. This is the characteristically
modern moment of blindness that yields no insight. Peggy's
mind falters in the face of this metaphysical nightmare: "But
I will not think, she repeated; she would force her mind to

21. Virginia Woolf, *The Years* (New York: Harcourt, Brace and World, 1965),
p. 388. Hereafter cited as *Years.*

become a blank and lie back, and accept quietly, tolerantly, whatever came." Peggy's mind is rescued from its incipient quietism by the emerging sounds of a force equally primordial —laughter:

> . . . she tried to think herself away into the darkness of the country. But it was impossible; they were laughing. She opened her eyes, exacerbated by their laughter.
>
> That was Renny laughing. He held a sheet of paper in his hand; his head was flung back; his mouth was wide open. From it came a sound like Ha! Ha! Ha! That is laughter, she said to herself. That is the sound people make when they are amused.
>
> She watched him. Her muscles began to twitch involuntarily. She could not help laughing too. [*Years,* p. 389]

Laughter is not only contagious, but, in essence, involuntary. Peggy's laughter is what Baudelaire identifies as "an expression, a symptom, a diagnostic": "Laughter is the expression of a double, or contradictory, feeling; and that is the reason why a convulsion occurs"[22] It is this double or contradictory feeling that laughter in Woolf's fiction invariably expresses, a laughter that simultaneously acknowledges and denies the abyss. Peggy's meditation describes, in all its essential outlines, the trajectory, "catastrophe," and denouement of the Woolfian imagination:

> But her laughter had had some strange effect on her. It had relaxed her, enlarged her. She felt, or rather she saw, not a place, but a state of being, in which there was real laughter, real happiness, and this fractured world was whole; whole, vast, and free. [*Years,* p. 390]

22. Charles Baudelaire, "On the Essence of Laughter, and, in General, on the Comic in the Plastic Arts," in *Comedy: Meaning and Form,* ed. Robert W. Corrigan (San Francisco: Chandler Publishing, 1965), p. 457.

The final, strange effect of Woolfian laughter is the enlargement, assimilation, and transfiguration of reality that occurs
whenever the mind half perceives and half creates a legitimate
human world that is whole, vast, and free. If Woolf sought to
base her fiction on a "feeling" for life, that feeling articulates
itself through the rhythms of comedy, a rhythm of feeling
that, as Susanne Langer has noted, is "not transmitted to us by
separate successive stimulations, but rather by our own perceptions of its entire Gestalt—a whole world moving into its own
future."[23]

Even as early as *The Voyage Out,* this rhythm of feeling,
this will to futurity, determines the pattern of Woolfian narrative. "What I wanted to do," wrote Woolf to Lytton Strachey,
"was to give the feeling of a vast tumult of life, as various and
disorderly as possible, which should be cut short for a moment
by the death and then go on again—and the whole was to have
a sort of pattern, and be somehow controlled."[24] The controlling pattern completes and announces itself after the death of
the novel's romantic heroine, Rachel Vinrace. As St. John
Hirst, the classicist of the novel, sadly contemplates her death,
he overhears the movements and voices of the hotel matrons,
"knitters" as they are pointedly characterized:

> He was terribly tired, and the light and warmth, the
> movements of the hands, and the soft communicative
> voices soothed him; they gave him a strange sense of
> quiet and relief. . . . Without any sense of disloyalty to
> Terence and Rachel he ceased to think about either of
> them. The movements and the voices seemed to draw to-
> gether from different parts of the room, and to combine
> themselves into a pattern before his eyes; he was content

23. Susanne Langer, *Feeling and Form* (New York: Charles Scribner's Sons,
1953), p. 347.
24. *The Letters of Virginia Woolf,* ed. Nigel Nicolson and Joanne Trautmann
(New York: Harcourt Brace Jovanovich, 1976), vol. 2, p. 82.

> to sit silently watching the pattern build itself up, looking
> at what he hardly saw.[25]

The heroine's quest for truth, for the real, for divine ultimates, which occupied the novel's foreground, fades from view, while the "background of organized British life," moves forward. Such a shift from depth to surface consoles. In the distance, complementing and commenting on Rachel's spiritual quest, were the figures of her Richmond aunts "at this very moment building things up, a solid mass, a background." The aunts, like the knitters of *The Voyage Out,* represent an authentic feminine activity, the old guard silently communicating their vision to the struggling young. From them descend Mrs. Dalloway, another worldly figure "building it up," and the Pargiters, survivors of the Victorian family, "spinners and sitters in the sun." As a narrative artist, Virginia Woolf combines and coordinates what Ralph Freedman calls "the relationship between the comedy of manners and the tragedy of life."[26] That relationship informs all of Woolf's fiction. It constitutes the pattern that repeats, evolves, readapts, and survives in the succession of novels.

But what of the mind that contrives means of linking the divided worlds of her narrative, of resolving the contradictory, double nature of her laughter? As Meredith observed: "Our English school has not clearly imagined society; and of the mind hovering above congregated men and women, it has imagined nothing."[27] It was of course the achievement of the modernists—James, Conrad, Joyce, Lawrence—to imagine the consciousness hovering above the human congregations. Except in those short stories marking the advent of her mature, unique narrative method, "The Mark on the Wall" and "An Unwritten Novel," Woolf perferred to dramatize the imagining

25. Virginia Woolf, *The Voyage Out* (London: Hogarth Press, 1915), p. 456.

26. Ralph Freedman, *The Lyrical Novel* (Princeton: Princeton University Press, 1963), p. 214.

27. Meredith, "Essay on Comedy," p. 10.

mind indirectly, perhaps because she detected in the "immense possibilities" of her new narrative style "the danger of the damned egotistical self."[28]

As a novelist Woolf never availed herself of what James termed "the romantic privilege of the 'first person'—the darkest abyss of romance this, inveterately, when enjoyed on a grand scale," having, like James, I suspect, an instinctive aversion to "the terrible fluidity of self-revelation."[29] Woolf's narrative persona is always semitransparent, half reflecting, half absorbing the light mirrored in her mind. Her writing "I" abides in the space or gap between the romantic "Subject," beguiled by its own imaginings into the very heart—or abyss—of loss, and the novelistic "Other"—the experiential realm of history, nature, society governed by invisible laws of causality, affiliation, dependence, and relation that the novelist both uncovers and legislates. The human scale of Woolf's novels is measured by the poetic intensities of the sovereign identity and its pathos, but the domain of her novels remains resolutely prosaic, an expanding surface on which are inscribed the impressions, some ephemeral, some lasting, of our life in time, the life of Monday and Tuesday.

"I think writing, my writing, is a species of mediumship," Woolf speculated in her diary; "I become the person" (*WD*, p. 274). The mimetic power and imaginative authority of Woolf's narrative presence derives from her negative capability in penetrating, becoming, and ordering the human and inhuman reality she contemplates. Hers is a species of mediumship descending from Keats's formulations concerning the chameleon poet who has no identity. And, of course, one cannot

28. In an early diary entry, Woolf remarks that her discovery of more elastic narrative forms (soon to bear fruit in her short stories, "Mark on the Wall," "Kew Gardens," and "An Unwritten Novel") may harbor the "danger" of "the damned egotistical self, which ruins Joyce and Richardson to my mind." See *The Diary of Virginia Woolf*, ed. Anne Oliver Bell (New York: Harcourt Brace Jovanovich, 1978), vol. 2, *1920–1924*, p. 14. This edition of the diaries hereafter cited as *DVW*.

29. Henry James, "Preface" to *The Ambassadors*, reprinted in *The Art of the Novel* (New York: Charles Scribner's Sons, 1962), pp. 320–21. I am grateful to my colleague, Jonathan Arac, for pointing out the relevance of this passage to me.

avoid, whether contemplating the ancestry behind Meredith's prosaic and comic flamboyancy or speculating on the poetics of Keats, the memory of Shakespeare.

It is the memory of this great ancestor, whose dramatic, narrative, and lyrical power is distributed throughout the English literary estate, that legitimates Woolf's status as a creator of fictional worlds and which authorizes what Woolf called her "philosophy of anonymity" (*WD,* p. 206). It is not a logical so much as a literary philosophy pervading all her pronouncements on art, but especially her prescriptions for women's fiction. Again and again her critical writings on women and fiction urge women to direct their attention "away from the personal centre which engaged it exclusively in the past" and to cultivate a greater impersonality that constitutes the basis of the poetic attitude. Again and again she envisions the time when women's gifts will be trained and strengthened and "the novel will cease to be the dumping-ground for the personal emotions."[30] To encourage the poetic spirit is to advise that women writers "look beyond the personal and political relationships to the wider questions which the poet tries to solve—of our destiny and the meaning of life."[31]

Woolf's theory of anonymity, which finds its representative hero in Shakespeare's mind, a mind of which we know conspicuously little, is more immediately indebted to E. M. Forster's essay, "Anonymity: An Enquiry," published by Leonard and Virginia Woolf's Hogarth Press. Forster's succinct formulation, echoing and transvaluing Pater, that "all literature tends toward a condition of anonymity, and that, so far as words are creative, a signature merely distracts us from their true significance"[32] describes the tendencies and conditions of Woolf's aesthetic. Objecting, like Woolf, that modern critics go too far

---

30. Virginia Woolf, "Women and Fiction," *Collected Essays,* vol. 2, p. 148.
31. Ibid., p. 147.
32. E. M. Forster, *Anonymity: An Enquiry* (London: Hogarth Press, 1925), p. 14.

in their insistence on personality, Forster argues that the creative impulse does not emanate from "the upper personality" which has a name, which is conscious and alert and differs vividly and amusingly from other personalities. Rather, the force that makes for anonymity and thus creativity resides in the "lower personality," which cannot be labelled with a name and which shares "something in common with all other deeper personalities."

> As it comes from the depths, so [the force that makes for anonymity] soars to the heights, out of local questionings; as it is general to all men, so the works it inspires have something general about them, namely beauty.[33]

In *A Room of One's Own,* Woolf's own "inquiry into what state of mind is most propitious for creative work," we hear an echo of Forster's contention that the evidence of authentic creative activity is in "this temporary forgetfulness, this momentary and mutual anonymity."[34] Great literature for Woolf, as for Forster, "tries to be unsigned," as Shakespeare's art remains unsigned; great literature resists the fatal and sterile prompting of the importunate letter "I":

> The reason perhaps why we know so little of Shakespeare —compared with Donne or Ben Jonson or Milton—is that his grudges and antipathies are hidden from us. We are not held up by some "revelation" which reminds us of the writer. All desire to protest, to preach, to proclaim an injury, to pay off a score, to make the world the witness of some hardship or grievance was fired out of him and consumed. Therefore his poetry flows from him free and unimpeded. [*Room,* pp. 58-59]

Where Woolf both expands and departs from Forster in her philosophy of anonymity is her belief that anonymity is a condition both imposed upon and sought by women writers.

---

33. Forster, *Anonymity,* p. 17.
34. Forster, *Anonymity,* p. 18.

In *A Room of One's Own,* she cites Currer Bell, George Eliot, and George Sand as examples of women writers plagued by "the relic of the sense of chastity that dictated anonymity to women even so late as the nineteenth century" (*Room,* p. 52). The impulse to veil and to conceal is, as Woolf claims in her essay "The Lives of the Obscure," in the great tradition of English women of letters.[35] But Woolf both satirically and seriously suggests that the instinct to conceal, the anonymity "that runs in the blood" of women of letters, is potentially a source of their strength:

> ey are not even now as concerned about the health of
>   fame as men are, and, speaking generally, will pass a
> tombstone or a signpost without feeling an irresistible
> desire to cut their names on it. [*Room,* p. 52]

The creative power of women differed, Woolf felt, from the creative power of men, but she insisted that the success and expression of that power depended on that impersonality or anonymity, that absence of special pleading, which lends to art "that curious sexual quality which comes only when sex is unconscious of itself." (*Room,* p. 96).

In her description of the poetic properties and powers of the creative mind, Woolf was, as Forster first remarked, essentially a fantasist.[36] Thus her theory of anonymity naturally formulated itself as poetic fable, the myth of androgyny. Two conditions determine Woolf's supreme fiction of the creative mind: it must be anonymous; it must be androgynous. Androgyny is predominantly a comic myth, as Plato suggested when he dramatized his poetic fable through the slightly drunken voice of the comic poet Aristophanes. Plato's myth, which recounts how primordial humans were compound

35. Virginia Woolf, "The Lives of the Obscure," *Collected Essays* (New York: Harcourt, Brace and World, 1967), vol. 4, p. 130.
36. E. M. Forster, *Aspects of the Novel* (New York: Harcourt, Brace and World, 1927), p. 19. Tellingly, Forster likened Woolf the fantasist and experimentalist to Sterne. "They [both] combine a humorous appreciation of the muddle of life with a keen sense of its beauty."

beings whom Zeus divided into halves, explains both the origin and the goal of the sexual instinct—to reunite through love. Woolf translates this androgynous myth of integration into a metaphor for that creative act in which a marriage of opposites is consummated and the undivided mind transmits its emotions without impediment. Carolyn Heilbrun's phrase, "the grace of androgyny,"[37] interprets the myth as a moment of redemption, in which we find, as Woolf says, "tokens of the fully developed mind" (*Room,* p. 103). As a philosophical, perceptual, and aesthetic ideal, the androgynous mind is Shakespearean and substantially comic, as George Meredith suggests in his essay on comedy.

> Comedy is an exhibition of [women's] battle with men, and that of men with them; and as the two, however divergent, both look on one object, namely, life, the gradual similarity of their impressions must bring them to some resemblance. The comic poet dares to show us men and women coming to this mutual likeness; he is for saying that when they draw together in social life, their minds grow liker; just as the philosopher discerns the similarity of boy and girl, until the girl is marched away to the nursery. Philosopher and comic poet are of a cousinship in the eye they cast on life; and they are equally unpopular with our wilful English of the hazy region and the ideal that is not to be disturbed.[38]

37. Carolyn Heilbrun, *Toward a Recognition of Androgyny* (New York: Knopf, 1973), p. 33. See also Mircea Eliade's *Mephistopheles and the Androgyne,* tr. J. M. Cohen (New York: Sheed and Ward, 1965). Eliade similarly argues that the androgyne's real significance is spiritual and symbolic, a symbolism degraded by decadent writers who only understood the androgyne as "a hermaphrodite in whom both sexes exist anatomically and physiologically." Eliade then contrasts the decadent image of the hermaphrodite to the "ritual androgyne" of antiquity that symbolically represented "the union of the magico-religious powers belonging to both sexes" (p. 100). For more recent researches into the political and social implications of the myth of androgyny, see *Women's Studies,* vol. 2, no. 2 (1974), whose entire issue is devoted to the concept of androgyny.

38. Meredith, "Essay on Comedy," p. 15.

Despite the wilfulness of hazy sentimentalists and patriarchal idealists, the comic, as Meredith says, will out. And it is
the daring of the comic poet to represent through the action
of comedy the gradual and inevitable congruence, however
initially divergent, of men and women as they look on life.
Meredith locates the heart of androgyny in a perceptual ideal
in which men and women, comparing their impressions of life,
discover a mutual likeness and a common fund of values.
Androgyny thus suggests a double triumph. It overwhelms
those stubborn, basically artificial divisions between men and
women and thus discovers the basis of a legitimate social order
governed by the law of equal association. And it also liberates
the mind of women from the most enduring form of cultural
and biological tyranny—the tyranny of sex. For it is fatal,
insisted Woolf, "for any one who writes to think of their sex.
It is fatal to be a man or woman pure and simple; one must be
woman-manly or man-womanly" (*Room*, p. 108).

Androgyny, as Carolyn Heilbrun puts it, releases and relieves
the mind "from the confines of the appropriate,"[39] especially
from those censoring and legislating powers that ordain and
govern the sphere of the appropriate both in fiction and in
life. Woolf insists on the distinction between androgynous
vision and confining, masculine convention. In *Women and
Fiction,* she writes:

> For a novel, after all, is a statement about a thousand dif-
> ferent objects—human, natural, divine; it is an attempt to
> relate them to each other. In every novel of merit these
> different elements are held in place by the force of the
> writer's vision. But they have another order also, which is
> the order imposed upon them by convention. And as men
> are the arbiters of that convention, as they have estab-
> lished an order of values in life, so too, since fiction is

39. Heilbrun, *Toward a Recognition of Androgyny,* p. x.

largely based on life, these values prevail there also to a
very great extent.[40]

As it is probable, Woolf concludes, that "both in art and life
the values of a woman are not the values of a man," the
woman novelist will be "perpetually wishing to alter the established values—to make serious what appears insignificant to a
man, and trivial what is to him important."[41]

Androgyny was for Woolf a serviceable myth that released
her from the confines of the appropriate and thus permitted
her to question, if not always alter, the established values. But
it also provided Woolf with another kind of relief—the "economic" relief that attends the mind's saving in the expenditure
on inhibition, Freud's account of the dynamics of laughter.[42]
As pure fantasy, androgyny frees the mind from its subservience
to the established body of biological and social "facts of life"
—the innate and inviolable difference between the sexes, patri-
archy as a "natural" and inevitable cultural order. As pure (in
Meredith's sense) comedy, androgyny promotes sexual equality
by conferring prestige on the "womanly" mind, while challenging the absolute hegemony of the "manly" mind in establishing and upholding human values and literary conventions.

The fable of androgyny and the philosophy of anonymity
together constitute the basis of Woolf's poetic attitude, that
"impersonality" in which are reconciled the competing claims
of narrative voice—the force of the writer's vision—and narrative authority—the order imposed by convention. They constitute, that is, those literary contrivances by which Woolf could
speak naturally out of the heart of her own unique experience
and yet still engage in what Auerbach has called "the multi-
personal representation of consciousness," or, more simply,

40. "Women and Fiction," p. 145–46.
41. Ibid., p. 146.
42. See especially Freud's theory of the mental economies involved in the comic
in his *Jokes and the Unconscious* in *The Standard Edition of the Complete Psychological Works of Sigmund Freud,* ed. James Strachey (London: Hogarth Press,
1975), vol. 8, pp. 118 and passim.

the representation of the one in the many. The success of her solution may be suggested in the question that Auerbach poses in examining the mimetic grounds of Woolf's style in *To the Lighthouse:* "Who is speaking in this paragraph?"[43]

It is a question still to be answered. Auerbach, as always, provides the beginning of an answer when he observes that the speaker presumably is the "author," but an author, he remarks with some surprise, if not exasperation, who "does not seem to bear in mind that she is the author and hence ought to know how matters stand with her characters."[44] The value and significance of Woolf's art is precisely in her refusal to make the world a witness to her convictions, the novel the court of her impassioned testimony. Woolf is an assiduous practitioner of the novelistic, necessarily ascetic habit of self-forgetfulness. Through her narrative moments of absentmindedness, in which she does not seem to bear in mind that she is an author, privileged with the prerogative of omniscience, the "ought to know" that is the special presumption of the fictionalizing mind, Woolf offers her own satiric critique of those presumptuous powers, ruling in art and in life, who contemplate their prejudices as if they were eternal verities. Her writing *is* a species of mediumship, a complex species emerging out of the auspicious mating of Shakespearean negative capability and the historical practice of feminine anonymity. Most critics of Woolf pay homage to the pathos of Woolf's repression without doing justice to the power and range of her mature and capable imagination. In recording the progress of her literary career, and in describing the formation of Woolf's distinct narrative identity, I will try to suggest the ways in which power and pathos combine to form, to paraphrase Keats's figure for excellence in literature, a "Woman of Achievement."

43. Auerbach, *Mimesis,* p. 531.
44. Ibid. Auerbach, of course, values Woolf's "unprejudiced and exploratory representations" of reality, arguing that through such surrender of the authorial presumption of certainty and omniscience, the modern novel preserves its independence from "the controversial and unstable orders over which men fight and despair" (p. 552).

2

Mrs. Dalloway

VIRGINIA WOOLF'S MEMENTO MORI

The Empty Center

The emergence of Woolf's distinctive literary identity can be dated, as Woolf herself dated it, to her fortieth year, just after the completion of *Jacob's Room:*

> There's no doubt in my mind that I have found out how to begin (at 40) to say something in my own voice; and that interests me so that I feel I can go ahead without praise. [*WD*, p. 46]

Woolf's diary entries for 1922 and 1923 speak exultantly of her newfound freedom of expression, her "excitement" in discovering new narrative methods to provide her novels with the encompassing unity they had previously lacked.[1] But three more authentic signs of Woolf's coming of age confirm her claim to literary ascendancy: her decreasing reliance on the motive of praise in her writing, essential to her project of forging an autonomous, yet nonegotistical voice; her whetted sense of competition with her contemporaries; the growing ambition of her narrative designs. The example of Joyce, also

---

1. See especially the diary entry for October 14, 1922, where Woolf claims that *Jacob's Room* "was a necessary step, for me, in working free" (*WD*, p. 51). A year later (October 15, 1923) she records her "great discovery": "It took me a year's groping to discover what I call my tunnelling process, by which I tell the past by instalments, as I have need of it" (*WD*, p. 60).

forty in 1922, looms large in her consciousness. While writing *Jacob's Room,* Woolf was justifiably anxious that "what I'm doing is probably being better done by Mr. Joyce,"[2] but by the time of *Mrs. Dalloway,* she was bold and confident enough to engage *Ulysses,* answering Joyce's patriarchal fiction with her own critique of history, memory, law, and the art of life.

It is in reflecting on her rivalry and friendship with Katherine Mansfield, recently dead, that Woolf makes a more balanced assessment of her powers as a writer and her feelings about the novel that will become *Mrs. Dalloway:*

> Have I the power of conveying the true reality? Or do I write essays about myself? Answer these questions as I may, in the uncomplimentary sense, and still there remains this excitement. To get to the bones, now I'm writing fiction again I feel my force glow straight from me at its fullest. After a dose of criticism I feel that I'm writing sideways, using only an angle of my mind. This is justification; for free use of the faculties means happiness. I'm better company, more of a human being. Nevertheless, I think it is important in this book to go for the central things. Even though they don't submit, as they should, however, to beautification in language. [*WD,* pp. 56-57]

To be free, to be happy, to be more completely human, to go for the central things—these are the imperatives and the perquisites that justify and motivate the writing "I." Yet the cen-

2. *WD,* p. 27. The diary entries for August and September of 1922 abound with references to *Ulysses,* including her famous reaction that *Ulysses* was an "illiterate, underbred book . . . the book of a self taught working man, and we all know how distressing they are, how egotistic, insistent, raw, striking, and ultimately nauseating." Woolf had only read a third of *Ulysses* at the time of this intemperate, distressingly snobbish criticism, and it should be noted that the criticism is introduced by a contentiousness, a "dutiful" conscientiousness of her own: "I should be reading *Ulysses,* and fabricating my case for and against" (*WD,* p. 46). She was not then, nor was she ever to be, a disinterested critic of Joyce, although her judgment of *Ulysses,* of course, was modified over time.

tral things, life and death, the objects of her imaginative desire, remain stubbornly resistant to the penetrating force of her mind. It is not so much that Woolf's center will not hold; it is that the imaginative center, where truth and beauty, life and death coexist as terms in the transparent equation of reality, eludes, as *Mrs. Dalloway* will dramatize, the spirit's grasp.

Mrs. Dalloway is a novel about "people feeling the impossibility of reaching the centre which, mystically, evaded them."[3] Reaching that center is the human categorical imperative because there is housed "the thing that mattered"—the privacy of the soul, the sanctuary of the sovereign "I." The feeling of impossibility, which contributes to the novel's vague but universal sense of malaise, of spiritual incapacity, of frustrated expectations, originates in the intuition that the passage to the center is blocked by real and phantom presences. For Miss Kilman, "It is the flesh"; for Septimus Smith and Clarissa Dalloway, the obscurely evil power of the "Other," personified in the alienist Bradshaw, to commit with impunity the "indescribable outrage—forcing your soul" (p. 281). Or "the overwhelming incapacity" may have its origin in the terror, the awful fear before life itself, "this life, to be lived to the end, to be walked with serenely" (p. 281).

The pervasive, middle-aged dysphoria of *Mrs. Dalloway* contrasts to the original euphoria of *Jacob's Room,* a novel that centered itself in "the obstinate irrepressible conviction" of youth—"I am what I am and I intend to be it."[4] But the hero's freedom to form and realize an absolute individuality—the I am what I am—proves illusory. "We start out transparent," reflects the narrator, "and then the cloud thickens. All history backs our pane of glass. To escape is vain."[5] The sense of

3. Virginia Woolf, *Mrs. Dalloway* (New York: Harcourt, Brace & World, 1925), p. 281. All further citations will be from this edition.
4. Virginia Woolf, *Jacob's Room* (London: Hogarth Press, 1960), p. 34.
5. *Jacob's Room,* p. 47.

futility that infects the moral and psychological atmosphere of *Mrs. Dalloway* may be a symptom of the malady of history itself, devitalizing and encroaching on the unique privacy of the soul. "When a child begins to read history one marvels, sorrowfully, to hear him spell out in his new voice the ancient words,"[6] observes the narrator. History not only reveals but repeats itself in Jacob, the eternal repetition that constitutes the "mother's sorrow."

Mrs. Dalloway incorporates the elegiac motifs of *Jacob's Room,* but it examines more closely and more fruitfully the limits of personal freedom, the use and abuse of history in the determination of the "modern" self, and the meaning as well as the source of human happiness. The June day on which the novel centers justifies its claims to importance by being the day during which Mrs. Dalloway realizes and recovers from the "illness" afflicting her heart. The therapeutic agency of the novel is what Nietzsche calls the "plastic power" of the creative individual, community, or culture, "the power of specifically growing out of one's self, of making the past and the strange one body with the near and the present, of healing wounds, replacing what is lost, repairing broken molds."[7] The novel's specific project is to unite in one body the memories of the past, symbolized by Bourton, the scene of Clarissa's youth and the legacy of a familial and national heritage, with the present and near, symbolized by the city of London, which incarnates "this moment in June."

The novel begins with a gaiety and an inconsequence that both belie and confirm the "momentousness" of the events that follow. Clarissa Dalloway sets out on her morning errands in a state of exhilaration: "What a lark! What a plunge!" This carefree plunge into the present moment "fresh as if issued to children on a beach" suggests the possibility of an unhistorical happiness, a happiness measured, as Nietzsche says, by the

6. *Jacob's Room,* p. 97.
7. Friedrich Nietzsche, *The Use and Abuse of History,* tr. Adrian Collins (Indianapolis: Second [Revised] Library of Liberal Arts Edition, 1957), p. 7.

ability to "go into" the present "like a number, without
leaving any curious remainder."[8] Experiencing such pleasure
initiates an impulsive forward motion in consciousness and life
that subsequent events, like some curious remainders, will
check or qualify. Intimations of the counter-motion immediately appear when Clarissa, recovering the image of the past at
Bourton, suddenly feels her light-hearted gaiety shadowed
by the solemnity of darker historical reflections:

> How fresh, how calm, stiller than this of course, the air
> was in the early morning; like the flap of a wave; the kiss
> of a wave; chill and sharp and yet (for a girl of eighteen
> as she then was) solemn, feeling as she did, standing
> there at the open window, that something awful was
> about to happen. [p. 3]

In a curious conflation of historical "times," the past eclipses
the present with its premonitions of a disastrous future. This
tension between the unhistorical happiness in plunging spon-
taneously into the present and the anxiety such spontaneity
produces determines the emotional rhythm or contratempo
of the novel.

This dialectic between unhistorical happiness and historical
memories and intuitions, related through the primary metaphor of an expanding and contracting spirit, is the source of
the novel's exquisite suspense and excitement. These "pulsa-
tions" produce the "excitement of . . . rising and falling"
(p. 32), an excitement associated with but not confined to
Clarissa's heart. To expand and contract is to rise and to fall,
build up and come down, like the "waves of that divine
vitality which Clarissa loved" (p. 9). These verticalities describe
the peaks and the depths of the novel's image of life as wave-
like motion: "So on a summer's day waves collect, overbalance,
and fall; collect and fall" (p. 58). Each moment, like Yeats's
"one throb of the artery," is an occasion for creation and

8. Nietzsche, *Use and Abuse of History,* p. 5.

decreation, an affirmation that generates its own negation. This metaphor has its base in a physiological reality. A permanently dilated heart, like a permanently contracted heart, is a sign or portent of death. Whatever is alive is throbbing; the pulse *is* the one "vital" sign of life.

The cumulative effect of these discrete moments of rising and falling, however, constitutes a constructive action. Waves collect as they rise. In the expansive moments of the "heart," such as Mrs. Dalloway's delight in the morning, her walk through London, her sewing ("building it up, first one thing, then another"), and her giving a party, life is collected, generating the illusion that life is a movement forwards as well as upwards. The contractive moments, most obviously symbolized in the suspenseful pauses that precede the tollings of Big Ben, solidify the seriousness of the narrative. Rising and falling as vertical motions have their counterparts in anticipation and retrospection as horizontal movements. These vertical and horizontal narrative lines intersect to form the temporal axis around which the novel revolves. They are the coordinates, however, of a structure whose center is hollow. "There is an emptiness about the heart of life" (p. 45), observes the narrator, just as Clarissa, on hearing of Septimus's suicide, exclaims, "Oh, in the *middle* of my party, here's death" (p. 279, emphasis mine). To reach the center is to find, like Rezia, "sheltering under the thin hollow of a leaf" (p. 99), or, like Septimus, to see in the pattern of rising and falling the image of a "hollow wave" (p. 32). In the middle, at the center, is emptiness, stasis, death.

The empty center that paradoxically manages to coordinate a structure of temporal relations also governs the nexus of personal relationships. The central relationship of the novel is between Clarissa and Septimus Smith, a relationship that only exists in terms of the novel's thematic and metaphoric texture. In orchestrating Clarissa Dalloway's spiritual recovery with the suicide of Septimus Smith, Virginia Woolf saw that her original intention in writing the novel—to depict "the world seen by

the sane and insane side by side"—would only be justified if
she could bring the two visions into conjunction. She solved
the narrative problem by splitting the traditionally indivisible
atom of narrative climax into its constituent parts—the catastrophe (or suicide) and the belated anagnorisis that reveals its
meaning. Through this purely formal device, Woolf could
dramatize the proximity of the mad and sane vision of the
world without obscuring or blurring the distinction that makes
madness and sanity adjacent, *never identical,* aspects of the
same reality. Thus Clarissa can, through Septimus's suicide,
reach the mystical center, the fatality buried in the heart of
the novel, but because she is sane, avoid succumbing to it
herself.

As the novel's initiatory and recurrent desire to plunge
modulates into the climactic action of Septimus Smith's fatal
"fall," the narrative discloses the mythic origin of its image of
fatality. Septimus Smith, "lately taken from life to death, the
Lord who had come to renew society" (p. 37), identifies the
ever receding, ever approaching "center" as "the meadow of
life beyond a river where the dead walk" (p. 36). The mythos
of voyage and solitary travelling that informs the novel's metaphoric surfaces is organized and revolves around the epic motif
of the descent into the underworld, conventionally the realm
wherein the secrets of history and human destiny are revealed.
Such descent myths operate powerfully, if subliminally, on
"the public-spirited, British Empire, tariff-reform, governing-
class spirit" (p. 116), the "Dalloway" spirit, adding a special
poignancy, perhaps illegitimate, to England's sense of national
mission. Clarissa's social faith, which Peter Walsh attempts
both to criticize and explain, rests on the metaphoric foundation that conceives of the British body politic as an imperilled,
foundering ship of State: "As we are a doomed race, chained
to a sinking ship (her favourite reading as a girl was Huxley
and Tyndall, and they were fond of these nautical metaphors),
as the whole thing is a bad joke, let us, at any rate do our
part" (p. 117).

The interpolation of this mythos also implies a more complicated relationship between *Mrs. Dalloway* and *Ulysses*, whose
resemblances have been examined by many commentators,[9]
a relationship not based exclusively on Woolf's revisionist
impulse to "re-do" the Viceregal cavalcade in *Ulysses* or to
compete with the patriarchal fiction of Joyce's one-day narrative with a feminine fiction of her own. Woolf's admiration for
the "Hades" episode in *Ulysses* suggests that *Mrs. Dalloway*
continues as well as reinterprets the modernist preoccupation
with Ulyssean narratives and Wasteland myths. There are, for
example, close symbolic analogues between "Hades" and *Mrs.
Dalloway*, particularly in their shared system of double and
warring images of heart—the "organ" of "Hades" as it is of
Mrs. Dalloway—and ghosts, the spectres of the past, both personal and impersonal, haunting the consciousness of characters
who have "been through it all."[10] Both narratives deal with the
profoundest memories of human loss that test, criticize, and
often mock "the atheist's religion" of their central characters:
the memory of Clarissa's sister, Sylvia, felled in the prime of
life resembling Bloom's recollections of his dead son, Rudy.
Both struggle with the knowledge, unprotected by myth, that
history and injustice are one.

   Where Woolf departs from Joyce is in her thorough skepti-
cism about the structures (Joyce's micro- and macrocosms)
Western culture has constructed on the "void incertitude"[11]
and in her radical inquiry into the grounds and legitimacy of

   9. See especially Diderik Roll-Hanson, "Peter Walsh's Seven-League Boots:
A Note on *Mrs. Dalloway*," English Studies, 50 (1968): 301–04. Avrom Fleishman
also explores some of the formal resemblances in his *Virginia Woolf: A Critical
Reading* (Baltimore: The Johns Hopkins University Press, 1975), pp. 70ff. Woolf
was reading *Ulysses* as she was writing *Mrs. Dalloway* (*WD*, pp. 46–49). Her admiration for the "Hades" chapter forms the basis of her defense of modernism in
"Modern Fiction," p. 107.
   10. See especially Robert Martin Adam's chapter on "Hades" in *James Joyce's
Ulysses: Critical Essays,* ed. Clive Hart and David Hayman (Berkeley: University of
California Press, 1974), pp. 99–106.
   11. James Joyce, *Ulysses* (New York: Random House, 1961), p. 207. The phrase
first occurs in "Scylla and Charybdis," the chapter whose organizing art is literature.

the authority commanded by the phantom powers of history, society, and religion over life itself. Because the center of life *is* empty, its territory is both haunted and humanly disputed. Contending for hegemony over the void incertitude are those "spectres which one battles in the night; . . . spectres who stand astride us and suck up half our life-blood, dominators and tyrants" (p. 17). The chief spectre for Clarissa in this passage is Miss Kilman, whose name is itself antithetical; there is the obvious pun on "kill-man," the vampire spirit that feasts on human vitality, but also "Doris," the gift of god, from the sea.[12] This "double" name accounts for the doubleness of Clarissa's feeling about the "mixed" gifts of the gods and about Miss Kilman herself: "for no doubt with another throw of the dice, had the black been uppermost and not the white, she would have loved Miss Kilman. But not in this world. No" (p. 17). History, Miss Kilman's specialty, carries the authority of irrevocability; unlike a game of chance, its course is irreversible.

The most important spectre of domination, then, is the ubiquitous power of time itself. The working title of the novel, *The Hours*,[13] mythologically the daughters of Themis, goddess of Order, and guardians of the gates of Heaven, conveyed the idea of an autonomous temporality that mediated between history and eternity. The impressive specificity of the finished novel's chronological sequence, its obsessive time-keeping, acknowledges the reign of the Hours, while systematically demystifying their authority. In a passage cancelled in the final revisions of the manuscript, Woolf had identified the "seat of time" in the island of Westminster:

> It might have been the seat of time itself, this island of Westminster, the forge where the hours were made, & sent out, in various tones and tempers, to glide into the

12. See the "Appendix on Names" in James Hafley's *The Glass Roof* (Berkeley: University of California Press, 1954), pp. 168–69.
13. *WD*, p. 56.

lives of the foot passengers, of studious workmen[,] desultory women within doors, who coming to the window looked up at the sky as the clock struck, as if to say, What? or Why? They had their choice of answers . . .[14]

The mythological project of fashioning the Hours devolves into the human order where time-keeping becomes an arbitrary, though necessary, convention. Westminster *might* have been the seat of time, had not the human congregation appealed to a higher authority to verify the meaning of this secular usurpation. The "choice of answers" available to the human subjects of time suggests Woolf's interest in decentralizing and displacing the power of time from its royal seat and distributing it among separate and multitudinous centers, all generating their own interpretations of time's meaning. Thus the comic dispute between St. Margaret's and Big Ben that "now, really & indeed, it was half past eleven." Thus the necessity to "think how not merely that time differed but that the tone of it was possessed of the strangest power; now militant and masculine; now curtly prosaic, & now in the voice of St. Margaret's flower in the mind. . . ."[15] The demystification of the reign of time as an incontestible order explains why, of all the experiences of time, prescience is the most suspect. Peter Walsh's famous predictions that Clarissa would marry a Prime Minister and stand at the top of the stairs is emblematic of Woolf's Shakespearean sense of prophecy as equivocation. Time is both what is and is not, what speaks, but, like the witches in Macbeth, speaks imperfectly.

The indeterminacy of time explains the transposition of the passage quoted above into its final form. The narrator's quasi-allegorical fantasy of the Hours yields to the more emotional resonances of the "tone" in which time speaks to Clarissa:

14. MS. in the British Museum, Vol. I, 5, 10, quoted by Avrom Fleishman in *Virginia Woolf: A Critical Reading*, p. 71.
15. Ibid.

> For having lived in Westminster—how many years now?
> over twenty,—one feels even in the midst of the traffic, or
> waking at night, Clarissa was positive, a particular hush,
> or solemnity; an indescribable pause; a suspense (but that
> might be her heart, affected, they said, by influenza)
> before Big Ben strikes. There! Out it boomed. First a
> warning, musical; then the hour, irrevocable. The leaden
> circles dissolved in the air. Such fools we are, she
> thought, crossing Victoria Street. For Heaven only knows
> why one loves it so, how one sees it so, making it up,
> building it round one, tumbling it, creating it every
> moment afresh . . . [pp. 4-5]

In the midst of day or in the dead of night may come that
indescribable pause intervening, perhaps blocking, the passage
from one moment to the next. But the association between
this disruptive pause in the continuous traffic of life and the
portentous feeling that something awful is about to happen
may be the feeling peculiar to the "affected" or diseased heart.
Clarissa herself dismisses the idea of an "irrevocable" hour as
her mind submits to the flux, the unstructured flow of moments that constitutes the vital and creative motion of life—
"making it up, building it round one, tumbling it" every
moment afresh. The shift from past tense to present par-
ticiples, verb forms of continual or continuing motion, intro-
duces a new feeling for time as a pure and fluid medium out of
which the mind creates, destroys, and recreates its own subjective order. Time is Janus-faced, an image of freedom and an
image of fate. As a series of occasions on which to make and
build up one's moment, time guarantees the freedom to create
life "each moment afresh." But that series is inscribed on "a
dial cut in impassive stone" (p. 44), on whose graduated face
Clarissa reads her irrevocable fate—"how it is certain we must
die" (p. 267).

This is the complex patterning that determines the dual and
decentralized structure of fate in *Mrs. Dalloway*. On the one

hand, time mediates between experience and the experiencing self:

> There was a mystery about it. You were given a sharp, acute, uncomfortable grain—the actual meeting; horribly painful as often as not; yet in absence, in the most unlikely places, it would flower out, open, shed its scent, let you touch, taste, look about you, get the whole feel of it and understanding, after years of lying lost. [p. 232]

Such is the Woolfian version of "spots of time." The experience ("a sharp, acute, úncomfortable grain") flowers over time and permits the experiencing self to feel and to understand the meaning of its singular life. The recovery of experience echoes the theme of Clarissa's recuperation and suggests the way in which spiritual reparation is to be achieved. The continuity between past acts and present feelings insures that over time the self is continuous and stable. Time contributes to the stability of personality in its role as the preserver, the advocate of the individual self in the uniqueness of its experience. On the other hand, time is the destroyer, the agent of mutability and change, the threat to continuity and "this interminable life." Between the woof of time the preserver and the warp of time the destroyer is woven—the self.

The Scenes of Inspiration

Also subject to Woolf's decentralizing and discriminating intelligence is the category of homogeneous space. Time presents the occasion, space the scene for that continual dilation and contraction that constitutes the source of the novel's exquisite suspense and delight. The authority of space is disseminated and distributed among three controlling metaphors of place: the London streets; the house; and, within the house, the final interiorization of subjective space, the "attic" room. Each setting provides its own unique consolation to the irrevocable decrees of time—how it is certain we must die.

The public spaces of London's streets represent what pastoral landscapes represented to the Romantics—the inspiriting scene that provides the "plaguy spirit" with intimations of its own immortality. Clarissa's youthful "transcendental theory" of life evolves out of her experience of urban place. In an important reminiscence, Peter Walsh recalls the occasion and logic of her theory:

> . . . Clarissa had a theory in those days—they had heaps of theories, always theories, as young people have. It was to explain the feeling they had of dissatisfaction; not knowing people; not being known. For how could they know each other? You met every day; then not for six months, or years. But she said, sitting on the bus going up Shaftesbury Avenue, she felt herself everywhere; not "here, here, here"; and she tapped the back of the seat; but everywhere. [p. 231]

Here space, the indivisible space of the self, is, like time, unseated from its confining locality of "here, here, here" and rendered, again like time, ubiquitous. This theory modulates into a kind of comic urban gothic in which Clarissa entertains the possibility that "the unseen part of us, which spreads wide, the unseen might survive, be recovered somehow attached to this person or that, or even haunting certain places after death . . . perhaps—perhaps" (p. 232). "Street-haunting" is one of Woolf's favorite metaphors for the "London adventure"[16] of the inquisitive spirit seeking in life the scene of its future haunts, projecting beyond its own death the prospect of its eternal attachments to people and places.

Clarissa Dalloway's own adventure in street-haunting confirms and persuades that the spirit will survive in space:

16. See her essay, "Street Haunting: A London Adventure," *Collected Essays*, vol. 4, p. 155.

Did it matter then, she asked herself, walking towards Bond Street, did it matter that she must inevitably cease completely? All this must go on without her; did she resent it, or did it not become consoling to believe that death ended absolutely? but that somehow in the streets of London, on the ebb and flow of things, here, there, she survived, Peter survived, lived in each other, she being part, she was positive, of the trees at home; of the house there, ugly, rambling all to bits and pieces as it was; part of people she had never met; being laid out like a mist between the people she knew best, who lifted her on their branches as she had seen the trees lift the mist, but it spread ever so far, her life, herself. [p. 12]

Transcending the ruins of time (the house rambling all to bits and pieces) and the imperfect knowledge that plagues all human relationships, is the power of the single life to disperse itself so far and so wide beyond its physical or visible boundaries that no one death can completely annihilate it. Clarissa's faith in the ubiquity of the spirit consoles her that death ends the seen, but not the unseen, essential part of human existence. This extension and investment of the self into its human and physical surroundings answers to a deep need in Clarissa, her need, as Peter Walsh says, to be "like something alive which wants to confide itself, to disperse itself, to be, with a tremor of delight, at rest" (p. 74). To be at rest, with its attendant tremor of delight, echoes the "indescribable pause" that precedes the tolling of the irrevocable hour and reinforces the notion that death represents an attenuation rather than a termination of life. It is this sense of life as "something central which permeated" that lends peacefulness to the images of death as a laying or a stretching out. Death seems to complete rather than disrupt a life whose inner dynamic has been one of dispersing and projecting the self out of the body that houses but cannot contain it.

Self-dispersal is both the augury of immortality and the antidote for temporal anxiety. Yet the antidote may have adverse as well as therapeutic effects on the diseased heart. The unforeseen consequence in "street-haunting" is to disperse and confide the self so widely that the seen and the unseen become radically disassociated. The crucial metaphor of invisibility, on which the whole structure of Clarissa's transcendental theory of being is based, is transposed into a metaphor for vacancy: "She had the oddest sense of being herself invisible, unseen; unknown; there being no more marrying, no more having of children now, but only this astonishing and rather solemn progress with the rest of them, up Bond Street, this being Mrs. Dalloway; not even Clarissa any more; this being Mrs. Richard Dalloway" (p. 14). The latent schizophrenia in Clarissa's divorce of body and spirit surfaces in the self-perception that she has become a public personage, appropriately labelled "Mrs. Richard Dalloway," that coexists but is not identical with the private person, Clarissa. Now the urban gothic is transformed into psychological gothic, the ghost haunting the mind is the insubstantial body itself: "this body, with all its capacities, seemed nothing—nothing at all" (p. 14). The body exists as a reminder of the prior claims Nature exerts over the spirit.

The chastising of the vagabond spirit is movingly represented in the "homecoming" scene when Clarissa returns from her morning excursion in street-haunting. She allows her "self" to be sheltered and enclosed within the protective confines of the house. The house provides a more humanized sense of space because, as Gaston Bachelard has remarked, "its councils of continuity are unceasing. Without it man would be a dispersed being."[17] But at the heart of the house, with its intimations of personal, social, and historical continuities, there exists the attic room and *its* councils of ritual isolation. This

17. Gaston Bachelard, *The Poetics of Space,* tr. Maria Jolas (New York: Orion Press, 1964), p. 7.

explains why Clarissa's withdrawal from the world and her subsequent exploration of interior space is conceived as an ascetic
rite of absolution and why her central confession consists in
acknowledging "the buds on the tree of life" for "the flowers
of darkness they are" (p. 43). It also explains why the ritual
of self-confrontation occurs at midday, the *hora demonium* in
which the human aspiration to penetrate the mystery of life is
simultaneously a recognition of the vanity of such knowledge. Clarissa's spiritual ascent thus culminates in an equivocal
epiphany: "There was the green linoleum and a tap dripping.
There was an emptiness about the heart of life; an attic room.
Women must put off their rich apparel. At midday they must
disrobe" (p. 45). The use of "must" implies that such penetrations into the interior constitute the categorical imperative for
the feminine consciousness, perhaps because men have abandoned—or delegated—responsibility for the house and its
mysteries to women. Given Clarissa's undisputed hegemony
over the "interior," it is surprising that the human lust for
mastery does not assert itself. As the room's two resident symbols of bed and mirror suggest, the feminine space provides the
scene, not of self-assertion, but self-abnegation (complicated
by the ritual reluctance to disrobe) and self-contemplation. In
bed, the soul is recumbent, allowing itself to be visited by the
spectres of its own failures and the admonishing voice of
Nature (who is invariably wise):

So the room was an attic; the bed narrow; and lying there
reading, for she slept badly, she could not dispel a virginity preserved through childbirth which clung to her
like a sheet. Lovely in girlhood, suddenly there came a
moment—for example on the river beneath the woods at
Clieveden—when, through some contraction of this cold
spirit, she had failed him. And then at Constantinople,
and again and again. She could see what she lacked. It
was not beauty; it was not mind. It was something cen-

tral which permeated; something warm which broke up
surfaces and rippled the cold contact of men and women.
For *that* she could dimly perceive. She resented it, had a
scruple picked up Heaven knows where, or as she felt,
sent by Nature (who is invariably wise). [p. 46]

Here the memory of place—Clieveden and Constantinople—
works to contain and localize the moments of failure that
occur "through some contraction of this cold spirit." The
bounding of failure in specific places is important, for it releases the idea of virginity from the bondage of general and
universal malaise. As a symbol of *sexual* failure, virginity is
confined to the marital bed, where it does indeed suggest the
lack of "something warm which broke up surfaces and rippled
the cold contact of men and women." But virginity is also an
exclusively feminine symbol of freedom and integrity. Thus
Clarissa's resentment of the scruples sent by Nature are later
transposed and defended in the great scene with Peter Walsh
when she involuntarily responds to his intrusive, if welcome,
appearance by hiding the dress she had been mending, "like a
virgin protecting chastity, respecting privacy." The encounter
between Peter and Clarissa, he brandishing his pen-knife, she
defending herself against his implicit criticisms, is a comic
variation of what Northrop Frye calls "the stock convention
of virgin-baiting." Deep within this convention, Frye explains,
"is a vision of human integrity imprisoned in a world it is in
but not of, often forced by weakness into all kinds of ruses
and stratagems, yet always managing to avoid the one fate
which really is worse than death, the annihilation of one's
identity."[18]

It is this deep, alternative understanding of virginity as a
symbol of spiritual inviolability that accounts for the complementary symbols of bed, where virginity is contemplated as an

18. Northrop Frye, *The Secular Scripture* (Cambridge: Harvard University Press,
1976), p. 86.

image of failure, and mirror, where virginity is contemplated as an image of integrity. Gazing into her mirror, Clarissa recovers a vision of intact identity in "seeing the delicate pink face of the woman who was that very night to give a party; of Clarissa Dalloway; of herself" (p. 54). Now the public personage, Mrs. Dalloway, coexists and is identical with the private person, Clarissa. In the complete transparency of this moment of integration, Clarissa can see her face, "with the same imperceptible contraction," in a more positive way:

> That was her self—pointed; dartlike; definite. That was her self when some effort, some call on her to be her self drew the parts together, she alone knew how different, how incompatible and composed so for the world only into one centre, one diamond, one woman who sat in her drawing-room and made a meeting-point, a radiancy no doubt in some dull lives, a refuge for the lonely to come to, perhaps. [p. 55]

The virginal contraction of spirit collects and concentrates the self into a diamond shape that acknowledges its status as a necessary social fiction "composed so for the world only into one centre." The different, often incompatible facets of that "diamond," identity, converge in a unified center, a meeting-point that assembles and composes, without annihilating, its separate parts into a whole. Thus the title of the novel, *Mrs. Dalloway,* which emphasizes the social radiancy and centrality of its heroine, yields to and is absorbed by its transformative ending—"It is Clarissa, he said"—an ending that is both the meeting-point and the terminal point of Clarissa Dalloway's quest for social and spiritual integration.

Frye suggests that the emblem for the virgin's closely guarded secret of invulnerability and preserved integrity is a "diamond set in a black horn, with the motto attached 'yet still myself' that appears in Sidney's *Arcadia.*"[19] Certainly it is

19. Frye, *Secular Scripture,* p. 86.

this radiant yet fragile clarity that is the source of the "integrity" of Clarissa's feeling for Sally Seton, a feeling that is not based so much on narcissistic identification as feminine allegiance, the "sense of being in league together, a presentiment of something that was bound to part them (they spoke of marriage always as a catastrophe)" (p. 50). Clarissa's presentiments prove true, and the "catastrophe" of division and separation is narratively rendered in their respective marriages. But beneath the romantic fable, grounded in the scruples sent by Nature, that virgins marry and live "happily" ever after, there persists a virginal integrity that remains the exclusive knowledge of the female and a powerful source of feminine bonding.

As Frye concludes, "the beleaguered virgin may be more than simply a representative of human integrity: she may also exert a certain redemptive quality by her innocence and goodness, or, in other contexts, by her astuteness in management and intrigue."[20] Woolf's portrait of the female artist of life, while incorporating the qualities of innocence and goodness, does not invoke them unconditionally. Knowing that these virtues ironically serve to promote the myth of innate feminine altruism, Woolf also emphasizes the guile of her feminine heroines, the strategy often adopted by the helpless or physically weak. The victory of guile is a comic victory, as Frye remarks, and in many ways assures a more lasting victory than the heroics of tragedy. The tragic, while making "the greatest impression on us," nevertheless often concludes with the death of the hero and the perception that strength is, after all, not invulnerable.[21] What is curious and innovative about Woolf's comic victory over violence, alienation, and the tragic recognition of the inhuman and absolute power of time, is that her heroine of life, Clarissa Dalloway, gradually absorbs the traditional emblems of tragic posturing into her own social bearing and demeanor. The various mock-epic similes of the novel

20. Frye, *Secular Scripture,* p. 87.
21. Ibid., pp. 87–88.

(such as the mock-heroic return from "battle" in which Lucy "disarms" Clarissa of her umbrella) assume more serious meaning in the novel's final sequence—the party itself.

The scene is the drawing-room that mediates between the public streets and the private rooms where we exist "alone, alone, alone." During the party, the criticisms of Peter Walsh ("the perfect hostess he called her") and Miss Kilman (that her life "was a tissue of vanity and deceit") are silenced by Clarissa's ability to act on her feeling for life. The metaphor verifying the connection between Clarissa's vision of life and life itself is the indispensable metaphor of the heart: "Like the pulse of a perfect heart, life struck straight through the streets" (p. 82), comments the narrator. Clarissa's "triumph" is announced in similar terms: ". . . walking down the room with him [the Prime Minister], with Sally there and Peter there and Richard very pleased, with all those people rather inclined, perhaps, to envy, she had felt that intoxication of the moment, that dilatation of the nerves of the heart itself till it seemed to quiver, steeped, upright" (p. 265). Clarissa's exultant posture recalls the "perfectly upright and stoical bearing" bred into the English by "this late age of the world's experience" and is associated with "the woman she admired most," Lady Bexborough, who opened a bazaar with the telegram announcing the death of her favorite son in her hand. It is the bearing of women of a certain class, conscious inheritors and continuers of the tradition of public service, hostesses who, reluctant to inflict their individuality, bury their private grief.

The Myth of Social Happiness

But Clarissa's upright bearing in the company of the Prime Minister also discloses a connection with a more ambiguous authority, miming as it does the posture of political power. Peter Walsh's prediction, complete with ironical twists, that Clarissa would marry a Prime Minister and stand at the top of the stairs, implies a real, perhaps unconscious fascination with power that manifests itself in Clarissa's lapses into snobbery. The correspondences between the public and private exercises of the will are dramatized when Clarissa, observing the talismanic disc of authority flashed by the royal car, consciously equates the power of the State, a power held "by force of its own lustre" (p. 25) with her own power to kindle and illuminate: "She stiffened a little; so she would stand at the top of her stairs." The symbolic presence of the "State" in *Mrs. Dalloway* is so imposing because the state possesses a special kind of power and authority. The state enjoys perpetuity in time and omnipresence in space (symbolized by the Union Jack and other portable symbols of imperial dominion). Thus as the motorcade embodying "the voice of authority" passes through the heart of London, it exerts a formidable and emotional common appeal: "for in all the hat shops and tailors' shops strangers looked at each other and thought of the dead; of the flag; of Empire" (p. 25). Paradoxically, the imminence of Royalty that makes the gathering crowd think "of the heavenly life divinely bestowed upon Kings" derives its own authority through the most fugitive of communal voices; it exists virtually by the power of rumor.

As the congregations of loyal subjects gather at the gates of Buckingham Palace, they cannot even locate the seat of the power they revere and obey, bestowing their emotion vainly, as the narrator satirically observes, "upon commoners out for a drive." Nevertheless, the "phantom" power of the state is perceived as absolute, making the community "ready to attend their Sovereign, if need be, to the cannon's mouth, as their ancestors had done before them." The revived memory of past violence, the renewed readiness to attend their Sovereign to more violence, accounts for the horror that Septimus experiences as the motor car passes him. The necessary collective myth of national unity, once centered in an absolute icon of authority ("this gradual drawing together of everything to one centre before his eyes"), terrifies him:

The world wavered and quivered and threatened to burst into flames. It is I who am blocking the way, he thought. Was he not being looked at and pointed at; was he not weighted there, rooted to the pavement, for a purpose? But for what purpose? [p. 21]

Septimus's presence in the novel is symbolically juxtaposed to the Prime Minister's to suggest that his "purpose" is to testify to the ambiguous status of social and political authority. The Prime Minister stands, with Clarissa, at the top of stairs, a visible symbol of the power of the ascendant classes, while Septimus occupies the threshold to that lower world where the myths of national destiny and identity originate. Like Forster's Leonard Bast in *Howards End,* Septimus embodies and characterizes the aspirations of the rising lower classes whose assimilation into the aristocratic upper order includes a radical reeducation in the established culture. As an English "type," Septimus, unlike the venerable Sir Hugh and the domineering Bradshaw, or even the aristocratic Lady Bruton, is drawn almost completely from the low-mimetic conventions of folktale and picaresque. He is a Dick Wittington figure who goes to London "leaving an absurd note behind him, such as great men have written, and the world has read later when the story of their struggles has become famous" (p. 127). The War, of course, provides the ironic culmination to Septimus's picaresque adventures. It is the European War that finally extinguishes his identity and exposes "the whole show"—friendship, helpless love for Isabel Pole, the England that consists almost entirely of Shakespeare's plays. And it is the war that transforms Septimus, the lower class upstart who failed in his effort to rise, into Septimus the scapegoat who assumes society's burden of guilt. The Prime Minister is a symbol of Empire without guilt, for all disgrace has been displaced onto Septimus, tormented by his sense of having committed "an appalling crime." Septimus thus obtains a double status in the novel, being both society's scapegoat and its "giant mourner" (p. 106).

It is he who most radically challenges, by the fixity of his vision and the oppressive weight of his guilt, the myth of social happiness.

Woolf's vision of society and the State is grounded in an irresolvable ambivalence: she recognizes that the basis for personal and historical continuity resides in the illusion of community and social order, but is plagued by the knowledge, never completely redeemed, that the power of social illusion is closely allied to delusion. This is the meaning of the airplane sequence that concludes the morning adventures of the novel and reveals, through its horribly deflationary denouement, that the communal symbols of aspiration, of shared dreams, of the spiritual determination to transcend the limits of material existence, are themselves written in corrupt and corruptible words. Even the narrator shares Bond Street's fascination with the looping airplane "sped of its own free will" and ascending "straight up, like something mounting in ecstasy, in pure delight" (p. 42). But haunting this apparition of sublimity and absolute freedom is a deep fear, the deepest fear of Clarissa herself, that grubbing at the roots of her soul, of every soul, is the monster hatred, that "the whole panoply of content [was] nothing but self love!" (p. 17).

It is this panoply of content—"all pleasure in beauty, in friendship, in being well, in being loved"—that the myth of social happiness upholds and sustains. It is through grubbing at the roots of this myth that Woolf makes her most searching criticism of the social order, partially through the self-inquisitions of Clarissa confronting her own hatred, loving her enemy Miss Kilman, partly through the sublime and unbearable madness of Septimus Smith, the "border case" (p. 127) who is the happiest man in the world and the most miserable.

Hatred in *Mrs. Dalloway* is both satisfying and real (p. 265), more satisfying, more real, and finally more lasting than love itself. The true poet, Goethe remarks, must learn to hate, and perhaps Septimus's failure as a poet to communicate the birth of a new religion and the cult of universal love originates in his inability to isolate and oppose the objects of his hatred. For him, it is human nature itself which is "the brute monster," personified in but not confined to the figures of Holmes and Bradshaw. He cannot disassociate, as Clarissa and the narrator can, monstrous ideas from the people who personify them, a telling and ultimately fatal confusion. Woolf's enlightened woman reserves her hatred "for ideas not people" (p. 190). Through such an act of discrimination, Clarissa registers her psychological victory over Miss Kilman. When Miss Kilman waits for Elizabeth at the top of the stairs, a usurping presence standing "with the power and taciturnity of some prehistoric monster armoured for primeval warfare," Clarissa allows the idea of Miss Kilman to diminish and watches her become "second by second merely Miss Kilman, in a mackintosh, whom Heaven knows Clarissa would have liked to help": "At this dwindling of the monster, Clarissa laughed" (p. 190).

Clarissa's laughter, sign of an internal triumph over hatred, triggers her defiant assault on the monster herself. "Remember the party," she cries out to her enemy, the triumphant cry of the soul that Kilman had wished to subdue (p. 189). Clarissa's laughter is also thoughtful laughter, as her subsequent meditations on the idea of love and religion, now divorced from the "body" of the departed Miss Kilman, reveal. In the novel's most sustained inquiry into the motives and principles of human action, Clarissa rejects love and religion, the traditional foundations for social law and the favorite masks of the authoritarian will, as moral or ethical absolutes. It is not just that love and religion, like all "causes," make people callous, but that they destroy, through the sheer force of their will to universality, Woolf's only absolute—the privacy of the soul:

Why creeds and prayers and mackintoshes? when, thought Clarissa, that's the miracle, that's the mystery; that old lady, she meant, whom she could see going from chest of drawers to dressing-table. She could still see her. And the supreme mystery which Kilman might say she had solved,

or Peter might say he had solved, but Clarissa didn't believe either of them had the ghost of an idea of solving,
was simply this: here was one room; there another. Did
religion solve that, or love? [p. 193]

The old lady, who throughout the novel represents an inviolable individuality, symbolizes the mystery and the per-
plexity complicating Clarissa's—and by extension Woolf's—
effort to create a stable, non-authoritarian community of
relations. No solution may be forthcoming, because of the
contrary and conflicting claims of liberty, the irreducible and
inalienable right of the soul to its privacy, and community,
which more often than not exists by virtue of an enforced or
passive conformity. The repeated references to Kilman's
mackintosh and to Septimus's shabby overcoat suggest the
authentic nature of this dilemma, echoing as they do John
Stuart Mill's famous analogy in *On Liberty:*

> Human beings are not like sheep; and even sheep are not
> undistinguishably alike. A man cannot get a coat or a
> pair of boots to fit him unless they are either made to his
> measure, or he has a whole warehouseful to choose from:
> and is it easier to fit him with a life than with a coat, or
> are human beings more like one another in their whole
> physical and spiritual conformation than in the shape of
> their feet?[22]

Mrs. Dalloway is, of course, filled with characters who, like
Clarissa, refuse to be suitably fitted with the life prescribed
for them, and even those, like Septimus, who cannot find a
coat made to his measure. Only the thoroughly socialized, if
"admirable" Sir Hugh, is blessed with a "very well-covered,
manly, extremely handsome, perfectly upholstered body" that
even Clarissa suspects is "almost too well dressed" (p. 7).
Love, religion, and the social faith that adorns the manners

---

22. John Stuart Mill, *On Liberty,* ed. David Spitz (New York: W. W. Norton &
Company, 1975), p. 64.

and the breeding of the English character exercise a powerful but dubious authority in the novel. They inspire both admiration (Peter, despite his "horrible passion," is "adorable," Kilman possesses an impressive historical mind, Hugh Whitbred is useful in drafting letters to the *Times*) and fear.

This fear is localized and personified in Bradshaw, who Rezia and Clarissa, besides the mad Septimus, both intuit to be obscurely evil. It is in the authoritarian figure of the benevolent thaumaturge that the individual and social lust to effect a tyrannical synthesis of physical and spiritual conformation is dramatized. Bradshaw administers and executes the law of social happiness. He insists that the mad regain their sense of proportion (for health is proportion), ordering bed rest, solitude, silence and rest "until a man who went in weighing seven stone six comes out weighing twelve" (p. 150). The long excursus on Bradshaw's twin goddesses, Proportion and Conversion, coming almost in the dead center of the novel and ironically reflecting on Clarissa's own *hora demonium* (Septimus's interview with Bradshaw occurs, like Clarissa's ritual disrobing, at midday) represents Woolf's most systematic and sustained attempt to demystify established structures of authority.

In his study of *Madness and Civilization,* Michel Foucault identifies these structures: "Family-Child relations centered on the theme of parental authority; Transgression-Punishment relations, centered on the theme of immediate justice; Madness-Disorder relations, centered on the theme of social and moral order."[23] Bradshaw is the resolute champion of all these orders, inspiring the respect of his colleagues, the fear of his subordinates, and the gratitude of his patients' families (p. 150). But he is an even more resolute defender of the inherited prerogatives of class in propagating the self-serving myth that the unsocial impulses of the defenseless, exhausted,

---

23. Michel Foucault, *Madness and Civilization,* tr. Richard Howard (New York: Vintage Books, 1973), p. 274.

and friendless are "bred more than anything by the lack of good blood" (p. 154). Class pride, however, is itself a metaphor for the fanaticism of all true believers, the self-righteous elect confidently asserting that "this is madness, this sense." Bradshaw, and the prosperous England whose will he executes, is not hesitant, like Clarissa Dalloway and Woolf herself, to define reality for others. Hence the quasi-incestuous relationship between his goddesses, Proportion and her sister Conversion, twin divinities masquerading as universal love, duty and self-sacrifice, yet secretly in love with their own stern countenances. It is this self-love that grubs at the roots of England's panoply of content and that provokes Conversion's desire "to impress, to impose, adoring her own features stamped on the face of the populace" (p. 151). In the heat and sand of India, in the mud and swamp of Africa, in the purlieus of London, comments the narrator, the dissenting, the dissentient, the dissatisfied receive the impress of the English will, bow to the overriding lust of Conversion "to stamp indelibly in the sanctuaries of others the image of herself" (p. 154).

Madness and the Work of Art

To cleanse the sanctuary and to cast from the temple its false idols of Proportion and Conversion is the special mission of the novel. Woolf dramatizes several self-defensive strategies by which the soul attempts to protect and secure its right to privacy. One is fantasy, "the better part of life," as Peter Walsh notes as he follows a young woman across Trafalgar Square, "making oneself up; making her up; creating an exquisite amusement, and something more" (p. 81). The object of Peter's fantasy emits her own curious kind of "excitement," whispering as she does "his name, not Peter, but his private name which he called himself in his own thoughts" (p. 79). But private fantasy, harmless and disinterested as it is, refreshing the soul with its promise of reckless, romantic adventure,

is only an exquisite amusement—and nothing more. As Peter
realizes, such fantasies cannot be shared: "It smashed to
atoms" (p. 81).

Besides fantasy, there are unconscious cosmic reveries, like
Clarissa's "star-gazing" and its opposite, "musing among the
vegetables" (p. 4). And there are actual dreams, like Peter
Walsh's diseased dream proclaiming "the death of the soul"
(p. 88). Staring out of that dream is the countenance of a
more benevolent female deity "showering down from her
magnificent hands compassion, comprehension, absolution"
(p. 86). This giant figure of divinized womanhood is metamorphosed, through the curious dream-logic of Peter's midday
visions, into the spectral figure of an "elderly woman who
seems . . . to be the figure of the mother whose sons have been
killed in the battles of the world" (p. 87). The wish content of
Peter's dream, also latent in the novel itself, is to restore the
privileged relationship between mothers and sons, fathers and
daughters. Sally Seton's maternal pride in her five sons, Elizabeth's devotion to her father contribute to the emotional
success of Clarissa's party. But the dream of restoring these
familial bonds is threatened by solitary experiences and private
fears: Clarissa, anxious about losing Elizabeth to Miss Kilman;
Rezia separated from her family, and of course, the radical
alienation of Septimus Smith. It is partially to escape his
mother that Septimus leaves home (p. 127).

The phantasmagoric visions of "the solitary traveller" find
their most complete expression in the madness of Septimus
Smith. Septimus is the eschatological figure in whom and
through whom the novel's revolutionary millennialism is
voiced. Disguised by his delirious and ecstatic prophecies of
universal love and the end of the reign of Death is the authentically subversive content of his vision: the unsettling and dis-
mantling of natural and social hierarchies, the levelling of the
great chain of being in which dogs turn into men (p. 102), the
unmasking of human nature as a breed of "lustful animals,

who have no lasting emotions, but only whims and vanities, eddying them now this way, now that" (p. 135). Septimus's creed of universal love is a deception of a deception, for illness, as Woolf remarked in her essay "On Being Ill," "often takes on the disguise of love, and plays the same odd tricks":

> It invests certain faces with divinity, sets us to wait, hour after hour, with pricked ears for the creaking of a stair, and wreathes the faces of the absent (plain enough in health, Heaven knows) with a new significance, while the mind concocts a thousand legends and romances about them for which it has neither time nor taste in health.[24]

In the hallucinations of illness (like Clarissa's influenza), in the delirium of frustrated passion (like Peter Walsh's fearful premonition of "death that surprised in the midst of life, Clarissa falling where she stood" [p. 75]), and in the apocalyptic fantasies of the mad Septimus (the world threatening to burst into flames), the line of division between the real and the imaginary is erased, disclosing the void incertitude. The buried anxiety of the novel is that the lunatic, the lover, and the poet *are* of imagination all compact in bodying forth the forms of things unknown.

This anxious intuition that the work of art and the hallucinatory forms of madness interpenetrate and communicate with frightening familiarity suggests a disturbing relationship between the narrator and Septimus, the visionary poet. His innumerable scribblings and his poetic testament, an immortal ode to Time, reflect on the narrator's romantic treatment of time as a structure of symbolic correspondences. He, like the narrator, is the transcriber of voices issuing from the land of the living and the dead. He exercises an enviable freedom with words and symbols and those meaningless sounds through which the beauty of the world is communicated. Viewing the soaring airplane inscribing letters in the sky, he can interpret

24. Virginia Woolf, "On Being Ill," *Collected Essays,* vol. 4, p. 194.

the beauty of the world which lies "beyond seeking and quest-
ing and knocking of words together" (p. 42):

> So, thought Septimus, looking up, they are signalling to
> me. Not indeed in actual words; that is, he could not read
> the language yet; but it was plain enough, this beauty,
> this exquisite beauty, and tears filled his eyes as he
> looked at the smoke words languishing and melting in the
> sky and bestowing upon him in their inexhaustible
> charity and laughing goodness one shape after another of
> unimaginable beauty and signalling their intention to
> provide him, for nothing, for ever, for looking merely,
> with beauty, more beauty! [p. 31]

If, as Peter Walsh speculates, "Nothing exists outside us
except a state of mind" (p. 85), it is just possible that the universal state of mind—the world itself—may be mad, that is,
without a determinate meaning or language of its own. In the
intemperate madness of Septimus, who questions, impiously,
life itself, the world reveals its beauty, a beauty that words
can't express nor reason explain. This is the special dispensation in being ill:

> Incomprehensibility has an enormous power over us in ill-
> ness, more legitimately perhaps than the upright will
> allow. In health meaning has encroached upon sound.
> Our intelligence domineers over our sense. But in illness,
> with the police off duty, we creep beneath some obscure
> poem by Mallarmé or Donne, some phrase in Latin or
> Greek, and the words give out their scent and distil their
> flavour, and then, if at last we grasp the meaning, it is all
> the richer for having come to us sensually first, by way of
> the palate and the nostrils, like some queer odour.[25]

In illness, sounds are released, legitimately perhaps, from
the meaning that has encroached upon them in health. Through

25. "On Being Ill," p. 200.

the queer power of synaesthesia enjoyed by the diseased imagination, Reason, the tyrant, is dethroned. Sound is set free, like the sound of St. Margaret's, to glide into the recesses of the heart and bury itself in ring after ring of sound (p. 74). Is this ring of sound the origin of "poésie pure," as Woolf's reference to Mallarmé suggests? Does the creativity of the poet lie in "taking his pain in one hand and a lump of pure sound in the other," just as, Woolf theorizes, "perhaps the people of Babel did in the beginning" when the first words were formed?[26] Or is the non-sense spoken by the mad no language at all, merely words languishing and dissolving into their constituent sounds —"ee um fah um so / foo swee too eem oo" (p. 124)—the sounds of the eternal, unreasonable world itself? Is the primal voice of the earth "a frail quivering sound, a voice bubbling up without direction, vigour, beginning or end, running weakly and shrilly and with an absence of all human meaning . . . the voice of no age or sex . . ." (p. 122)?

These unanswerable, not rhetorical questions suggest that the language of madness and the language of art may be continuous or contiguous discourses through which the mind, burdened with its visions of beauty and truth, communicates with and about the world. This does not mean, as Michel Foucault observes, speaking of the peculiar status of madness in the "modern" art of Nietzsche, Van Gogh, and Artaud, "that madness is the only language common to the work of art and the modern world." What it does mean, he argues, is that

> through madness, a work that seems to drown in the world, to reveal there its non-sense, and to transfigure itself with the features of pathology alone, actually engages within itself the world's time, masters it, and leads it;

26. "On Being Ill," p. 194. See J. Hillis Miller's "Virginia Woolf's All Soul's Day," in *The Shaken Realist: Essays in Modern Literature in Honor of F. J. Hoffman,* ed. O. B. Hardison, Jr., et al. (Baton Rouge, 1970), pp. 114–15. Miller identifies and expands on the meaning of the "song of love" in *Mrs. Dalloway,* a song whose sounds only yield to sense when translated by the reader, never the character who overhears it.

by the madness which interrupts it, a work of art opens a void, a moment of silence, a question without answer, provokes a breach without reconciliation where the world is forced to question itself. What is necessarily a profanation in the work of art returns to that point, and, in the time of that work swamped in madness, the world is made aware of its guilt.[27]

The suicide of Septimus Smith constitutes the necessary profanation in *Mrs. Dalloway,* its illegality, its impiety, through which the world of the novel, assembled at its meeting-point in Clarissa Dalloway, is made aware of its guilt: "Somehow it was her disaster—her disgrace" (p. 282). In the time in which Clarissa's body ("Always her body went through it first") and mind succumb to the profound darkness and experience the suffocation of blackness symbolized by Septimus's death, Clarissa begins to question herself:

A thing there was that mattered; a thing, wreathed about with chatter, defaced, obscured in her own life, let drop every day in corruption, lies, chatter. This he had preserved. Death was defiance. [p. 280]

With the clock striking the hour, the words "Fear no more the heat of the sun" come back to her, words that earlier in the day had disclosed to her the real time of the world, sounds of that eternal spring sighing throughout the novel's summer's day:

So on a summer's day waves collect, overbalance, and fall; collect and fall; and the whole world seems to be saying "that is all" more and more ponderously, until even the heart in the body which lies in the sun on the beach says too, That is all. Fear no more, says the heart. Fear no more, says the heart, committing its burden to some sea, which sighs collectively for all sorrows, and renews, begins, collects, lets fall. [pp. 58-59]

27. Foucault, *Madness and Civilization,* p. 288.

The Lawgiver

But Clarissa, unlike Septimus, does not drown in the world's time. The lines from Imogen's dirge in *Cymbeline* connecting the visionary madness of Septimus to Clarissa's diseased heart, a heart which wishes to commit its burden to the sea, only seems to be saying "that is all." For just as Imogen is not really dead, so Clarissa's desire to succumb, to let fall, is surmounted by the "waves of that divine vitality which Clarissa loved" (p. 9). The sequence of the world's time that "begins, collects, lets fall" is not a single action, but a series of actions that repeat and renew this pattern. Septimus is the "drowned sailor" desperately trying to return to the shores of life (p. 140), but his fatal plunge is echoed and transfigured by Clarissa's plunge into dark seas:

> . . . she entered, and felt often as she stood hesitating one moment on the threshold of her drawing-room, an exquisite suspense, such as might stay a diver before plunging while the sea darkens and brightens beneath him, and the waves which threaten to break, but only gently split their surface, roll and conceal and encrust as they just turn over the weeds with pearl. [p. 44]

Clarissa can dive into deep seas, but she can also rise to the surface. For her, the waves that threaten to break "just turn over." This "turn" of the waves absorbs and transforms the profoundly tragic rhythm of the world—the tragic rhythm of rising that always concludes with a "fall"—into a comic arc. Clarissa, like Imogen, only feigns death. In her plunge into dark seas she does not drown but undergoes a Shakespearean sea-change:

> For this is the truth about our soul . . . our self, who fish-like inhabits deep seas and plies among obscurities threading her way between the boles of giant weeds, over sun-flickered spaces and on and on into gloom, cold,

> deep, inscrutable; suddenly she shoots to the surface and
> sports on the wind-wrinkled waves; that is, has a positive
> need to brush, scrape, kindle herself, gossiping. [p. 244]

Clarissa's ability to dart to the surface and sport on the wind-wrinkled waves like a "creature floating in her element" (p. 264) distinguishes her from Septimus, who goes "on and on into gloom." She undergoes a sea-change, metamorphosed into a mermaid "lalloping on the waves." Septimus is the dying god, his "body . . . macerated until only the nerve fibres were left. It was spread like a veil upon a rock" (pp. 102-03).[28]

Thus while Septimus apprehends and is sacrificed to the "ghastly beauty" of the world, it is Clarissa who comprehends the soul's divine, precious truth. Woolf can affirm Septimus's tragic posture, his ceremonial baring of the body on the sacrificial rock, only as an act of expiation and atonement, not as the sublime rebellion of the apocalyptic imagination. Like Joyce, she resists the apocalyptic urge to uncover and expose the bare rock of the world and its inhuman time and grounds her supreme fiction of the earth on the comic myths of eternal return, eternal renewal. Her art is the art of lying, the art that creates those necessary fictions that conceal the void incertitude, the Conradian art that finds its ultimate justification in the lie that saves. Only Miss Kilman prides herself in her incapacity to tell lies (p. 187), but her commitment to "truth" is associated with her demythifying desire to unmask, to demoralize, to master the "soul" of Clarissa and the life she, unlike Miss Kilman, loves. The failure to comprehend the characteristically modern forms of Woolf's romanticism, the romanticism of Joyce, Lawrence, and Conrad, has led many critics to misrepresent Woolf's illusionism. Philip Rahv's criticism of the novel is in many ways representative:

---

28. For a more detailed discussion of Septimus's mythic affinities to the dying god, Adonis, who is associated, like Septimus, with the vital spirit of trees, see Jean Wyatt, "*Mrs. Dalloway:* Literary Allusion as Structural Metaphor," PMLA, vol. 88, no. 3 (May, 1973): 443.

> Septimus is the mysterious stranger, the marked man, the
> poet upon whom an outrage has been committed. . . .
> This apparition haunted Mrs. Woolf, but she always
> strove to escape from it. She felt more at home with Mrs.
> Dalloway.[29]

Woolf's achievement, as Forster appreciated,[30] was in convey-
ing the sublimity of Septimus's apocalyptic visions, without
sentimentalizing his madness. If she evaded the spectral apparition, it was a conscious evasion effected by adhering to the
sanative and prescriptive formulae of comic art. *Mrs. Dalloway* is not a work of madness, but a work of art, and as
Foucault reminds us, "where there is a work of art, there is
no madness."[31]

The point at which the narrative disassociates even as it
emerges from the mad imaginations of Septimus is in its interpretative appropriations of the dirge from *Cymbeline,* "Fear
no more the heat of the sun / Nor the furious winter's rages."
For Septimus, "the message hidden in the beauty of words" in
Shakespearean art is loathing, hatred, despair: "The secret signal which one generation passes, under disguise, to the next is
loathing, hatred, despair. Dante the same. Aeschylus (translated) the same" (p. 134). Of course, it is precisely through such
a secret and covert transmission of signals on which the narrator relies to effect the climactic and transformative identification of Clarissa with Septimus: "She felt somehow very like
him, the young man who killed himself" (p. 283). But the
message Septimus meant to communicate—"how Shakespeare
loathed humanity—the putting on of clothes, the getting of
children, the sordidity of the mouth and the belly!"—is misin-

29. Philip Rahv, "Mrs. Woolf and Mrs. Brown," *Literature and the Sixth Sense*
(Boston: Houghton Mifflin, 1969), p. 328.

30. E. M. Forster, *Two Cheers for Democracy,* p. 243.

31. Foucault, *Madness and Civilization,* pp. 288–89. For a sentimental and
rather confused study of the relation between madness and art in the novels of Virginia Woolf, see Roger Poole's *The Unknown Virginia Woolf* (Cambridge: Cambridge University Press, 1978).

terpreted and transvalued by Clarissa: "He made her feel the beauty; made her feel the fun. But she must go back. She must assemble. She must find Sally and Peter" (p. 284). Septimus either cannot feel the fun of life, the crime for which he stands self-condemned, or he feels the beauty of life too much. His tears, the tears of the "giant mourner" shed for all the sorrows of the world, are emblems of that morbidity that "is fatal to art, fatal to friendship," as Peter Walsh notes (p. 229). Clarissa's feelings about suffering are of a different order. She trans-mutes her feelings of pain and loss into the art of life. Having penetrated into the heart of human corruption, she revives, and, obeying the summons of recall, returns to Sally and Peter, her "companions in the art of living" (p. 83).

This is the "normal outcome" in the work of mourning, which consists, as Freud writes, not in defying, but in defer-ring to reality:

> In what, now, does the work which mourning performs consist? . . . Reality-testing has shown that the loved object no longer exists, and it proceeds to demand that all libido shall be withdrawn from its attachments to that object. This demand arouses understandable opposition— it is a matter of general observation that people never willingly abandon a libidinal position, not even, indeed, when a substitute is already beckoning to them. This opposition can be so intense that a turning away from reality takes place and a clinging to the object through the medium of a hallucinatory wishful psychosis.[32]

The dirge, Woolf suggests in her interpolations from *Cymbeline,* may be the original form of human art, the imagination's first radical testing of reality, the first necessary dissimulation by which the mind compromises and transforms its grief. The dirge artfully mourns the dead; its art soothes and consoles by

32. Sigmund Freud, "Mourning and Melancholia," *Standard Edition,* vol. 14, pp. 244-45.

disguising, and thus mocking, the verdict of reality. Certainly the work of mourning is the primary labor performed by the feminine imagination. Feminine art always seeks to restore the oppressed and mournful to the reality of ordinary life with its chatter, its gossip, its fun.

Even Septimus appreciates the compassionate presence of this feminine power as he watches and listens to Rezia as she sits sewing flowers on Mrs. Filmer's hat, building it up, first one thing, then another, the slow, painful process, as Freud describes mourning, of carrying out the command of reality:[33]

> Mrs. Peters had a spiteful tongue. Mr. Peters was in Hull. Why then rage and prophesy? Why fly scourged and outcast? Why be made to tremble and sob by the clouds? Why seek truths and deliver messages when Rezia sat sticking pins into the front of her dress, and Mr. Peters was in Hull? Miracles, revelations, agonies, loneliness, falling through the sea, down, down into the flames, all were burnt out, for he had a sense, as he watched Rezia trimming the straw hat for Mrs. Peters, of a coverlet of flowers. [p. 216]

The female art consumes and transforms the apocalyptic hallucinations of the grief-stricken mind, its sobs, its trembling revelations, into "a coverlet of flowers." Flowers are the primary materials of feminine art, the transient, evanescent flowers of life and of darkness. But they are also emblems of the figurative powers of the feminine imagination, the flowers of the female mind that blossom for Rezia after Septimus's death when, half dreaming, there comes to her the "whisperings, . . . the caress of the sea . . . murmuring to her laid on shore, strewn she felt, like flying flowers over some tomb" (p. 228). For Septimus, Rezia herself is the flowering tree of life through whose branches he glimpses the face of the lawgiver:

33. Freud, "Mourning and Melancholia," p. 245.

She was a flowering tree; and through her branches looked out the face of a lawgiver, who had reached a sanctuary where she feared no one; not Holmes; not Bradshaw; a miracle, a triumph, the last and greatest. Staggering he saw her mount the appalling staircase, laden with Holmes and Bradshaw, men who never weighed less than eleven stone six, who sent their wives to Court, men who made ten thousand a year and talked of proportion; who different in their verdicts (for Holmes said one thing, Bradshaw another), yet judges they were; who mixed the vision and the sideboard; saw nothing clear, yet ruled, yet inflicted. "Must" they said. Over them she triumphed. [pp. 224-25]

The last and greatest triumph in *Mrs. Dalloway* is in inaugurating, in the time of the novel, the reign of the feminine lawgiver who has reached the sanctuary where she fears no one. The lawgiver may be Nature, who is invariably wise. She may be that "state of mind" that exists outside us that Peter Walsh endows with womanhood (p. 85). She may be Maisie Johnson sardonically advising that "life had been no mere matter of roses," but who transmutes the matter of her life through the work of mourning, imploring pity, "Pity for the loss of roses" (p. 40). The most imposing avatar of this female lawgiver who, staggering, mounts the appalling staircase, is the nameless old lady who reappears intermittently throughout the novel, the last time in connection with Septimus's death. She remains nameless, perhaps because, like the hostess, she is reluctant to inflict individuality. She exists as a psychic projection, a metacharacter whose function is to embody the dignity of our solitude and to suggest the infinite mystery about ourselves as "alone, alone, alone." She is indisputably the antitype of Clarissa and Septimus, both "lost in the process of living" (p. 282) in different ways. She preserves throughout the narrative her fascination for Clarissa as the one who does not suffer the "death of the soul." The attic room in which she

moves is the sanctuary whose light is glimpsed at the moment
it is extinguished.

It is in clearing and defining this sacred inner space before it
is overcome by darkness, defaced in corruption, that makes *Mrs.
Dalloway* such a healthy work of the imagination. Possessed of
the sanctuary, the lawgiver dispenses of her law, the law of
natural, mutual, and voluntary association. Happiness, as
Clarissa intuits, cannot be legislated by acts of parliament (p. 5).
It must be created through "pleasure-making," the pleasure-
making symbolized by Clarissa Dalloway's party:

> But to go deeper, beneath what people said (and these
> judgements, how superficial, how fragmentary they are!)
> in her own mind now, what did it mean to her, this thing
> she called life? Oh, it was very queer. Here was So-and-so
> in South Kensington; some one up in Bayswater; and
> somebody else, say, in Mayfair. And she felt quite con-
> tinuously a sense of their existence; and she felt what a
> waste; and she felt what a pity; and she felt if only they
> could be brought together; so she did it. And it was an
> offering; to combine, to create; but to whom?
>
> An offering for the sake of offering, perhaps. Anyhow
> it was her gift. [pp. 184–85]

The degenerate, despotic utopias of Holmes and Bradshaw
can only exist by enforcing the law of compulsive physical and
spiritual conformity. Such utopias represent totalitarian social
forms in which no exit, no protest is possible; their moral
closure never admits of an opening. Men must not weigh less
than eleven stone six and must accept, without appeal, the partial judgment that "this is sense, this madness" as the final,
irrevocable decree of the goddess Proportion. Clarissa's ideal
comic society is fashioned by another kind of symmetry, the
symmetry of beauty, not the crude beauty of the eye, as Peter
Walsh puts it, but beauty anyhow:

> It was straightness and emptiness of course; the sym-
> metry of a corridor; but it was also windows lit up,

a piano, a gramophone sounding; a sense of pleasure-
making hidden, but now and again emerging . . . [p. 248]

The symmetry of beauty, and the pleasure it arouses, is the
symmetry, the unbroken straightness, of the will exercising its
right to moral choice. It is this symmetry that discloses and
encloses that empty but unobstructed corridor that leads to
the privacy of the soul and its freedom. Clarissa's party preserves the principle of voluntary, unenforced participation by
acknowledging the gratuitousness of its existence. She does
not, like Holmes and Bradshaw, inflict her vision of life on the
dissatisfied, the lonely, the weak. She offers for the sake of
offering, refusing to force people to be free or to force them
to be happy.

This crucial disassociation of the creative will from the cor-
rupting impulse for mastery is the triumph of feminine art, of
Clarissa's "exquisite sense of comedy" (p. 118). Even though
she needs, as Peter Walsh realizes, "people, always people to
bring it out" (p. 118), she never invades the sanctuary, never
forces the soul. In giving her party to "kindle and illuminate,"
she never uses the imperative "must," but, in imitation of that
original moment of creation, prefers the authoritative, yet self-
absenting word, "let."[34] All pleasure and all beauty can only
be created and communicated through such gratuitous offer-
ings, as Richard's gift of flowers suggests and as Septimus's
death testifies. In taking his life, Septimus protests that

It was their idea of tragedy, not his or Rezia's (for she
was with him). Holmes and Bradshaw like that sort of

34. Clarissa justifies her party before Love and Religion by the example of her
own life: "Had she ever tried to convert any one herself?" As she thinks about the
old woman opposite who will be excluded from the party in which life will be
kindled and illuminated, she respects the old woman's choice: "Let her climb
upstairs if she wanted to; let her stop; then let her, as Clarissa had often seen her,
gain her bedroom, part her curtains, and disappear again into the background"
(p. 191). Morris Philipson argues that the justification for Clarissa Dalloway's party
consists in "the literary artist's search for the intelligible equivalents in social inter-
course to consummatory sensory experience." See "*Mrs. Dalloway:* What's the Sense
of Your Parties," *Critical Inquiry,* vol. 1, no. 1 (September, 1974): p. 148.

> thing. . . . He did not want to die. Life was good. The sun
> hot. Only human beings—what did *they* want? . . . Holmes
> was at the door. "I'll give it you!" he cried, and flung
> himself vigorously, violently down on to Mrs. Filmer's
> area railings. [p. 226]

Septimus's gift, the thing that human beings want, the thing
that matters, is life itself, the mixed gift of life and death
Nature gratuitously bestows. But Septimus's gift is forced
from him. His offering is associated with the ritual sacrifices
of tragedy and not the festive exchange of gifts by which
comedy traditionally celebrates and cements its achieved social
concord. Clarissa may be glad that Septimus had thrown it
away, her guilt modulating into self-reproach as she remembers
the shilling she had thrown into the Serpentine. But she is
for the party.

For Woolf, the world is the theatre of "free play" in which
beauty is scattered and tossed to the winds; and society is but
a fortuitous, haphazard collection of So-and-so in Kensington,
So-and-so in Mayfair. She feels, like Clarissa, that this dispersed
spectacle of life can and should be collected and assembled
and created into new, more human forms. Ultimately, the
justification for art as mere gift derives its authority from the
banal yet profound cliché that in giving, one receives. Clarissa's
offering to life is the self-rewarding gift, the "extraordinary
gift, that woman's gift, of making a world of her own wherever
she happened to be" (p. 114). This power of making a world
of her own is the power exercised by the narrator who, even
more than Nature or the old woman ascending the stairs, is the
lawgiver of the novel. She is nameless, never inflicts her individuality, yet succeeds in combining and creating out of the
diffuse matter of life a work of art. As the dreamer who
dreams the world of the novel, the narrator is like her characters, engaged in reverie, imagining their memories, trans-
cribing their dreams.

The difference between the dreamer and the dreamed ones
of the novel consists in what Gaston Bachelard sees as "the

radical difference" between the ordinary dream and the conscious reverie:

> . . . while the dreamer of the nocturnal dream is a shadow who has lost his self (*moi*), the dreamer of reverie, if he is a bit philosophical, can formulate a *cogito* at the center of his dreaming self (*son moi rêveur*). Put another way, reverie is an oneiric activity in which a glimmer of consciousness subsists. The dreamer of reverie is present in his reverie. Even when the reverie gives the impression of a flight out of the real, out of time and place, the dreamer of reverie knows that it is he who is absenting himself— he, in flesh and blood, who is becoming a "spirit," a phantom of the past or of voyage.[35]

In the presence of the omniscient, though insubstantial narrator of *Mrs. Dalloway,* Woolf was beginning to formulate and implement her philosophy of anonymity in which the creative mind consciously absents itself from the work it creates. Through this dissolution of the importunate, egotistical narrative "I," the narrative consciousness becomes pure spirit, a phantom of the past or of the voyage it imagines. Through this dissolution, then, the work of mourning and of dreaming in withdrawing, testing, and, in the normal outcome, returning to the real, become one and join forces against the madness which represents the *actual* flight of the mind out of time and place and the confines of the real. In the cooperative labor of mourning and dreaming, Woolf began to discover and recover the "center" that, mystically, had evaded her in her apprentice works. As *To the Lighthouse* demonstrates, Woolf would transform the work of mourning into an elegy for her lost parents, those lawgivers in whose countenances, beautiful and stern, she would see reflected her own face.[36]

35. Gaston Bachelard, *The Poetics of Reverie,* tr. David Russell (Boston: Beacon Press, 1969), p. 150.

36. For an excellent reassessment of Woolf's work in relation to her life, see Phyllis Rose, *Woman of Letters: A Life of Virginia Woolf* (New York: Oxford University Press, 1978).

3

To the Lighthouse

VIRGINIA WOOLF'S WINTER'S TALE

The "Old Man"

"Books," insists Virginia Woolf in *A Room of One's Own,*
"continue each other, in spite of our habit of judging them
separately (p. 84). Like T. S. Eliot, Woolf is intent on tracing
literary lines of descent. In his search for origins, however,
Eliot need only select his favorite ancestors in a tradition already established. The female writer is literature's waif. This
explains why in surveying the past and present prospects of
women and fiction Woolf is faced with the most awesome of
terrors—the blank page. While she acknowledges Austen, the
Brontës, and George Eliot as great originals, she denies them
the status of great originators (*Room,* pp. 79–82). The lack of
an established and living tradition for the individual female
talent forces Woolf to invent one. In place of the luminous
example of Shakespeare, she imagines and then adopts as her
literary ancestor Shakespeare's sister, a poet whose distinctive
voice was reduced by social conventions and economic necessity to an ignominious silence.

A Room of One's Own, of course, argues persuasively for
economic and social independence as the prerequisites for the
emergence and survival of women's fiction. But throughout
Woolf's often comic polemic, and especially in her peroration,
she reminds her audience that for her sexual politics functions
as a metaphor for literary succession, which establishes itself

along patriarchal or matriarchal lines. "For," writes Woolf, "we think back through our mothers if we are women" (*Room*, p. 79). Woolf's organizing metaphor suggests that the parental structure of literary influence, with all its attendant Oedipal anxieties, is not confined to post-Miltonic poets nor, more generally, to literature's designated heirs. Fathers have their favorite sons, but they also have daughters, however dispossessed. Moreover, Woolf's analysis helps reemphasize the motive in Oedipal literary struggles—the rivalry over the mother.[1] As Woolf's argument develops, her focus shifts subtly but unmistakably from the poet's relation to the received tradition to the poet's relation to "the world of reality" and it becomes increasingly clear that she is less interested in the mother as precursor than in the mother as Muse. In this respect, women writers may be more fortunate, since the Muse is one of their own sex, her mysteries closer, finally, to what Woolf deems the mind's essentially feminine "fountain of creative energy." So much, at least, is the belief of Virginia Woolf when, in the final visionary moments of *A Room of One's Own*, she exhorts her female audience to look past Milton's bogey, to "face the fact . . . that our relation is to the world of reality and not only to the world of men and women," so that "the dead poet who was Shakespeare's sister will put on the body which she has so often laid down" (p. 118). That female incarnation of what Woolf sees as the "continuing presences" of past poets is her real hope for assuring the per-

1. Ezra Pound, in a capricious moment, shares such an Oedipal joke with T. S. Eliot:

Song fer the Muses' Garden

> *Ez Po and Possum*
> *Have picked all the blossom,*
> *Let all the others*
> *Run back to their mothers*
>   *Fer a boye's bes' friend iz hiz Oedipus,*
>   *A boy's best friend is his Oedipus.*

Selected Letters of Ezra Pound, 1907-1941, ed. D. D. Paige (New York: New Directions, 1950), p. 272.

petuation of the common life shared by all creative talents, male and female. Thus by a metaphoric sleight of hand, Woolf has translated the central ceremony of literary investiture—the incarnation of the poet—into a truly androgynous phenomenon. Now the dutiful son must share with the dutiful daughter the special privileges of the Muse. In *A Room of One's Own,* Woolf urges its possibility. But in *To the Lighthouse,* a novel about the liberation of the poetic voice, she had encountered unforeseen complications.

The centrality of Mrs. Ramsay in *To the Lighthouse* would seem to confirm Woolf's habit of thinking back through her mother. The imaginative genesis of the novel, however, proves differently. Having just completed *Mrs. Dalloway,* Woolf records the progress made in expressing her personal voice and foresees a future fiction.

> I feel indeed rather more fully relieved of my meaning than usual— . . . Anyhow, I feel that I have exorcised the spell which Murry [John Middleton Murry] and others said I laid myself under after *Jacob's Room.* The only difficulty is to hold myself back from writing others. My cul de sac, as they called it, stretches so far and shows such vistas. I see already the Old Man. [*WD,* pp. 66-67]

Out of a visionary glimpse of an old man, not a woman, issued Woolf's *To the Lighthouse.* The Old Man is, in one sense, Virginia Woolf's slangy nickname for a disappearing God. It may also be her irreverent, though buried, assault on Milton's bogey.[2] Woolf's mockery of the patriarchal, possibly senescent guardians of creation belies the force of her obsession. As her vision clears, the Old Man, the universal father, becomes particularized as her own father, Leslie Stephen.

> This is going to be fairly short; to have father's character done complete in it; and mother's; and St. Ives; and child-

---

2. See Sandra M. Gilbert's interesting discussion of this peculiar phrase in "Patriarchal Poetry and Women Readers," *PMLA* (May, 1978): 368.

hood; and all the usual things I try to put in—life, death,
etc. But the centre is father's character, sitting in a boat,
reciting We perished, each alone, while he crushes a dying
mackerel. [*WD,* p. 75]

It is then, as much the ghost of the father as the mother that
constitutes the novel's center. Woolf admitted as much in a
diary entry dated November 28, her father's birthday.

Father's birthday. He would have been 96, 96, yes,
today; and could have been 96, like other people one has
known: but mercifully was not. His life would have entirely ended mine. What would have happened? No writing, no books;—inconceivable.

I used to think of him and mother daily; but writing
the *Lighthouse* laid them in my mind. And now he comes
back sometimes, but differently. (I believe this to be true
—that I was obsessed by them both, unhealthily; and
writing of them was a necessary act.) [*WD,* p. 135]

The repeated mention of her father's age suggests how imposing the figure of the Old Man was to Woolf's personal and
imaginative life. His continuing life would have augured her
creative death: "No writing, no books." For Woolf the passage
of thought back through the mother—the creative source—is
blocked by the father. The Old Man, the Victorian patriarch, is
not so easily dethroned. The daughter must either be silenced
or perform the "necessary act." Woolf's belief that the writing
of her obsession was essential to her psychic and imaginative
health suggests that writing initially functions for her as exorcism, a verbal rite that casts out the resident ghosts haunting
the mind. The Woolfian artist is the spiritual medium that
mediates between the living and the dead on the hallowed
ground where death and life intersect. Her act, hovering in the
fictional space (her cul de sac?) between mimesis and invoca-
tion, is a summoning of ancestral ghosts.

The emphasis on the relationship between words, writing,
and the death of a beloved also suggests that Woolf's novel is

linked at its origin to the "consolatio" of the elegiac mode:
"I have an idea that I will invent a new name for my books to
supplant 'novel.' A new —— by Virginia Woolf. But what?
Elegy?" [*WD,* p. 78] Woolf's term is still the best for describing the experimental form of her novels after the more traditional narratives of her apprenticeship, *The Voyage Out* and
Night and Day. The narrative ground of *Jacob's Room, Mrs.
Dalloway, To the Lighthouse,* and *The Waves* is haunted by
memories of the dead.[3] Commemorating the dead is, however,
the secondary function of these elegiac narratives. Their primary function is to liberate the elegiac mourner from the
dejection of mortality that is death to the imagination. Coleridge's prescription for the decorum of poetic elegy holds true
for elegy as a narrative form: "It may treat any subject, but it
must treat of no subject for itself; but always and exclusively
with reference to the poet himself."[4] *To the Lighthouse* is an
elegiac narrative that treats its subject—the dead mother and
father—exclusively in terms of the surviving daughter, the
implied, anonymous narrator of the novel. Like Milton's
"Lycidas," the novel establishes an authentic line of succession
to which the poet is finally proclaimed the legitimate heir.
Woolf's elegy thus occasions a double celebration: the dead are
transfigured (they come back, but differently) and the living
descendant discovers an independent voice and a genuine
artistic vocation.

The ghosts of the parents, then, are summoned, like the
ghostly couple in Woolf's short story, "A Haunted House," to
reveal their buried treasure, what Woolf calls simply "the light

3. The sudden death of Virginia Woolf's brother, Thoby Stephen, is reflected in
Jacob's Room and *The Waves,* where it is transmuted into the generalized theme of
heroic elegy, the death of the young hero. For the effect of the suicide of Katherine
Maxse on the writing of *Mrs. Dalloway,* see Quentin Bell, *Virginia Woolf: A Biography* (New York: Harcourt Brace Jovanovich, 1972), p. 87. Woolf's aesthetic,
however, demanded that the personal sources of her art be converted into more
impersonal meditations on death and human loss.
4. Samuel Taylor Coleridge, *Specimens of the Table Talk of Samuel Taylor
Coleridge* (London: John Murray, 1876), p. 275.

in the heart."[5] It is the repossession of that spiritual light, the artist's rightful heritage, that purges the novel's haunted ground. The primary movement of elegy, as Potts has argued, is light out of darkness.[6] It is also the primary creative movement in Genesis and the mythos that informs the Oedipal progress from blindness to insight. As elegy, *To the Lighthouse* interprets Woolf's own family romance as a parable of creation, a fable of knowledge. The novel originates in a forbidding vision of an Old Man that eclipses the light of the mind, but it is sustained by the vision of the mother: the shade of Mrs. Ramsay, in Lily Briscoe's intuition of her, "putting her wreath to her forehead and going unquestioningly with her companion, a shade across the fields" of death.[7] Finally it is the mother who illuminates life's darkest places, and her child who communicates that light to the world.

The Oedipal Dream

The Oedipal origins of *To the Lighthouse* determine not only its subject, but its structure. The form of the novel is contained in the dream of a child. James Ramsay is assured by his mother that, weather permitting, "the wonder to which he had looked forward, for years and years it seemed, was, after a night's darkness and a day's sail, within touch" (p. 9). Mrs. Ramsay, sympathetic to childhood dreams, does qualify her son's hopes, however: "If it's fine tomorrow." Yet what she warns as nature's possible constraint on desire is misunderstood. Her words—"if it's fine"—are transposed to "as if it were settled." The novel as a whole vindicates the child's confidence that he will realize his dreams. The expedition does

5. Virginia Woolf, *A Haunted House* (New York: Harcourt, Brace and World, 1949), pp. 3–5.

6. Abbie Finlay Potts, *The Elegiac Mode* (Ithaca, N.Y.: Cornell University Press, 1967), p. 37.

7. Virginia Woolf, *To the Lighthouse* (New York, Harcourt, Brace and World, 1955), p. 270. All subsequent citations are from this edition.

take place after a night's darkness and a day's sail. Yet what to James only seems years and years of waiting actually becomes, in the narrative time of the novel, the ten years that lapse in "Time Passes." The illusion of prolonged anticipation becomes a reality, and the night's darkness that intervenes between the desire and its fulfillment is protracted in the visionary night of the novel's middle section. Nor is the day's sail without its frustrations; the Ramsay boat is often suspended in its motions by the sea's "horrid calm."

James's expedition, then, like all quests, is completed only after a series of delays, trials, ordeals (the becalmed sea). Yet the most serious threat to the imagination's adventures is the resistance of "facts uncompromising," represented by Mr. Ramsay's abrupt, "But it won't be fine." The father's retort initially frustrates the expedition. Mr. Ramsay, the Old Man, is the anti-quester who mocks James's desire, reproving his reverie as the most infantile form of imagination—daydream. So abrupt and so violent is his initial appearance that the language within the novel responds with reciprocal violence: "Had there been an axe handy, or a poker, any weapon that would have gashed a hole in his father's breast and killed him, there and then, James would have seized it. Such were the extremes of emotion that Mr. Ramsay excited in his children's breasts by his mere presence" (p. 10). Innocent reverie is translated into its opposite—"guilty" patricidal fantasy excited and activated by the extremes of emotion that inform the novel's psychological and creative dialectic. This fantasy relocates the dramatic ground of the novel. The conflict is no longer between James's desire and the reality that frustrates it—facts uncompromising—but between masculine wills competing for authority. Such unspoken hostility between father and son masks a central conflict of the novel.

For Ramsay's initial act of aggression proves traumatic. The memory of thwarted desire will haunt James when, years later, on the final sail to the lighthouse, his childhood dream becomes a nightmare. When the Ramsay boat is becalmed, James becomes anxious that his father will look up and reprove him. "And if he does," James thinks, "I shall take a knife and strike him to the heart" (p. 273). But James, as he sits staring at "that old man reading," realizes that his symbolic role as patricidal avenger is inappropriate to the old man, "very sad," who once inspired his hatred. Without knowing it, James seeks a new Oedipal image "to cool and detach and round off" his hot anger:

Suppose then that as a child sitting helpless in a peram-bulator, or on some one's knee, he had seen a waggon crush ignorantly and innocently, some one's foot? Sup-pose he had seen the foot first, in the grass, smooth, and whole; then the wheel; and the same foot, purple, crushed. But the wheel was innocent. So now, when his father came striding down the passage knocking them up early in the morning to go to the Lighthouse down it came over his foot, over Cam's foot, over anybody's foot. One sat and watched it. [p. 275]

The name Oedipus in Greek means swollen foot. In the child-hood tragedy James stages in his mind, the crushed foot is linked to paternal tyranny. The Oedipal encounter between father and son does not take place at the crossroads, but in a garden, romantically linked here to the lost world of child-hood. The garden, though happy, is not innocent in desire. As James imaginatively reenters the garden, a figure, distinctly female, begins to emerge.

. . . he could see . . . a figure stooping, hear, coming close, going away, some dress rustling, some chain tinkling.
    It was in this world that the wheel went over the person's foot. Something, he remembered, stayed and darkened over him; would not move; something flour-ished up in the air; something arid and sharp descended even there, like a blade, a scimitar, smiting through the

leaves and flowers even of that happy world and making it shrivel and fall.

"It will rain," he remembered his father saying. "You won't be able to go to the Lighthouse."

The Lighthouse was then a silvery, misty-looking tower with a yellow eye, that opened suddenly, and softly in the evening. Now— [p. 276]

The faltering rhythms of this interior reverie imitate the motion of James's mind as it struggles to complete the Oedipal "play" of his emotions.[8] The phrases that interrupt the emotional continuity of his thoughts—"like a blade, a scimitar"—isolate the object of his fixation (something that "stayed and darkened over him; would not move"). The aggressive, dominating power of the father, metaphorically represented as a flourishing weapon, is associated with the avenging, punitive force that makes James's happy world shrivel and fall. The divine father and the natural father become conflated in James's mind as he attributes the terrible omnipotence of the one to the other. He now remembers, in the Freudian sense, the traumatic words of judgment that exiled him from paradise: "It will rain," echoing "But it won't be fine," the father's first words in the novel. The tyranny of paternal authority runs counter to the child's instinctual desire for the veiled feminine figure and the paradise she promises—the "misty-looking tower" with an eye that suddenly and softly

8. In her notebooks, Woolf plotted the play of James's Oedipal emotions as follows:

> James hated him
> felt the vibration in the air
> felt the emotion
> a bad emotion?
> All emotion is bad
> felt his mother's emotion
> What her emotion was
>   [Lighthouse Notebook 1/31/26]

Quoted by Harvena Richter, *The Inward Voyage,* pp. 225–26.

opens. The Old Man has a wife, James has a mother. In the eternal "Now" of his mythic memory, James is hopelessly divided between them. The Oedipal child must kill his father in order to possess his mother—and to reclaim a paradise lost.

Like the Romantics, Woolf interprets both the Christian and Oedipal myths of the Fall as fables of identity. In the novel's romantic psychomachia, the world that shrivels and falls has no reality except in James's mnemonic reconstruction of it: "But all the time he thought of her, he was conscious of his father following his thought, surveying it, making it shiver and falter. At last he ceased to think" (p. 278). More menacing than the impotence of desire is the paralyzing spectre of the father "following his thought." James does not fall because he transgresses divine or natural law; he falls when he submits to that intimidating presence whose priority cannot be denied. James's reverie declines from active dreaming to mental torpor and, finally, to the extinction of thought itself.

James's Oedipal "complex" of feelings is refracted in the mirror of the novel's family romance. Lily's painting and Mr. Ramsay's scrutiny of her progress are posited as "opposing forces" in the novel's creative dialectic. Minta Doyle, Paul Rayley, even Charles Tansley, Ramsay's academic heir, have also attached their affections and, in varying degrees, relinquished their power of self-determination to the novel's archetypal mother and father. The divided loyalties generated by the Oedipal competition to win the praise and secure the recognition of Mr. and Mrs. Ramsay excites "extremes of emotion." "I feel," wrote Woolf in "A Sketch of the Past," "that strong emotion must leave its trace; and it is only a question of discovering how we can get ourselves again attached to it, so that we shall be able to live our lives through from the start."[9] It is not the mother or father who bequeathes the

9. Virginia Woolf, "A Sketch of the Past," in *Moments of Being: Unpublished Autobiographical Writings,* ed. Jeanne Schulkind (New York: Harcourt Brace Jovanovich, 1976), p. 67.

child an image of its destiny, of its life "lived through from the start." It is the emotion generated by their compelling, if invisible, presence in the continuing life of the child that discloses the passage into the past and toward the future (to the lighthouse).

In making this subtle distinction between the Oedipal emotion and the Oedipal precursor Woolf is more careful than many of her critics in analyzing her own anxiety of influence. She never falsifies her genuine Oedipal feelings by allegorizing the parental figures as, respectively, the claims of the imagination over reason, or the artistic over the philosophic vision of the world. She credits the father, Mr. Ramsay, with his own kind of imagination. He, too, is capable of envisioning a "fabled land where our bright hopes are extinguished, our frail barks founder in darkness" (p. 11). Mr. Ramsay is also a romantic voyager, exploring the horizon of the unknown with his far-sighted vision, while his wife, constantly described as short-sighted, confines her romances to the green world of her garden. Both perceive of life and nature as essentially hostile realities to be withstood and transformed by the sheer effort of human will and human imagining. One is the genius of the shore, the other of the garden, offering their protection against "the reign of chaos." But like all governing spirits, each assumes a terrible aspect when its power over life is challenged. Woolf's elegiac tribute acknowledges both the just and unjust exercise of parental authority. If *To the Lighthouse* is cast in the form of an Oedipal dream, the dream work is primarily executed in the mind of the narrator, who records, embraces, and resolves all contradictions in thought and feeling.

The Fisherman and His Wife: The Myth of Eden

"But in what garden did all this happen?" wonders James, trying to reconstruct his happy world. His sister Cam, caught between her impulse to submit to her father or to keep her pledge to "resist tyranny to the death," looks longingly at the receding shoreline and thinks, "They have no suffering there" (p. 253). Both remember a world free from divisions of feeling, an island paradise that circumscribes and contains the innocent visions of childhood. Theirs is not a true remembrance of things past, only a mythification of them. That mythic recovery of the irrecoverable past is articulated by the shape of the novel itself—a circle that contains its end within its beginning. The form of *To the Lighthouse* images fate as the *uroboros,* the snake with the tail in its mouth, the psychic symbol, as Neumann has argued, "of the origin and of the opposites contained in it."[10] The novel's circular structure represents reality as the "*uroboric* totality" or "Great Round" out of which life is individuated and to which it is destined to return.

Presiding over the Great Round of existence is the novel's archetypal mother, Mrs. Ramsay. She is the primary focus of all feeling in the prewar idyll of "The Window," an iconic figure of idealized desire whose "royalty of form" derives not from the authority commanded by her moral being, but from the power of her extraordinary beauty. As a type of the Great and Good Mother who contains and preserves the beauty of the world in a "circle of life," Mrs. Ramsay inspires the novel's pastoral imagery, an imagery emanating from a "naive" vision of a beneficent, prolific, and artful Nature: "The graces assembling seemed to have joined hands in meadows of asphodel to compose that face" (p. 47). William Bankes's homage to her beauty invokes, necessarily, the figure of Nature's graces. Such pastoral figures reflect what Neumann designates as "the elementary character" of the eternal feminine that emphasizes the maternal aspect of the archetype and renders all consciousness, whether male or female, "childlike and dependent in their relation to it."[11] Only the fully mature artistic con-

10. Erich Neumann, *The Great Mother: An Analysis of an Archetype,* tr. Ralph Manheim (Princeton: Princeton University Press, 2nd edition, 1963), p. 18.
11. Neumann, *The Great Mother,* p. 26.

sciousness of Augustus Carmichael—the stern classicist who
invokes a Virgilian vision of history and nature in the novel—
distrusts her beauty and remains outside her sphere of influence. All other social and familial relations in "The Window"
find their primary model in the transparent "participation
mystique" of mother and child that constitutes "the original
situation of container and contained."[12] Woolf's narrative
honors the life-sustaining role of the mother as the foundation
of social life; yet it also acknowledges that dependence on the
mother is a real threat to the growth and transformation of
unreflecting life into autonomous consciousness. Paradoxically, only the estranged, self-reflective mind can penetrate
into the pathos that always informs the bonds uniting mother
and child, the pathos of inevitable separation and death embodied in the myth of Demeter and Persephone which, as in
The Winter's Tale, is the underlying season-myth in *To the
Lighthouse.* The myth of Persephone also projects the mother-
child relation as the primary aspect of nature's Great Round,
but represents death as a phase in the self-regenerating cycles
of life. Like *The Winter's Tale, To the Lighthouse* is centered in the relation between the "dead" mother and the
"lost" daughter, between things dead or dying and things
struggling to be born, a relation finally revealed and reconciled
through art.

The originating relation between mother and child, "objects
of universal veneration" (p. 81), is commemorated in Lily
Briscoe's painting, where it is abstracted and stabilized by
Christian iconology. Lily represents the "participation mystique" between mother and child in terms of a third relation,
invisible but implied, to the father. The mother in the Christian family romance is venerated primarily as a figure of intercession, mediating between earthly child and the heavenly

12. Ibid., p. 29. See also Jane Lilienfeld, "The Deceptiveness of Beauty: Mother
Love and Mother Hate in *To the Lighthouse*," *Twentieth Century Literature,* 23
(October, 1977): pp. 345–76.

father who decides its fate. The double relation of container and contained that informs the "pagan" archetype of the Good Mother is a source of ambivalence because it expresses the domination of nature over spirit. But in the Christian vision, the heavenly mother is the patron of marriage, of the conscious and moral relation embodied in the Holy Family.[13] By depicting Mrs. Ramsay as a triangular shape, Lily interprets her subject in terms of the mediated or "triangular" desire that, as René Girard has cogently demonstrated, directs the course of the novel's "metaphysical desire" and determines its central metaphor for the devious art of human relationships—the psychological circle.[14] Mrs. Ramsay's role as both the object and mediator of human desire is stressed throughout "The Window," though the full meaning of her human art is imperfectly understood, even by Lily, until years later when she finally comprehends and transcends the triangular circuits of mediated desire. Mrs. Ramsay's part in effecting Paul and Minta's engagement and her dreams for Lily and William Bankes establish her precedence in the social and emotional lives of the community centered around her. Of course, the

13. In Mrs. Ramsay's stories about Joseph and Mary, two quarrelling rooks who settle in the trees outside the Ramsays' bedroom, Woolf makes gentle fun of the Holy Family motif. Her son Jasper, who rather enjoys his mother's quaint stories, nevertheless finds great pleasure in shooting at the birds, while Rose, "who was bound to suffer," objects to his aggressive sport: "Don't you think they mind," she asks Japser, "having their wings broken?" (pp. 123 and passim).

14. René Girard, *Deceit, Desire and the Novel: Self and Other in Literary Structure*, tr. Yvonne Freccero (Baltimore: Johns Hopkins University Press, 1965), p. 300. Arguing that all great novels "always spring from an obsession that has been transcended," Girard describes the mechanism of novelistic transcendence: "The novelist's self-examination merges with the morbid attention he pays to his mediator. All the powers of a mind freed of its contradictions unite in one creative impulse" (p. 300). Certainly, such is the dialectic at play in "The Lighthouse" as Lily struggles to complete her picture and as Woolf struggles to bring her self-examining, at times morbidly self-searching narrative to a conclusion.

For a different reading of Lily's painting and its dominant psychological shapes, see Allen McLaurin, *Virginia Woolf: The Echoes Enslaved* (London: Cambridge University Press, 1973), pp. 189-200. McLaurin's reading, which investigates the influence of Roger Fry's theories of representation in Woolf's novels, is excellent, although he often trusts too extensively on the interchangeability of painterly and literary "effects."

first marriage is a failure and the second never materializes. As in Joyce's *Ulysses,* Woolf's treatment of the family romance is essentially comic, stressing the imperfect coincidence between her literary figures and their mythic ground, between her "characters" and their informing archetypes, all the while exploiting their psychological force and authority as models of imitation.

Nowhere is the distance separating figure and ground more comic—and distressing—than in Mrs. Ramsay's attempt to govern life. Lily, a virgin who would "urge her own exemption from the universal law" of marriage that Mrs. Ramsay blindly enforces, rebels against her dependence on maternal approval: "Then, she remembered, she had laid her head on Mrs. Ramsay's lap and laughed and laughed and laughed, laughed almost hysterically at the thought of Mrs. Ramsay presiding with immutable calm over destinies which she completely failed to understand" (p. 78). Mrs. Ramsay's "godlike simple certainty" is both a source of consolation and of comic frustration in the novel. One of the Jobian complaints against her is that, like all given or created divinities, she remains mindless of or deaf to the cries of unhappy or struggling life. Her serene act of knitting, the sign of her creative urge to unite the separate strands of life into a seamless unity, is simultaneously a sign of her terrible power. Her knitting makes her the mother who spins destiny, a faint but persistent echo of the Fates of antiquity who spun, measured, and cut the threads of human life. As the potential arbiter and mistress of human fate, Mrs. Ramsay incarnates the complementary and negative aspect of the eternal feminine, whose will is indomitable and whose activity does not release but entangles human lives in Nature's artful web.

The paradoxical and ambivalent nature of the feminine will is dramatized in the transaction Mrs. Ramsay conducts with life:

> A sort of transaction went on between them, in which she was on one side, and life was on another, and she was always trying to get the better of it, as it was of her; and

> sometimes they parleyed (when she sat alone); there were, she remembered, great reconciliation scenes; but for the most part, oddly enough, she must admit that she felt this thing that she called life terrible, hostile, and quick to pounce on you if you gave it a chance. There were the eternal problems: suffering; death; the poor. . . . (and the bill for the greenhouse will be fifty pounds). [p. 92]

The deeply-embedded feminine pessimism Louise Bogan detects in Woolf's sensibility finds its voice in Mrs. Ramsay's dialogue with life.[15] She bargains from a position of dread, and from the tone of these parleys one surmises that the great reconciliation scenes negotiated result in precarious balances of terror. Her "sense of life" motivates little positive action besides occasional visits of charity, cultivating her greenhouse, and insisting that "people must marry; people must have children."

The greenhouse and marriage are the rallying points for the female opposition to life. The conservatism of the eternal feminine continually works to perpetuate, never to transcend or revise the eternal round of existence. In opposing the life she deems hostile and threatening to the human order, Mrs. Ramsay merely succeeds in becoming an instrument of its recreation. The presumption of Mrs. Ramsay's thoughts is in arrogating a power that properly resides in untransformed Nature—reproduction, symbolized in her mania for marriage and child-bearing—and having done so, imagining fairy tale existences for those she has willed into life: "And yet she had said to all these children, You shall go through it all." Mrs. Ramsay's wish for her children—be they children or flowers—is that they persist in their first childhood: ". . . she had often the feeling, Why must they grow up and lose it all? And then she said to herself, brandishing her sword at life, Nonsense.

15. Louise Bogan, *The New Republic,* May 29, 1950, p. 18.

They will be perfectly happy" (p. 92). Nothing, she feels, makes up for the loss of childhood. The refrain that accompanies her reverie, "(and the bill for the greenhouse will be fifty dollars)," suggests the green world she provides to compensate for that loss. As an ultimate judgment against life, Mrs. Ramsay's thoughts are understandable, but her solution—to perpetuate childhood—is, after all, a regressive form of desire.

Mrs. Ramsay and not life reveals herself slightly tyrannical in these negotiations, and to emphasize the spiritual traps of the mother, the narrative frames Mrs. Ramsay's reveries with a fairy tale, the Grimms' "The Fisherman and his Wife," which she is reading to her son.[16] The fairy tale is a fable of sexual competition and embattled wills. A fisherman catches an enchanted fish—just as Ramsay will catch a dying mackerel—which he would release, but which his wife insists on using to improve their human lot. The plot turns on the successive wishes of the wife, each of which, when granted, generates a still greater desire. The wife first demands that their sty be turned into a manor, the manor into a castle. Her imperial dreams culminate in her desire to be Holy Roman Emperor. With the granting of each wish, a corresponding disruption occurs in the natural order, symbolized by the increasing turbulence of the sea. Those passages describing the sea in turmoil are those cited in Mrs. Ramsay's reading.

The parallel between Mrs. Ramsay's dreams and those of the fisherman's wife are highlighted in the verse that summons the enchanted fish (p. 87):

> Flounder, Flounder, in the sea,
> Come, I pray thee, here to me;
> For my wife, good Ilsabil,
> Wills not as I'd have her will.

The refrain recapitulates the conflict between sexual wills that is the implicit subject of the fairy tale. The wife's determina-

16. *The Complete Grimms' Fairy Tales* (New York: Pantheon Books, 1972), pp. 103–12.

tion to realize her dreams tyrannically overrides her husband's objections that such desires breed chaos. The imperial feminine will deems itself superior to all laws of nature, all restraints of reason. The arrogance of power, usually associated with the male in Woolf's fictional psychology, finds its most hubristic form in the female. In the fairy tale, the final wish of the fisherman's wife is to be God. Certainly, such is the unconscious, implied wish of Mrs. Ramsay in her solipsistic reveries when she dreams of ruling and reforming a world she feels to be unjust and much mismanaged. Nor does the masculine will ever approach the demonic presumption of the imperious feminine will. Even the most prideful masculine fantasies expressed in the novel confine themselves to historical and cultural dreams of eminence. Ramsay's preoccupation with human destiny is limited to anxious brooding over the future reputation of the Waverley novels and the historical verdict on the character of Napoleon, whose own imperial, titanic will stopped short of cosmic divinity.

The self-seeking, self-regarding motives disguised in the apparent beneficence of the maternal will belies the myth of innate feminine altruism. Left to her own devices and her own imaginations, the eternal feminine would, "like God himself" (p. 115), occasionally interfere with Nature's orderly design. Even Lily Briscoe, a more sexually neutral character, is prone to such feminine temptations. Musing over her picture, Lily stirs the plantains on the lawn with her brush, disturbing the horde of ants crawling among them:

> She raised a little mountain for the ants to climb over. She reduced them to a frenzy of indecision by this interference in their cosmogony. [p. 294]

This comic instance of *imitatio dei* ("this interference in their cosmogony") is directly followed by the problem of "seeing" Mrs. Ramsay and tracing the labyrinthine divagations of her will: "Fifty pairs of eyes were not enough to get round that one woman with, she thought. Among them, must be one that

was stone blind to her beauty" (p. 294). Lily, blinded by the
luminous beauty of the mother, cannot discern that her own
unconscious motions provide the best commentary on Mrs.
Ramsay's "thoughts, her imaginations, her desires": "What did
the hedge mean to her, what did the garden mean to her, what
did it mean to her when a wave broke?" (p. 294). The multiple
and often antithetical meanings generated by the mother's
imagination are expressed in the green world of hedge and
garden she creates to insulate the community centered in her
from the breaking of the waves. The garden, the work of the
feminine will, belongs, however, to the tradition of the Renaissance gardens of bliss.

As the presiding genius of the earthly paradise, the Good
Mother is transfigured and apprehended in her opposite—the
siren or Circean demigoddess whose enchantments lure the
unsuspecting towards death. "Steer, hither steer your winged
pines, all beaten Mariners" (p. 179) is a line Mrs. Ramsay
casually reads aloud in her husband's presence, unaware that
she is singing a siren's song. The line is from William Browne's
"Siren Song," a poem which merits quoting because it qualifies the sentimental vision of Mrs. Ramsay's maternal art by
hinting at its demonic aspect:

> Steer hither, steer your winged pines,
>   All beaten mariners!
> Here lie Love's undiscovered mines,
>   A prey to passengers;
> Perfumes far sweeter than the best
> Which makes the Phoenix' urn and nest.
>   Fear not your ships,
> Nor any to oppose you save our lips;
>   But come on shore
> Where no joy dies till love hath gotten more.
> For swelling waves, our panting breasts
>   Where never storms arise,

> Exchange; and be awhile our guests:
>> For stars, gaze on our eyes.
> The compass Love shall hourly sing,
> As he goes about the ring,
>> We will not miss
> To tell each point he nameth with a kiss.
>> Then come on shore,
> Where no joy dies till love hath gotten more.[17]

The siren sings of "Love's undiscovered mines," promising the mariners the security of a "shore / Where no joy dies till love hath gotten more." The exchange of the sea's treachery for the sensual paradise is the promise of the alluring siren who, like Mrs. Ramsay, enthralls the imagination by "the deceptiveness of beauty, so that all one's perceptions, half way to truth, were tangled in a golden mesh" (p. 78). The feminine power to create a circle of life now describes the great round of a wanton nature, the ceaseless and indiscriminate regeneration of life that is only found in a lower paradise. Now the ring of desire is transformed into the chain of necessity, symbolizing the mysteries of nature's negative transformations. And the artful web spun by the mistress of destiny ensnares and entangles the imagination in the deceptive beauty of appearances, the veil of Maya.

In the novel's interpolation of the Grimms' cautionary tale, Mrs. Ramsay is the wife whose beauty and promise of sheltered life would lure the husband-mariner from his appointed destiny as the Ulyssean adventurer into the unknown. Mr. Ramsay's insistence that the sea represents the true condition of man corrects and complements Mrs. Ramsay's pastoral imaginings. Woolf's portrait of the father represents him as the hero of thought, the rationalist and philosophic realist who

17. William Browne, *Inner Temple Masque,* reprinted in *Elizabethan Lyrics,* ed. Norman Ault (New York: Capricorn Books, 1960), pp. 462–63.

delineates the boundaries between subject and object that the maternal will trespasses in its search for unity. Despite the undercurrent of burlesque, Mr. Ramsay's agonies in exploring the alphabet of thought, the A to Z that represents the inexorably linear, temporal nature of reality are signs of an authentic destiny:

> It was his fate, his peculiarity, whether he wished it or not, to come out thus on a spit of land which the sea is slowly eating away, and there to stand, like a desolate sea-bird, alone. It was his power, his gift, suddenly to shed all superfluities, to shrink and diminish so that he looked barer and felt sparer, even physically, yet lost none of his intensity of mind, and so to stand on his little ledge facing the dark of human ignorance, how we know nothing and the sea eats away the ground we stand on—that was his fate, his gift. [pp. 68-69]

Woolf's vision of the male fate is inevitably Victorian, just as her vision of the sea that comprises our "final destiny" is predictably Arnoldian. Like the speaker of "Dover Beach," Ramsay stations himself on the shore "where ignorant armies clash by night." The isolation and desolation of his outpost contrasts to "the house . . . full of children sleeping . . . shaded lights and regular breathing" that represent "the best of life" to the feminine will. For the female imagination is pietistic and ultimately comic in its faith in regeneration, custom, and transfiguration. The feminine vision absorbs the individuating fact of death in its own ecstatic auguries of transfiguration, even as Lily's knowledge of Mrs. Ramsay's death is transformed into a vision that portends resurrection: "For days after she had heard of her death she had seen her thus, putting her wreath to her forehead and going unquestioningly with her companion, a shade across the fields" (p. 270). The apotheosis of Mrs. Ramsay into a nature goddess, signalled by the royal gesture of self-coronation, is testimony to the feminine faith in transfiguration, a faith beyond the arguments of reason and the evidence of facts uncompromising.

No such transfiguration is conceivable for the male, whose sense of life remains tragic: "We perished each alone." Mr. Ramsay's vision is without shade or shadow ("it spared no phantoms"), opposing the instinctive piety of his wife ("We are in the hands of the Lord," a sentiment Mrs. Ramsay knows to be false even as she murmurs it) with his own stern agnosticism. The real distinction between husband and wife lies in the tragic starkness of his vision and the comic abundance of hers. This is the generic difference between his "fatal sterility" and her "delicious fecundity"—in the "nature" of the world each envisions. Both the fisherman and his wife are united by their common cause against the "fluidity out there." But each responds to the flux differently. Mrs. Ramsay, in the novel's symbolic topography, is at the center of a circle of life which encloses a green world of gardens and marriage. That circle is located in the heart of nature, in a hollow, on an island. Ramsay's station is at the circumference of that circle, on the shore, the very point where the sea is eating the ground we stand on. He positions himself at the edge of the floods, a "stake driven into the bed of a channel." Implied in the figurative relation of fisherman and wife is that Ramsay centers himself in the floods, the flux of life, without being overwhelmed. He demystifies the romantic, essentially feminine mystique of death by drowning. As a male principle he embodies the resistance to engulfment that the maternal will commends. Both he and his wife have destinies linked to the sea, but in the nautical metaphor the novel employs to distinguish various ways of sailing over the seas of life, he is the leader of the doomed expedition who would die standing, she the reluctant mariner who "would have whirled round and round and found rest on the floor of the sea" (p. 127). The egotistical man, Mr. Ramsay presses the claims of the individual over the undifferentiated flow. He upholds the authority of "I-I-I" over the anarchy of oceanic feelings.

If the fisherman and his wife have real differences of opinion, they are still married. Differences of will are not as important in *To the Lighthouse* as the love that reconciles those differences. Mr. and Mrs. Ramsay's love is an example of united wills in the private sphere: "Directly one looked up and saw them, what she [Lily] called 'being in love' flooded them" (p. 72). Being in love is an ideal state, like matrimony, of cooperating wills. In the novel's evocation of ideal love, Ramsay's is the responsible vision that makes Mrs. Ramsay's irresponsibility possible.

> . . . she let it uphold her and sustain her, this admirable
> fabric of the masculine intelligence, which ran up and
> down, crossed this way and that, like iron girders spanning the swaying fabric, upholding the world, so that she
> could trust herself to it utterly, even shut her eyes, or
> flicker them for a moment, as a child staring up from its
> pillow winks at the myriad layers of the leaves of a tree.
> [p. 159]

The masculine intelligence is the rational foundation on which human order, dry land itself, rests. This order is inclusive of what is generally called culture—science, mathematics, history, art, the social questions. The female transformative power, which seeks its expressive images in dream and fancy, leans on and trusts to this masculine solidity and can contemplate nature's infinite variety ("the myriad layers") without anxiety (like a child). Once the male organizes the flux and erects that fortress, civilization, nature does seem to murmur a cradle song to soothe the dreaming maternal will.

The cooperation of male and female wills underlies the novel's veiled myth of marriage as Eden, a paradisaical state in which the relationship between subject and object, self and world is spiritualized into the union of lover and beloved. Love translates the imagination out of "fallen" reality into "that unreal but penetrating and exciting universe which is the world seen through the eyes of love" (p. 73). Love projects a world of perfect correspondences that the lover can perceive in absolute, although transient intuitions of meaning. In this unreal universe objects become signs and signs become symbols—of the self. In Eden, nature becomes an extended metaphor of creation:

> It was odd, she thought, how if one was alone, one leant to inanimate things; trees, streams, flowers; felt they expressed one; felt they became one; felt they knew one, in a sense were one; felt an irrational tenderness thus . . . as for oneself. There rose, and she looked and looked with her needles suspended, there curled up off the floor of the mind, rose from the lake of one's being, a mist, a bride to meet her lover. [pp. 97-98]

The bride rising from the depths is feminized desire, compared to a mist in its suffusive drive to merge with the object it contemplates through love. The lover in this liaison is the fertilizing power that transforms inanimate things into intimate, meaningful expressions of the self. Out of this mating of mind and its world is generated the thing that endures, which is also the thing that signifies and satisfies the self's quest for meaning: "It is enough! It is enough!"

The love between men and women, husbands and wives, is a recurrent metaphor for mental ecstasy and successful creation throughout *To the Lighthouse,* from Mrs. Ramsay's private raptures to the communal feast in honor of Paul and Minta's emerging love. But the novel's most moving celebration of marital love is Ramsay's final benediction of human community, the refrain he intones at the conclusion of the dinner party (p. 166):

> Come out and climb the garden path,
>   Luriana Lurilee.
> The China rose is all abloom and buzzing with
>   the yellow bee.

The verse celebrates an Arcadian vision of generation and fecundity. The child's paradise, James's naive dream of a happy garden, does fall before the oppressive figure of the father, but *To the Lighthouse* canonically interprets the child's exile as a *felix culpa*. The child falls, but the garden remains, now purged of profane desire. The father, like Cronos, is a paradoxical figure, a merciless tyrant who eats his children but whose reign is memorialized as the golden age of man.[18]

Comedy's Agape

Ramsay's is a necessary tyranny, for his authority legitimizes familial love by repressing its erotic, essentially Oedipal components. Once the father socializes the libido, love is purged of its destructive desires, and the mother is released to perform her proper function. The father can only maintain order in the private sphere. It is the mother who translates private love into communal love—*agape*. The dinner over which Mrs. Ramsay presides is an expression of the total form of love, a secular equivalent of the love feasts of religious communities. The female toil is to give shape, order, and direction to the community which centers around her but lacks expression: "Nothing seemed to have merged. They all sat separate. And the whole of the effort of merging and flowing and creating rested on her" (p. 126). Resisting creative union in love are the separate selves that compose the party and are not aware of their relation to the social composition. The egotistic "I" that resists the impulse to merge and flow with life is here a negative attribute. For Virginia Woolf, the ideal self has a finely developed sense of decorum. It knows when to resist, when to submit. In a social context, the male principle of resistance is not heroic, but stubborn. To resist nature's rhythms is

18. See Robert Graves, *The Greek Myths: 1* (Baltimore: Penguin Books, 1972), p. 40.

necessary, but to impede the flow of social rhythms is bar-
barous. Mrs. Ramsay's appeal to Lily Briscoe—

> I am drowning, my dear, in seas of fire. Unless you apply
> some balm to the anguish of this hour and say something
> nice to that young man there, life will run upon the rocks
> [p. 138]

—demonstrates her concern with social, not sea life, with
human rather than marine rhythms. The familiar pulse she sets
beating "as the watch begins ticking" is a mechanical one, the
tick of a watch rather than the heartbeat, and like the watch,
an artifact, must be continually rewound.

The conscious artifices Mrs. Ramsay employs to mask and
merge self-assertive, dissident impulses into a unified order of
life testify to the pragmatic comic guile of the feminine imagination. Mrs. Ramsay's "social manner" derives its authority
and efficacy from its generic origin in the comic vision. Her
social art exploits the stylization of speech and gesture that
devolve from comedy's filial dependence on its parent forms—
rite, pageant, and feast. The language of these social rituals,
like the official language of diplomacy, is rooted in a necessary
conventionality. To obtain unity, one must "speak French":

> Perhaps it is bad French; French may not contain the
> words that express the speaker's thoughts; nevertheless
> speaking French imposes some order, some uniformity.
> [pp. 135-36]

The acknowledged conventionality of social discourse creates
a common ground of exchange in which private utterance is
translated into a public speech that may "not express the
speaker's thoughts" yet does silence "the strife of tongues"
that is the most divisive threat to dialogue. As the linguistic
analogy implies, Woolf trusts to the formulaic properties of
language, however trivial, non-sensical, or abused in common
usage, to communicate the unapprehended harmonies and

agreements that comic art can best discover. It is by articulating the shared relations of social life that the comic imagination creates a whole out of its stubborn, disparate parts.

The meaning of this comic work of art is inalienable from the structure of relations it articulates. The community Mrs. Ramsay brings into existence is not created *ex nihilo, in imitatio dei.* The work of the imagination, like the work of Eden, is to give an ordered and visible expression to the concord wrought by love. The aesthetic composition that discovers the material forms languishing in nature finds its concrete symbol in the fruit bowl prepared by Rose. The cornucopia, which makes Mrs. Ramsay think of a "trophy fetched from the bottom of the sea" (p. 146) visually reasserts the vital relationship between nature's boundless fertility and the "delicious fecundity" of the feminine imagination in containing that abundance within a determinate form. This fertile union of art and nature, of which Eden is the preeminent and perennial example, is reenacted whenever the external order of nature or society mirrors the internal harmonies of that unreal, but penetrating universe which is the world seen through the eyes of love. As the artist's *agape* or unifying power infuses each member of the community, the empty rituals of social life revive their ancient connection with nature's transformative mysteries. The dinner table, previously a masculine symbol of the philosophical problem in discriminating subject, object, and the nature of reality, assumes, in its feminine character, a numinous aspect. It becomes a sacred site, the altar for communion rites by which love is distributed throughout the community of belief.

The positive transformations of the feminine will, ritually commemorated in the preparation of foods (the Boeuf en Daube, a "triumph" of feminine art), attest to the power of maternal love to nourish and sustain life. In the ritual moment of transfiguration, signalled by the radiance of Minta's sexual glow, love gives birth to the illusion that is both the triumph and the mockery of the human community it has brought into

being. The doubleness of the novel's social vision is incorporated and inspired by the doubleness of the love the worship-
pers, under Mrs. Ramsay's aegis, celebrate: "for what could be
more serious than the love of man for woman, what more
commanding, more impressive, bearing in its bosom the seeds
of death; at the same time these lovers, these people entering
into illusion glittering eyed, must be danced round with
mockery, decorated with garlands" (p. 151). The mother
creates the illusion of self-generating, self-containing life, the
great round of existence that bears within itself the "seeds of
death." It is not love that dies, but the illusions it generates,
and for this reason those out of love can afford to mock the
maternal vision they revere. Mockery is also part of ritual, its
mode of insuring that the human order will not relapse into
the compacted center of unorganized, unconscious life.
Mockery places the community celebrating the power of love
"trembling on the verge" of that circle of life that excludes
and is unaware of them. On the threshold between nature and
culture that mockery delineates, those out of love can share in
the dream of love without being absorbed into it; they can
regard the hollowness of the illusion without denying its
human necessity: "there is nothing more tedious, puerile, and
inhumane than this; yet it is also beautiful and necessary"
(p. 155). Only Paul and Minta, whose love will die, and Prue,
"just beginning, just moving, just descending" into the dream,
are unaware of the fatality of love. For Prue, who will marry
and die in childbirth, life is a condensed allegory on the processes of love. But ignorant of the destiny love holds for her, she
too greets "the sun of the love of men and women" (p. 164).

That sun soon sets. The mother's twilight vision of a community rescued from impending darkness and division eva-
nesces the moment it is achieved: "it had become . . . already
the past" (p. 168). The mother's vision is constrained by its
own fixation on surfaces and the cycles of mutability. When
Mrs. Ramsay joins her husband in the study after dinner, she
needs to "go deeper" than her own vision of life permits, to

get, as she says "something" from him. Though they sit in
silence, something does communicate itself from him to her.
This "something" that extends and deepens her consciousness
is "the life . . . the power of it," of Scott's novel, *The Antiquary,* which Mr. Ramsay, to his great pleasure, is reading. The
episode Ramsay reads concerns the sorrow of Mucklebackit
over the death by drowning of his fisherman son, thus sum-
marizing and expanding on the theme of drowning and re-
absorption into nature that always accompanies, as if by qualification, the celebration of the maternal will. The central
figure in the funeral scene alluded to is not the drowned
corpse, nor the bereaved father, but the "crazed old woman"
who mourns the loss of the young fisherman. Like Mrs.
Ramsay, the old woman of Scott's novel sits weaving, mechani-
cally "twirling her spindle" either unaware or uninterested in
the life around her. The allusion is important, for it uncovers
the obsessive force in Woolf's elegy on the lost mother, now
remembered and imagined as an old woman, consort to the old
man or father. Scott's description of the old woman prefigures
Mrs. Ramsay's eventual status in the community she weaves
and holds together:

> Thus she sat among the funeral assembly like a connect-
> ing link between the surviving mourners and the dead
> corpse which they bewailed—a being in whom the light of
> existence was already obscured by the encroaching shad-
> ows of death.[19]

The child's fixation on the old man, whose death is desired, is
transferred to the old woman, whose death is inevitable. In the
child's vision of the lost mother, a vision shared by the narrative commemorating her, Mrs. Ramsay is the link between the
mystical "body of life" of the community she has created and
which will survive her and the body of death. The proleptic

19. Walter Scott, *The Antiquary* (Boston and New York: Houghton Mifflin
Company, 1912), vol. 2, chapter 31, p. 4.

shadows that obscure the old woman's "light of existence" subtly penetrate Mrs. Ramsay's mind as she reads a sonnet by Shakespeare:

> From you have I been absent in the spring,
> When proud-pied April, dressed in all his trim,
> Hath put a spirit of youth in everything,
> That heavy Saturn laughed and leapt with him;
> Yet nor the lays of birds, nor the sweet smell
> Of different flowers in odor and in hue,
> Could make me any summer's story tell,
> Or from their proud lap pluck them where they grew,
> Nor did I wonder at the lily's white,
> Nor praise the deep vermilion in the rose;
> They were but sweet, but figures of delight,
> Drawn after you, you pattern of all those.
> > Yet seemed it winter still, and you away,
> > As with your shadow I with these did play.[20]

In the novel's narrative time, the day is mid-September. But in its larger temporal configurations, *To the Lighthouse* is a winter's tale. It concerns itself with the death of the beloved queen mother and her resurrection through art. The luxuriant pastoral landscapes of "The Window" cannot make the narrator, any more than the sonneteer, "any summer's story tell." The flowers in both literary gardens are but "figures of delight," patterns or emblems that ultimately derive their beauty and their significance from the original figure of delight, or cynosure, Mrs. Ramsay.[21] Only in her physical presence does the beauty of the natural world assert itself. The final couplet of the sonnet prefigures the eventual eclipse of the luminous autumnal vision of "The Window." Lily's insight that love is solemn because it bears within it the seeds of death is thematically expanded in Woolf's evocation of this Shakespearean

---

20. William Shakespeare, *Sonnets,* ed. Douglas Bush and Alfred Harbage (Baltimore: Penguin Books, 1970), Sonnet 98.
21. Cf. Avrom Fleishman, *Virginia Woolf: A Critical Reading,* p. 128.

vision of love. The death of Mrs. Ramsay will inaugurate a winter mood of negation, and the seeds of death will blossom into the flowers of darkness that overrun her garden in "Time Passes."

Time's Chorus

I, that please some, try all, both joy and terror
Of good and bad, that makes and unfolds error,
Now take upon me, in the name of Time,
To use my wings. . . . Let me pass
The same I am, ere ancient'st order was
Or what is now received. I witness to
The times that brought them in; so shall I do
To th' freshest things now reigning, and make stale
The glistering of this present, as my tale
Now seems to it. Your patience this allowing,
I turn my glass and give my scene such growing
As you had slept between.

                                         [*The Winter's Tale,* IV, i]

Time's chorus in *The Winter's Tale* is the best gloss on the imaginative action of "Time Passes." In both interludes, the unity of time, by which a tale of family jealousy, division and atonement is compressed into two momentous days, is suspended. The mirror held up to life is turned, exposing its opaque back. This lapsus in representation Shakespeare compares to that eclipse of consciousness that occurs when sleep overcomes the mind, sealing it off from the light by which the world is perceived or reflected.

"Time Passes" is an extension of that visionary night when consciousness is overwhelmed and submits to the darkness that surrounds it. "Well, we must wait for the future to show," says Mr. Bankes at the close of the day, echoing Time's injunction "let Time's news / Be known when 'tis brought forth." As night envelops the sleepers, all human shapes and natural forms become blurred and eventually undifferentiated from the "profusion of darkness" flooding the world:

> Not only was furniture confounded; there was scarcely anything left of body or mind by which one could say "This is he," or "This is she." Sometimes a hand was raised as if to clutch something or ward off something, or somebody groaned, or somebody laughed aloud as if sharing a joke with nothingness. [p. 190]

Sharing that joke with nothingness is the narrator, the only waking consciousness left on the deserted island, herself disembodied, a voice whistling in the dark. The narrator is the one sleeper "tempted from his bed to seek an answer," searching for some "image with semblance of serving and divine promptitude [to bring] the night to order and [to make] the world reflect the compass of the soul" (p. 193). But all that remains in the world are the broken fragments of vision, empty forms "from which life had parted":

> What people had shed and left—a pair of shoes, a shooting cap, some faded skirts and coats in wardrobes—those alone kept the human shape and in the emptiness indicated how once they were filled and animated; . . . how once the looking-glass had held a face; had held a world hollowed out in which a figure turned, a hand flashed . . . [p. 194]

The human shape is neither reflected nor imprinted in the looking-glass art holds up to life. There are no vital signs in this universe of death, emptiness, vacancy. The estrangement between consciousness, which seeks order, and nature, which languishes in its disorder, is rendered in the double narration of "Time Passes." The lyrical sequences are soliloquies in which time's mirror is turned inward, reflecting the struggles of the narrative consciousness to reimagine a human order.

The bracketed portions represent the victory of the narrator in rescuing humanly decisive events from the vast stretches of indifferent time that surround them. The death of Mrs. Ramsay, Prue's marriage, Prue's and Andrew's deaths, and the war are recorded in a series of brackets which typographically enclose and thus preserve historical or human moments from the chaos of undifferentiated existence that threatens to absorb them. The toil of the narrator is reduced to an elementary yet necessary function: to record or chronicle, to mark time according to the human measure of passage—marriage, childbirth, death, human loss (the death of Mrs. Ramsay) and human achievement (the publication of Carmichael's poems). Such moments are protected from "the insensibility of Nature" that observes only her own relentless rhythms, without aim or direction.

The narrative mind approaches autism in the face of this insensibility of nature. The visionary nadir of the novel occurs at the moment when the sights affirmed to be "tokens of divine bounty"—"the sunset on the sea, the pallor of dawn"— are overshadowed by "the silent apparition of an ashen-coloured ship" (p. 201). The narrator enters into a Coleridgean nightmare in which a ship, James's symbol of romantic voyaging, becomes a ship of fools or a ship of death, and the bland surface of the sea is stained "as if something had boiled and bled, invisibly, beneath" (p. 201). In contemplating the spectral ship Life-in-Death and the sea of corruption, the narrator is forced to interrogate her own orderings, to acknowledge the groundlessness of her "sublime reflections" that the beauty outside mirrored the beauty within. Her mind despairs in imagining that which has no conceivable image, the vitalism of nature, or, as it is traditionally called, the sublime:

> Did Nature supplement what man advanced? Did she complete what he began? With equal complacence she saw his misery, his meanness, and his torture. That dream, of sharing, completing, of finding in solitude on

the beach an answer, was then but a reflection in a
mirror, and the mirror itself but the surface glassiness
which forms in quiescence when the nobler powers sleep
beneath? Impatient, despairing, yet loth to go . . . to pace
the beach was impossible; contemplation was unen-
durable; the mirror was broken. [pp. 201-02]

The "Nature" of the sublime is that which diminishes
human power relative to its own. Sublime Nature does not
"share the dreamer's solitude," but intensifies his consciousness of alienation. Sublime Nature does not exalt the dreamer
but mirrors in her complacent gaze "his misery, his meanness,
and his torture." The mirror that reflects the human dream of
order is but a surface glassiness that does not intensify, but
anaesthetizes "the nobler powers" of the mind. This is a
rationalist critique of imagination as baseless dream and comes
close to identifying vision with the irrational or unconscious
power. This self-critical impulse issues from that part of the
narrative consciousness obsessed and paralyzed by the figure
of the father, whose insistence on "facts uncompromising"
constitutes a perpetual restraint on the child's imaginative
freedom. With the mother, Mrs. Ramsay, dead, those finely
wrought, necessary feminine illusions—what Woolf calls
"beauty"—can no longer claim an equal authority with masculine "Truth." Truth, in its limited, masculine sense of factual
reality, breaks the mirror of beauty:

Listening (had there been any one to listen) from the
upper rooms of the empty house only gigantic chaos
streaked with lightning could have been heard tumbling
and tossing, as the winds and waves disported themselves
like the amorphous bulks of leviathans whose brows are
pierced by no light of reason, and mounted one on top of
another, and lunged and plunged in the darkness or the
daylight (for night and day, month and year ran shape-
lessly together) in idiot games, until it seemed as if the

universe were battling and tumbling, in brute confusion
and wanton lust aimlessly by itself. [pp. 202–03]

When the mirror breaks, the imagination suffers an apocalyptic night in which all Nature reverts back to that "gigantic
chaos" in which no shape, form, or light presents itself to the
inquisitorial mind searching for semblances, orderings, meanings in and for itself. This is the dream that is a nightmare, an
unreal and penetrating universe populated with terrifying
forms, a universe energized by wanton lust, not love, a universe that confounds the dreams of reason with its own brute
confusions. Imagination finds its daimon symbolized in the
biblical Leviathan, the body of death that swallows up the
created forms of life. And it finds its nihilism expressed in a
Schopenhauerian vision of Nature as the pure and wanton will
that mocks the human idea of order. In the "idiot games" of
nature the narrator finds a metaphor for her own mad, light-
deprived mind that beholds, but cannot transform, the vital
chaos it contemplates.

The novel's most powerful symbol of this human debacle is
the ruined garden. Cast out of Eden, man falls into history, the
nightmare from which he vainly tries to awake. Nature's wanton
ways go unopposed: "Nothing now withstood them; nothing
said no to them" (p. 208). The mortal "No" to the indiscriminate and wanton will of nature could have been the imagination's "yes" to its own power to order, contain, and restrain
the "fall" of Nature. The refusal to oppose Nature's decline
into disorder, a sign of a corrupt or enervated will, motivates
a grammatical declension from the merely passive to the
optative mood:

Let the wind blow; let the poppy seed itself and the carnation mate with the cabbage. Let the swallow build in
the drawing-room, and the thistle thrust aside the tiles,
and the butterfly sun itself on the faded chintz of the
arm-chairs. Let the broken glass and the china lie out on

the lawn and be tangled over with grass and wild berries.
[p. 208]

This demonic litany invoking the powers of darkness and disorder is a direct and ironic inversion of the sexual benediction
that concluded the dinner party. One summons to paradise,
where art orders nature in determinate forms, the other enjoins
acceptance and resignation to the fallen, unregenerate world.

But in the circular paradigm of *To the Lighthouse* all falling
is a prelude to rising, all death a necessary stage of regeneration. Rising out of the universal silence are the "witless" songs
of Mrs. McNab, the inarticulate yet unyielding voice of opposition and resistance to Nature's insensibility. The hope that
speaks through her "dirge" is precisely this feminine faith in
the triumph of cyclical over linear time, the comic over the
tragic view of natural and human history. Her "dream of a
lady" springs from the female's natural and abiding faith in
resurrection, the spring that must follow winter. In that dream
is preserved the "everlasting yea" that silences doubt in action
and overcomes despair in the energy of labor. Her dirge modulates into a hymn to human toil by which the imagination
issues its own ultimatum to Nature: "Be no longer a chaos, but
a World."[22] The reclamation of the garden becomes the heroic
work of the resurgent will that, as in Carlyle's *Sartor Resartus,*
finds its ideal world, its "kingdom wherein to rule and create,"
in "this poor, miserable, hampered, despicable actual": "Up,
up! Whatsoever thy hand findeth to do, do it with thy whole
might. Work while it is called Today; for the Night cometh,
wherein no man can work."[23]

The rescue of the garden from the vast pool of time threatening to reclaim it is not, however, without its cosmic suspense:

For now had come that moment, that hesitation when
dawn trembles and night pauses, when if a feather alight

22. Thomas Carlyle, *Sartor Resartus* (Garden City, N.Y.: Halcyon House, 1942),
p. 197.
23. Ibid.

in the scale it will be weighed down. One feather, and the house, sinking, falling, would have turned and pitched downwards to the depths of darkness. [p. 208]

Not just the garden, but creation itself is suspended in the balance between eternal night and the breaking day, between Nature's insensibility and man's conscientious toil. The cosmic precariousness of the creative moment in which imagination dictates to chaos, "Be a World," is conveyed in that feather weight that could tip the scales, consigning the visible universe to darkness and oblivion.

This cosmic suspense repeats itself in a human register in Lily Briscoe's existential waking-up scene that concludes "Time Passes." As Lily sleeps on her first night at the Ramsay home, the voices of the night enjoin her to "accept this, be content with this, acquiesce and resign" (p. 214). But Lily resists the stupefying songs of nature and is released from the spell cast on her mind. Once disenchanted, she is delivered from the final and fatal plunge into the abyss, that night wherein no man can work:

She clutched at her blankets as a faller clutches at the turf on the edge of a cliff. Her eyes opened wide. Here she was again, she thought, sitting bolt upright in bed. Awake. [p. 214]

"The Grace of Androgyny"

The last word—Awake—ends the demonic sleep that commenced in "Time Passes" and reveals the intervening passage of time to be a nightmare, both real and imagined. Far from being a "break of unity in [the] design" (*WD*, p. 79), "Time Passes" is a condensation and inversion of the novel's completed structure. It is a dream within the dream that constitutes the novel's total form. It is also the nightmare that ruins the dream of peace "the dreamers dreamt holily, dreamt wisely, to confirm" (p. 213). The dream work of "The Lighthouse" then becomes the work of reconfirming the dream of peace that is the legacy of the mother.[24]

But the dream work is made difficult by the radical discontinuity between the prewar idyll celebrated in "The Window" and the present, postwar moment of "The Lighthouse." The war and the death of Mrs. Ramsay are experiences linked in the communal mind the novel represents. The collapse of Britain as an imperial power, foreshadowed in Ramsay's constant quotation of Tennyson's "The Charge of the Light Brigade," is associated with the collapse of Mrs. Ramsay's imperial dream of peace. In some sense, "Time Passes" elaborates Woolf's claim that "On or about December 1910 human nature changed,"[25] although in the novel her conscious hyperbole is historically defensible in viewing the world war as the event that permanently disassociated the sensibility of modern man.

Lily Briscoe wakes from the nightmare, then, only to encounter the waking nightmare of the shaken present. Like the rest of the survivors of "Time Passes," she cannot recapture nor move beyond the dream of the past. Musing on the lawn, only one moment presents itself to Lily's mind, a moment with Mrs. Ramsay on the beach, writing letters: "Why, after all these years had that survived, ringed round, lit up, visible to the last detail, with all before it blank and all after it blank, for miles and miles?" (p. 254). Lily's memory rings round a

24. Technically, the dream work, as Freud defines it in *The Interpretation of Dreams,* consists in translating the latent "dream-thoughts" into the dream's manifest content, a work performed through the condensation, displacement, symbolic representation, and secondary revision of the dream-thoughts. My discussion of "The Lighthouse" is dependent on Freud's useful observation that the dream-content produced through the work of dreaming is "like a transcript of the dream thoughts," a pictographic script (Freud's analogy) in which characters or inscriptions must be read or interpreted according to their symbolic relation and not according to their pictorial value. Lily, as I will demonstrate, clearly thinks of her own painting as a heiroglyphic script which seeks to encode the "dream-thoughts" she attributes to Mrs. Ramsay. See Freud, *The Interpretation of Dreams, Standard Edition,* vol. 4, p. 277.
25. "Mr. Bennett and Mrs. Brown," in *Collected Essays,* vol. 1, p. 320.

moment in time, tracing a circle of life with Mrs. Ramsay at its center. But the numinous figure of the mother inhabits "a centre of complete emptiness" (p. 266); she is a vivid memory, a presence by virtue of an absence. Lily's hope, the hope of all mourners, persists that "the space would fill; those empty flourishes would form into shape; . . . Mrs. Ramsay would return" (p. 268). "About life, about death, about Mrs. Ramsay"—Lily feels that if the three can be brought into conjunction, their relations would reveal the mystery of the world: "If only she could put them together, she felt, write them out in some sentence, then she would have got at the truth of things" (p. 219).

The ideal sentence would compose an epitaph, linking life and death in the image of "one life." But that sentence is never composed, nor are the "sacred inscriptions" written by Mrs. Ramsay and secured in the sanctuary of her being ever read or decoded. *To the Lighthouse* assumes a more expansive form than epitaph—the elegy, whose primary subject, as Coleridge reminds us, is not the figure of the beloved dead, but the tormented life of the poet who survives. "To want and not to have—to want and want" is the elegiac cry of frustrated desire, expressing the grief and anger the living feel toward the dead who abandon them.

Ramsay's repeated quotations of the final lines of Cowper's "The Castaway" incorporate this elegiac grief in the novel's underlying myth of the fisherman and his wife. In Cowper's poem, the elegist equates the physical peril of the castaway with the interior condition of the poet who "of friends, of hope, of all bereft / His floating home forever left."[26] The despairing but courageous self of Cowper's elegy resembles and illuminates Ramsay's mind as he hears MacAlister's tale of the "great storm" in which three ships sank. Ramsay, like the other survivors of "Time Passes," is an emotional castaway

26. William Cowper, "The Castaway," from *Cowper: Verse and Letters,* selected by Brian Spiller (Cambridge, Mass.: Harvard University Press, 1965), pp. 138–40.

whose sole remaining delight is "to trace" the semblance of his grief "in another's case." So Ramsay "relished the thought of the storm and the dark night and the fisherman striving there" (p. 245) because he finds in that story a confirmation of his personal, tragic sense of life. Cowper's emphasis on destiny and fatality dovetails with Ramsay's continuous meditations on our final destiny, how we perished each alone. The sudden reversal that concludes "The Castaway"—"But I beneath a rougher sea / And whelmed in deeper gulphs than he"—redefines the structure and content of tragic destiny. The survivor, not the victim of death, becomes the authentic tragic figure. The tragic fate is not death, but the engulfment of the self by forces that extinguish hope, but not life.

Ramsay, like all honest mourners, mourns for himself. His elegiac lamentations begin in self-pity and conclude in self-justification. Elegy can displace, but it can never disguise its origin in the indomitable egoism of the living. Woolf's understanding of the psychology of mourning accounts for her generally sympathetic portrait of the father as supreme Egoist. In the tradition of Meredith, she would and does allow that, for all his petty tyrannies and self-indulgences, the Egoist is fundamentally a comic figure who "surely inspires pity":

> He who would desire to clothe himself at everybody's expense and is of that desire condemned to strip himself stark naked, he, if pathos ever had a form, might be taken for the actual person. Only he is not allowed to rush at you, roll you over and squeeze your body for the briny drops. There is the innovation [of comedy].[27]

Ramsay's constant demands for sympathy, the immense pressure of his concentrated woe, the horror of his effusive lamentations are tolerated in the novel because, for all his overweening egoism, Ramsay embodies, as Meredith says, the very form of pathos. That is why it is to Lily's immense discredit

27. George Meredith, *The Egoist* (New York: W. W. Norton, 1979), p. 6.

sexually to stand dumb in the presence of his desolation. But it is also why her cheerful remark, "What beautiful boots!" actually consoles Ramsay, for the remark, comically inappropriate to the scope of his self-pity, represents a redeeming innovation of comedy. Mr. Ramsay smiles at the non sequitur and animatedly protests that "Bootmakers make it their business to cripple the human foot" (p. 229). The Oedipal preoccupation with damaged feet is comically absorbed and displaced in Ramsay's momentary lapse into the particulars of ordinary existence. Obsession is disguised and forgotten in this renewed interest in immediate life, ushering Lily into "a sunny island where peace dwelt, sanity reigned and the sun for ever shone, the blessed island of good boots" (p. 230). Ramsay's egoism, which like the Oedipal fable is a source of the novel's underlying pathos, is transformed through the sane and peaceful perspectives of comic art. The innovation of comedy is to represent the pathos of egoism, while delimiting its power to rush and roll over all other life. From the father, the daughter inherits the egoism and self-concern necessary for her own survival; from him she learns the potential tragedy of her own life. But she trusts to her innately comic vision to humanize her own elegiac self-reflections.

It is by focusing on the pathos of the living, not the dead, that the turn or reversal of fortune in *To the Lighthouse* depends: "And it struck her, this was tragedy—not palls, dust, and the shroud, but children coerced, their spirits subdued" (p. 222). Lily's insight that the tyranny of the grieving father, not the death of the mother, constitutes the real childhood tragedy is crucial to the resolution of the novel's elegiac theme. Throughout *To the Lighthouse* the Ramsay children are forces of healthy and necessary subversion. They all share a "mute questioning of deference and chivalry"—those normative values of romance cherished by the primal mother and father. Their subversive spirit of inquiry corresponds to life's ceaseless questioning and reformulation of itself. The father's attempt to subdue that spirit is the true threat to life. It is he who would block and shut life off from its renewing source— the will of children, which is inseparable from the will to futurity. James's and Cam's pledge to resist his tyranny to the death unites them in a rebellious compact against the father who opposes change and obstructs life. Their compact, in turn, designates a new social contract, a new covenant between the living and the dead, the past and the present.

But like all comic romances, *To the Lighthouse* is funda- mentally conservative in its vision of a renovated order. James's ascendancy in the novel's final pages marks a success- ful beginning to a bloodless psychic and social revolution. In the Oedipal logic on which the novel relies, the hatred of the father is a measure of the idealization of him.[28] The child must kill in order to become the person he loves. James is both the royal pretender and the authentic heir to his father's king- dom: "Loneliness . . . was for both of them the truth about things" (p. 301). This tragic insight shared by father and son is embedded in the heart of the novel. That we perish each alone is an inviolable, "profound" truth that is absorbed by the novel's essentially feminine, comic surface. This fact uncom- promising is veiled by the beautiful and necessary illusion of regeneration. *To the Lighthouse,* in this formal respect, re- verses the structural pattern of *Mrs. Dalloway.* In the previous novel, Clarissa's climactic recovery and transcendence over death is projected through the image of a nameless old lady. In *To the Lighthouse* the locus of transformation shifts from old age to youth, where it naturally belongs.

Thus when James assumes the symbolic tiller of his father's boat, he inherits the place and the authority of the master

28. The psychological struggle embodied in the family romance to displace or replace the real father is, as Freud concludes, "only an expression of the child's longing for the happy, vanished days when his father seemed to him the noblest and strongest of men and his mother the dearest and loveliest of women." See Freud, "Family Romances," *Standard Edition,* vol. 9, pp. 240–41.

mariner. The old man's praise, "Well done," acknowledges James's accession to manhood, while Ramsay, himself reinvigorated by his new alliance with resurgent life, becomes "like a young man" (p. 308). Roles are reversed and exchanged, sealing the familial restoration. The inauguration of a new familial order is mirrored by the vision within. The figure of the "old man reading," the image of James's traumatic Oedipal fixation on the forbidding father, becomes in Cam's mind an image of the masculine strength and protection on which the trusting feminine spirit can rely: "He read, she thought, as if he were guiding something. . . . And she went on telling herself a story about escaping from a sinking ship, for she was safe, while he sat there" (p. 283). Guided and protected by the paternal vision of facts uncompromising, Cam can daydream, make up stories, without being lost in the waters of annihilation. The "rising" of Cam's imaginative power paradoxically involves a "falling" into the sexual roles and attitudes prescribed by the mother. Like her mother before her, Cam defers to and honors her father's vision when, "dabbling her fingers in the water," she murmurs, "dreamily, half asleep, how we perished, each alone" (p. 284). Cam's tribute to the father prepares for the reconciliation of father and child. Lily, who observes the family's successful expedition, completes the comic action with the words of divine atonement: "It is finished" (p. 309).

A comic resolution could almost be defined, argues Northrop Frye, "as an action that breaks out of the Oedipus ring, the destruction of a family or other close-knit social group by the tension and jealousies of its members."[29] The novel's linear movement toward the lighthouse represents an imaginative effort to separate its Oedipal origin from its psychological end —to break and thus break out of the Oedipal ring of anxious and conflicted desire. The narrative action "is finished" when Ramsay steps on the rock, an action that precipitates the completion of Lily's picture. The line Lily draws in the center

29. Frye, *Secular Scripture,* p. 137.

of her canvas recapitulates Ramsay's movement from vision to fulfillment, but it also expresses a relation between opposite points of reference, connecting and binding them in a determinate, encompassing form. The Oedipal ring, a symbol of ritual and imaginative bondage, is transformed into the Great Round, the "uroboric totality" which unites life and death.

Lily's final brush stroke is thus the novel's most positive image of the imagination's leap into liberty, its triumph over anxiety. Despite Lily's fears that "women can't paint, women can't write," she strikes out against the oppressive spectres of self-doubt:

> She looked at the steps; they were empty; she looked at her canvas; it was blurred. With a sudden intensity, as if she saw it clear for a second, she drew a line there, in the centre. [p. 310]

The novel, like *The Winter's Tale,* concludes in the *heuresis* or "finding again" of the mother by the daughter. The mother, who had cast a "triangular shadow over the step" (p. 299) is reembodied and restored to life in the work of art through which "is built up a whole structure of the imagination" (p. 258).

Yet the work of art itself expresses more than this genealogical affinity between Mrs. Ramsay's fecundity and Lily's creative powers. Lily's picture represents the novel's completed effort to reconcile antithetical visions of reality. It captures the light of a butterfly's wing—the beauty of the world wrought by the fecund feminine will—burning on a framework of steel—the structure the rational intelligence of the masculine will imposes on the fluidity of nature. The dialectics of plot had previously centered the conflicting, partial, and contradictory perspectives of embattled sexual wills: mother versus father, father versus son, male versus female. Only in the dream do such opposites attract and merge. As Freud observed, the word "no" does not exist in dreams: "They [dreams] show a particular preference for combining two contraries into a unity or for representing them as one and the same thing."[30] To represent opposites as the same thing is the dream work whose product is, like Lily's picture, the thing that endures, even if it leaves no material trace or is hidden from public inspection.

To the Lighthouse, then, concludes as a fable of an artistic "rite de passage" in which Lily, the productive dreamer, masters the female anxiety centered in fears of sexual and creative inadequacy, the fears that earlier had made the creative "passage from conception to work as dreadful as any down a dark passage for a child" (p. 32). Lily is forty-four when her passage from conception to finished work is completed. Virginia Woolf, the child victimized by a tyrannical, forbidding, yet beloved old man, is also forty-four when she moves from her original conception of a novel rooted in the ambivalent memories of childhood, through the dark passages of elegy, to her masterwork on the Victorian family romance.

Appropriately, it is a child triumphant, James Ramsay, the sensitive boy attached to his mother but sharing his father's vision, who solves the Oedipal puzzle riddling the novel. It is he who realizes that getting to the lighthouse means arriving at the end of a dark passage where the dream work, the work of representing opposites as the same thing, is finally accomplished. As he looks up at the lighthouse, James understands that as one thing it symbolizes antithetical realities.

> James looked at the Lighthouse. He could see the white-washed rocks; the tower, stark and straight; . . . So that was the Lighthouse, was it? [pp. 276–77]

The father's vision, stark and straight, as austere as that angular table that represents for Lily the energies of Ramsay's splendid mind, "satisfies" James. Yet the knowledge of facts

30. Sigmund Freud, "The Antithetical Sense of Primal Words," *Standard Edition,* vol. 11, p. 155.

uncompromising no longer opposes, but complements the feminine vision:

No, the other was also the Lighthouse. For nothing was simply one thing. The other Lighthouse was true too. It was sometimes hardly to be seen across the bay. In the evening one looked up and saw the eye opening and shutting and the light seemed to reach them in that airy sunny garden where they sat. [p. 277]

The word "No" in James's reverie provides the rhetorical link between two opposites about to be reduced to a unity. The father's linear and purposive image of the world, by which knowledge is represented in the consecutive alphabet from A to Z, is true. But so is "that other Lighthouse" that James and his mother see from their sunny, happy garden, a garden in which thought does not proceed along a keyboard of linearity. Through what Carolyn Heilbrun has aptly called the special "grace of androgyny,"[31] the child now sees with the father, but thinks back through the mother.

Woolf's struggles with her ending indicate her sensitivity to the decorums of her fable:

At this moment I'm casting about for an end. . . . The last chapter which I begin tomorrow is In the Boat: I had meant to end with R. climbing on to the rock. If so, what becomes of Lily and her picture? Should there be a final page about her and Carmichael looking at the picture and summing up R.'s character? . . . If this intervenes between R. and the lighthouse, there's too much chop and change, I think. Could I do it in a parenthesis? So that one had the sense of reading the two things at the same time? [WD, p. 98]

As Woolf's diary makes clear, both in the original and final stages of composition, Ramsay's character, singled out for

31. Heilbrun, *Toward a Recognition of Androgyny*, p. 33.

summation, remained central to Woolf's vision of the childhood past. Her decision to discard the proposed "simultane-
ous" double ending and to focus instead on the completion of
Lily's canvas, is structurally consonant with the elegiac priorities of her narrative. Ramsay's successful voyage to the lighthouse, undertaken to commemorate the memory of his dead
wife, concludes the narrative action, but not the elegiac meditation, which must always refer to the resolutions achieved in
the artist's imagination.

The real "grace of androgyny" thus yields a more significant sign of election—"the recognition," as Heilbrun argues,
"of the daughter as the true inheritor."[32] The work of dreaming and the rites of mourning are aesthetically transformed
into elegy, the literary form centered in antithesis and contradiction, absence and presence: "Elegy is the form of poetry
natural to the reflective mind," writes Coleridge. "Elegy presents everything as lost and gone or absent and future."[33]
The either/or of life resolves itself in the dreamed elegy in
which the child lives through her life from the start. The world
of childhood, lost and gone, abides in the world of the present.
To the Lighthouse moves from a dream of childhood through
a nightmare of bereavement into the dream of freedom. That
freedom, of course, is the freedom to continue in the future—
writing books. The creative self, the dutiful daughter having
found her mother and made peace with her father, no longer
mourns, but is free to dream again. Put another way, books do
continue each other in the career of Virginia Woolf. The bereaved and obsessed self of *To the Lighthouse* becomes the
dream self of *Orlando*—the androgyne.

32. Heilbrun, *Toward a Recognition of Androgyny*, p. 32.
33. Coleridge, *Table Talk*, p. 275.

4

Orlando

THE COMEDY OF ANDROGYNY

The Sexual Fantasy

Orlando began as a private joke but concluded as a public comedy of historical and literary manners. The transformation of coterie humor, whose simple and one-dimensional "joke" revolved around a comic biography of Virginia Woolf's intimate, Vita Sackville-West,[1] into a pan-historical fantasy satirizing sex roles, literary styles, social fashions, and political factionalism is, in many ways, part of *Orlando*'s intrinsic subject. The public expression of a private vision is a sign of accomplished professionalism in *Orlando,* a fantasy that is finally connected to reality by its closing reference to October 11, 1928, the date of publication that delivers the book to

---

1. See Frank Baldanza, "Orlando and the Sackvilles" *PMLA* (1955) 274–79, for a comprehensive survey of the source materials incorporated into Woolf's comic biography. For an account of the friendship between Woolf and Sackville-West, see Joanne Trautmann's recent monograph, *Jessamy Brides: The Friendship of Virginia Woolf and Vita Sackville-West,* Pennsylvania State Studies #36 (University Park, Pa.: Pennsylvania State University, 1973), especially pp. 40–48. Vita Sackville-West's reaction to Woolf's comic biography is expressed in her letter of October 11, 1928: "It seems to me that you have really shut up that 'hard and rare thing' in a book; that you have a complete vision and yet when you came down to the sober labour of working it out, have never lost sight of it nor faltered in the execution." She then engagingly confesses to Woolf: "Also, you have invented a new form of Narcissism,—I confess,—I am in love with Orlando—this is a complication I had not foreseen." See the Appendix of *The Letters of Virginia Woolf,* ed. Nigel Nicolson and Joanne Trautmann (New York: Harcourt Brace Jovanovich, 1977), vol. 3, p. 574.

the world.[2] Orlando's "ecstasy" on the banks of the Serpentine, in which she comprehends and fulfills her poetic destiny, is coincident with the "fate" of the book she inspires. It is as if Woolf belatedly discovered that publishing *Orlando* was the raison d'être of her writing. Such a reversal of priorities suggests that for Woolf the communicative function of *Orlando*—what may be designated as the "social character" of its comedy—eventually superseded the personal, cathartic, exhibitionistic, or commemorative feelings that prompted her to put pen to paper. As Lily Briscoe completes her painting, she fears, perhaps knows, that "it would be hung in attics; it would be destroyed," but it does not matter to her because "I have had my vision." To possess and then express a vision is primary; to address an audience, an "Other," is a secondary, even unnecessary condition in the life of Lily's art. But Orlando's manuscript demands readers: "It wanted to be read. It must be read. It would die in her bosom if it were not read" (p. 272). Orlando may give birth to the text, but its life can only be nurtured and sustained by being read. To relieve her poem of its desire for "life," Orlando, a confirmed solitary, must return it to the human world, for "human beings had become necessary," if only because they possess the power to read.

By submitting to the "fate" prescribed by her manuscript and allowing what has been written privately to be read publicly, Orlando's own vision is socialized. But she can only rejoin the human world by relinquishing her proprietary rights over the cherished product of her creation. For Orlando's poem, "The Oak Tree," the *summa* of her long literary labors, is no longer properly hers once it has been delivered into print. Her attempt to bury her published poem, putting it beyond the range of the public's "chatter and praise and blame," proves abortive, because "No luck ever attends these symboli-

2. Virginia Woolf, *Orlando* (New York: Harcourt, Brace and World, 1928). All further citations will be to this edition.

cal celebrations" (p. 324). "The Oak Tree," like the country estate of which it is a synecdoche, is given over to the public domain in the last chapter of the book, a restitution that signals Orlando's own return to historical and consequently human time. Relieved of her manuscript, Orlando "felt a bare place in her breast where she had been used to carry it—she had nothing to do but reflect upon whatever she liked—the extraordinary chances it might be of the human lot" (pp. 281-82).

Once Orlando entrusts her manuscript to the reading public, the "extraordinary" chances of her life are humanized, but not demystified. Ordinary life replaces Orlando's own timeless, androgynous existence as the realm of fantastic happenings, a surer ground to test her luck with symbolical celebrations. As the creative Orlando makes her way through the modern world, her fantastic perceptions are increasingly replaced by visions of everyday things that are "all precisely life-size" (p. 282). Yet even amid the increasing "actuality" of *Orlando*'s narrative terrain, there persists, as Elizabeth Bowen has remarked, "a touch of hallucination about 'reality,' "[3] a magical touch by which Orlando confers to "words of no beauty, interest or significance in themselves" a symbolical meaning, proving, at least to Orlando's satisfaction, "that when the shrivelled skin of the ordinary is stuffed out with meaning it satisfies the senses amazingly" (p. 315). That the day's routine and the phenomena of the ordinary become the final and lasting source of amazement in Woolf's fantastic fiction is a fitting denouement to her comic biography of the creative spirit. Like all classic comedy, *Orlando* educates pleasure and wild imaginings to the reality principle, while simultaneously instructing reality in the pleasures of fancy and imagination. Publication becomes an apt comic symbol for the processes recorded in

3. Elizabeth Bowen, "Afterword" to *Orlando* (New York: New American Library, 1960), p. 222.

Orlando, a symbolic literary ritual through which the imaginary is inducted, through print and through the artifact of the book itself,[4] into material reality.

Perhaps the final accommodation of reality in the last chapter of *Orlando* explains why Woolf worried that *Orlando* "fell" between two stools, "too long for a joke, and too frivolous for a serious book" (*WD,* p. 122). Brevity is indeed the soul of wit, and extending the joke to accommodate a sober reality may not redeem its essentially frivolous nature. Woolf, in a less self-critical mood, justified *Orlando* in a slightly different way: "I want fun, I want fantasy"—such was the "perfectly definite, indeed overmastering, impulse" in *Orlando,* she writes (*WD,* p. 134). Mastering such an overmastering impulse may have ruined the quick joke, but it undoubtedly retrieved her humorous fantasy from sheer frivolity and delivered it to an authentically, if comically, serious subject: "I want (and this was serious) to give things their caricature value. And still this mood hangs about me. I want to write a history, say of Newnham or the women's movement, in the same vein. The vein is deep in me—at least sparkling, urgent" (*WD,* p. 134). No one will question that the vein of caricature is sparkling in Woolf, but how account for its urgency, its overmastering power in the economy of her mind? Woolf's own explanation that caricature was among "the offices to be discharged by talent for the relief of genius: meaning that one has the play side; the gift when it is mere gift, unapplied gift, and the gift when it is serious, going to business" (*WD,* p. 134) confuses rather than clarifies the issue. Even the most rudimentary psychology of play expands on the insights of Huizinga, Callois, or Piaget, that the office "discharged" by play is to effect a mastery over reality, to procure freedom for the

4. Avrom Fleischman argues that *Orlando* is "a literary biography not merely in recounting the life and times of a writer, but in transforming that account into literature itself, making her biography a literary object which is her adequate symbol." See his *Virginia Woolf: A Critical Reading,* p. 139.

player.[5] In this sense, Jacques Ehrmann is certainly right in arguing that however gratuitous, nonutilitarian, or "unserious" play may appear to be, the play side of the mind, what Woolf calls mere gift, unapplied gift, is never completely disinterested: ". . . the ethnologists . . . have taught us that the 'pure' gift is in fact an exchange. One gives, one spends *in order to* receive. The so-called liberty of the gift is in fact liberality; the generosity, the gratuitousness of play are ways of *acquiring* prestige and power."[6] If, as I shall argue, Woolf "plays" with literature in *Orlando* in order to test, acquire, and defend her own literary power and prestige, then we can see why she thought that the vein of caricature, the "play side" of *Orlando*, provided the serious justification for the merest of her gifts.

Both the urgency and seriousness of caricature as a species of Woolf's comic, playful expression in *Orlando* springs from an aggressive impulse directed against all she perceives as threatening to the integrity and freedom of the self—the pretentious, the powerful, the potentially tyrannical. Caricature relies primarily on the technique of degradation, unmasking or distorting its objects in order to belittle them. Caricature attempts to reduce great things to small through an aesthetic transformation that diminishes a perceived danger by subjecting it to the formal play of imagination.[7] Such was Hobbes's initial insight into comic pleasure when he defined the effect of comic perception as a "sudden glory"[8] that confirms feel-

5. See especially Johan Huizinga, *Homo Ludens: A Study of the Play Element in Culture* (Boston: Beacon Press, 1955) and Roger Caillois, *Les Jeux et les hommes* (Paris: Gallimard, 1958) for extended treatments of the psychology of play.

6. Jacques Ehrmann, "Homo Ludens Revisited," in *Game, Play and Literature* (Boston: Beacon Press, 1968), p. 43.

7. See Ernst Kris's discussion of these techniques in "The Psychology of Caricature," *Psychoanalytic Explorations in Art* (New York: International University Presses, 1952), pp. 194–203. See also John Graham's "The 'Caricature Value' of Parody and Fantasy in *Orlando*," reprinted in *Virginia Woolf: Twentieth Century Views,* ed. Claire Sprague (Englewood Cliffs, N.J.: Prentice-Hall, 1971), pp. 101–16.

8. Thomas Hobbes, *Leviathan* (London, 1651), part I, chap. 6.

ings of superiority. *Orlando* begins with such a moment of
"sudden glory." Its opening scene reveals the eponymous hero
"in the act of slicing at the head of a Moor" (p. 13), a shrunken
head which in shape and color resembles a football. In Orlando's adolescent game, the violence inherent in his aristocratic, chivalric ancestry is comically contained and displaced
through a diminished image (a shrunken head) of a formidable
danger ("a vast Pagan . . . in barbarian fields"). His play
mimics the actions of his fathers who "had struck many heads
of many colours off many shoulders, and brought them back
to hang from the rafters" (p. 13).

The comic inventions of *Orlando* in its masculine first half
are linked to events of extreme elemental violence (The Great
Thaw that ends the first chapter) or extreme psychological
violence (the betrayals by Sasha, his first love, and Sir Nicholas
Greene, his literary mentor). This pattern of violence culminates, of course, in the Turkish insurrection that precedes the
most violent transformation in Orlando's life—his metamorphosis into a woman. These playful encounters with reality, in
which a magnified external threat is comically reduced, gradually teach Orlando to be master of himself and lord of creation.
Such sublimations of inner and outer violence inform the
comic fantasies of prestige in *Orlando,* just as Orlando's play at
the book's beginning is preparatory for his coming into his
aristocratic and poetic "estate."

The best example of Woolf's serious determination to give
all things their caricature value is her exaggerated, ruthlessly
literal interpretation of *Orlando*'s dominant comic theme—
human sexuality. Sex confusion is the prime topos of comedy
in dramatizing the conflict between the instinctual self and
the civilized, conventional world it must negotiate in. *Orlando*'s
mischievous first line, "He—for there could be no doubt of his
sex—though the fashion of the time did something to disguise
it—" is conventionally allied to the transvestitism common
to Shakespearean comic romances. The certitude of Orlando's sexual identity is immediately qualified even as it is

asserted. This shadow of doubt concerning Orlando's sexual nature prepares for his attraction to the genuinely epicene Sasha, his deception by the sexual masquerades of the Roumanian Archduchess Harriet Griselda of Finster-Aarhorn and Scandop-Boom, who later reveals herself to be a man, and, of course, his own miraculous sex-change. The sexual charades that provide the richest source of social satire in *Orlando* climax in a comic scene of "protestation and demonstration" in which Orlando, now a woman, and Shel, her lover, are unmasked simultaneously:

"You're a woman, Shel!" she cried.
"You're a man, Orlando!" he cried. [p. 252]

Orlando's quest for "Life and a lover" (p. 185) terminates in a comic anagnorisis, the recognition of androgyny as a source of sudden glory, a triumph over the most rationalized, institutionalized and internalized form of violence known to Woolf—the tyranny of sex. Sex in *Orlando* is never treated as an indisputable fact of biological and social life. Sex is a disguise Nature adopts to confuse—at times amuse—her children. In *The Subjection of Women* John Stuart Mill entertained doubts that in a state of culture men and women were capable of discerning the innate differences—if any—between the sexes.[9] Mill's doubt becomes Woolf's fantastic certainty in her most ambitious, daring, and irreverent comedy.

The admission of that fantastic certainty into the formal territory of biography, the generic mantle with which *Orlando* disguises its aggressive license in its representations of reality, is negotiated by a lacuna in the biographical narrative. The biographer, chronically obsessed with verifying the objectivity of his account of the life and times of Orlando, is suddenly

9. John Stuart Mill, *The Subjection of Women: Essays on Sex Equality*, ed. Alice Rossi (Chicago: University of Chicago Press, 1970), p. 202. Mill writes: "I have said that it cannot now be known how much of the existing mental differences between men and women is natural, and how much artificial; whether there are any natural differences at all; or supposing all artificial cause of difference to be withdrawn, what natural character would be revealed."

confronted with a hiatus in the historical documents that have
accumulated around his subject. The biographer laments that
revolution and fire, historical and natural forms of violence,
"have so damaged or destroyed all those papers from which
any trustworthy record could be drawn, that what we can give
is lamentably incomplete": "Just when we thought to elucidate
a secret that has puzzled historians for a hundred years, there
was a hole in the manuscript big enough to put your finger
through" (p. 119). Woolf punctures the representational fabric
of her "objective" biography, creating a "hole" through which
enters a new Orlando, transformed into a woman. She then
proceeds to mend or cover over the gap that separates the
masculine from the feminine part of her fiction by having her
biographer admit that "often it has been necessary to speculate, to surmise, and even to make use of the imagination"
(p. 119). The irony of "even" is, of course, confined to the
surface of this highly imaginative and conjectural chronicle.
The deeper, obscurer irony in the biographer's embarrassed
speculations pertains to the "secret" or hidden truth that the
conscientious, if ostensibly disingenuous tone assumed by the
biographer works to conceal. What the objectivity of the biographer hides is the radical subjectivity and indeterminism that
invariably attends the treatment of sex in social and political
life and in fiction itself. Sex is not a fact, but a space in the
psychic life, a hole or lapsus in identity onto which are projected the imagoes, archetypes, or stereotypes comprehended
in the terms male and female. This is "the truth and nothing
but the truth" proclaimed by the apocalyptic trumpets that
announce the transformation of Orlando, whose sex seemed
indubitable, into a woman.

Orlando's sex-change occasions a momentary hesitation in
the narrative in which the biographer pauses to make certain
statements about the incontrovertible, though inexplicable,
event he is forced to admit into his "trustworthy record." His
subsequent statements are mutually contradictory, if internally
self-consistent: "(1) that Orlando had always been a woman,

(2) that Orlando is at this moment a man" (p. 139). The biographer's inability or reluctance to endorse either explanation for the miraculous event is what Todorov identifies as an inherent feature of fantastic literature. For Todorov, the fantastic necessarily resides in the space or "pause" between two interpretations of an extraordinary occurrence, one a rationalistic explanation favored by fictions wedded to the canons of realism, one a poetic perspective that accepts the supernatural or unnatural as part of reality.[10] Orlando as a fantastic character, however, is not plagued by such hermeneutical uncertainty principles. Her serene act of self-contemplation as she gazes, without shame or surprise, at her transformed body, contrasts comically and pointedly with the biographer's embarrassed discomposure. He can only advise to "Let biologists and psychologists determine" the status of Orlando's sex, contenting himself and his readers with a sufficient, if partial view of Orlando's new sex: "It is enough for us to state the simple fact; Orlando was a man till the age of thirty, when he became a woman and has remained so ever since" (p. 139).

The biographer's bald assertion of an incontestable fact that blithely, if uneasily dismisses any rationalistic objection that such changes "are against nature" is made even more ironic—and playful—by the historical topicality of its comedy. Orlando's sexual transformation occurs at the dawn of the eighteenth century, a joke at the expense of the spirit of the age of reason. Woolf's timely laughter may be aimed at the metaphysics best expressed in Pope's poetic dictum that whatever is, is right. Pope's assumption, at any rate, is the assumption on which Orlando and her biographer proceed.

The Quest for a Serviceable Style

Orlando's metamorphosis is fantastic because it violates natural law. It is comic because, as fantasy, it transgresses

10. Tzvetan Todorov, *The Fantastic,* tr. Richard Howard (Cleveland: Press of Case Western University, 1973), pp. 25 and passim.

human law. The comic agon between law and an unlawful nature is appropriately invoked when Orlando, now a woman, returns from Turkey to her native England. There the mystery of Orlando's sexual identity, which her biographer could not elucidate, is referred to the courts. Orlando's sex becomes an issue to be litigated, a matter for social and legal deliberation rather than biological fact. All her estates are put in abeyance as a series of suits are instigated to decide the question of her "highly ambiguous condition, . . . whether she was alive or dead, man or woman, Duke or nonentity" (p. 168). Woolf's feminist satire surfaces in the ambiguous syntax of this sentence whose serial construction parodies the language of law. To be alive is to be a man is to be a titled aristocrat. To be dead is to be a woman is to be a social nonentity. The series also questions Orlando's status in the fiction: is she alive or did she die in the Turkish insurrection; is she a man or a woman; is she a duke or a nonentity because of her changed sexual status? It is finally a legal judgment that decides Orlando's ontological, sexual, and social status, but it is, of course, on the determination of sex that all the mysteries devolve. Orlando's legal battles eventually conclude in a compromise when Lord Palmerston, some hundred years later, pronounces her "indisputably, and beyond the shadow of a doubt . . . Female" (p. 255), disinherits her children by Pepita, and entails her estates to any future male heirs. Sex becomes a legal fiction, like paternity and property rights, a notion Woolf had hinted at when the trumpets announcing Orlando's sex change bruited "The truth, the truth and nothing but the truth," a cliché convenient in matters of law, but inapplicable in matters of fiction where shadows of doubt invariably complicate perceptions of reality.

The comic adjudication of Orlando's sex does not so much reveal the truth and nothing but the truth about innate differences between men and women as demystify and de-objectify the assumptions commonly held about sexual natures. Male and female are roles sanctioned by society, roles one may adopt or dismiss at one's whim—or hazard. Orlando initially challenges society's rigid law of sex by surreptitiously taking an androgynous holiday, enjoying her escapades about Gerrard Street and Drury Lane:

> She had, it seems, no difficulty in sustaining the different parts, for her sex changed far more frequently than those who have worn only one set of clothing can conceive; nor can there be any doubt that she reaped a twofold harvest by this device; the pleasures of life were increased and its experiences multiplied. [pp. 220-21]

Orlando's protean sexuality is a device, like transvestitism, to maximize experience, to double one's pleasure. At times Orlando, the androgynous actress, performs her role absent-mindedly, as in her clumsy ministration of tea for Pope, an awkwardness the biographer claims inspired his famous line, "Women have no characters at all."[11] But Woolf's more profound borrowing from Pope's "Epistle to a Lady" may be its peroration on Woman as Heaven's "last best work," last because in framing woman Heaven "but forms a softer Man," best when Heaven

> Picks from each sex, to make its Fav'rite blest,
> Your love of Pleasure, our desire of Rest,
> Blends, in exception to all gen'ral rules,
> Your taste of Follies, with our Scorn of Fools,
> Reserve with Frankness, Art with Truth ally'd,

11. Of course, it is Martha Blount who is credited with the line. Moreover, it is worth pointing out that when Pope speaks of the "Particular Characters" or the "General Characteristick" of women he is not concerned with what Mill theoretically designates as woman's "natural character" stripped of all artificial cause. Artificial causes and affectations are precisely what Pope means when describing and anatomizing women's characters as "the Affected, the Soft-natur'd, the Cunning, the Whimsical, the Wits and Refiners, the Stupid and Silly." See the "Argument" of "Epistle II: To a Lady" *The Poems of Alexander Pope,* ed. John Butt (New Haven: Yale University Press, 1963), p. 559.

> Courage with Softness, Modesty with Pride,
> Fix'd Principles, with Fancy ever new;
> Shakes all together, and produces—You.
>   [Moral Essays: Epistle to a Lady, ll. 273–80]

Implicit in Pope's portrait of the estimable woman is the vision of androgyny; the ideal feminine identity blends, combines, and consolidates, "in exception to all gen'ral rules," both the "Particular Characters" and the "General Characteristick" of each sex. Martha Blount and Orlando are exceptional figures precisely because they lack stable sexual "characters" by which women are easily distinguished from the other sex. It may take, as Pope hints, "Sense, Good Humour, and a Poet" to describe what Woolf calls the "true self . . . compact of all the selves we have it in us to be" (p. 310). Pope's estimable woman and Woolf's androgynous heroine, both of whom can imaginatively incorporate and embrace the varied and often contradictory sexual selves "we have it in us to be," remain fundamentally "literary" characters, partly the productions of wish-fulfilling fantasy, partly the fond portraits of old friends, partly the satiric, good-humoured investigations of sexual and social manners.

The pleasure derived from such fanciful and good-humoured characterizations of the androgynous identity is akin to the pleasure derived from all comic art—the comic "relief" that results from a saving on the expenditure of inhibition.[12] Androgyny, as I have argued, is essentially a comic myth directed primarily, but not exclusively, against the tyrannies of sex. As such its representation constitutes for Woolf the revenge of the repressed. Herbert Marder was among the first to observe that the masque that inaugurates, and in a sense legitimizes, the patent artifice of Orlando's sex-change represents an

12. See especially Freud's views on jokes and the comic in his *Jokes and the Unconscious, Standard Edition,* vol. 8, pp. 118 and passim.

imaginative movement from repression to freedom.[13] The dismissal of Purity, who veils life and urges "Speak not," of Chastity, who freezes life, and of Modesty, to whom increase is odious (p. 135), is performed as a ritual of exorcism, a casting out of the mind of those psychic censors who prohibit and deny. These spectres housed in the feminine psyche are replaced by a more virile personification of Truth, embodied in the naked form of Orlando who, like Adam, awakens from her sleeplike trance and finds her dream is true. The masque is an allegory tracing the progress from repression to a resurgent creativity.

The best gloss for that allegory can be found in "Professions for Women," an essay written comtemporaneously with *Orlando* and containing Woolf's seminal ideas about women and fiction later expressed more fully in *A Room of One's Own.* Woolf typically resorts to an imaginative scene to dramatize the aesthetic problems confronting a woman whose humanity and imagination traditionally have been circumscribed, restricted, and dwarfed by the single fact of her sex. She exhorts her audience to imagine "a girl sitting with a pen in her hand . . . letting her imagination sweep unchecked round every rock and cranny of the world that lies submerged in the depths of our unconscious being."[14] But the unimpeded flow of imagination as it casts about in the depths of the unconscious is checked by the "thought of something, something about the body, about the passions which it was unfitting for her as a woman to say. . . . She could write no more."[15] What blocks the feminine imagination Woolf purports to be a common obstacle for women writers: "They are impeded by the extreme conventionality of the other sex. For though men sensibly allow themselves great freedom in these respects, I

13. Herbert Marder, *Feminism and Art* (Chicago: University of Chicago Press, 1968), p. 114.
14. "Professions for Women," *Collected Essays,* vol. 2, p. 287.
15. "Professions for Women," p. 288.

doubt that they realize or can control the extreme severity
with which they condemn such freedom in women."[16]

To realize the freedom enjoyed by men is the comic intent
of *Orlando,* a fiction that is concerned more than any other
work by Woolf with writers and the act of writing.[17] Such intent does not contradict the caricature value of her fiction,
for, as Ernst Kris argues, the object and target of tendentious
comedy "is even now held in esteem, *is even now represented
in the superego.*"[18] Literature and men of letters are subjected
to comic irreverence primarily when they support or embody
the assumptions and rites—the "conventionality," to use
Woolf's comprehensive term—a male-dominated "sacred fraternity" (p. 82) has imposed on the literate body. The desire
to overcome that conventionality, either by subterfuge or
through the direct disparagement of parody and caricature,
informs the comic processes of *Orlando.* Literature as an
activity or an arena for the imaginative transformation of
reality is itself immune from direct attack. Woolf's literary
satire is confined to the notion of "period." It observes a
progress through a history of styles—Elizabethan, Restoration,
Augustan, Romantic, Victorian, and modern. As literary history, *Orlando* records the quest for a serviceable style, a quest
that tests and often rejects the language, conventions, and
modes that historically have composed the British tradition.

Like all quest fictions, *Orlando*'s quest requires, as a condition for success, a series of trials testing the resilience and
authenticity of Orlando's—and by extension Woolf's—poetic
vocation. *Orlando* is both a satiric literary history and a
"work-in-progress"[19] that includes, as part of its formal process, the trial of self-examination, a self-parody in which Woolf

16. Ibid.
17. See John Graham, "The 'Caricature Value' of Parody and Fantasy in *Orlando,*" p. 102.
18. Kris, *Psychoanalytic Explorations in Art,* p. 186.
19. Cf. James Nohrnberg, *The Analogy of the Faerie Queen* (Princeton: Princeton University Press, 1976), p. 647. I am particularly indebted to his discussion of
midpoint conjugations in works that present themselves as "works-in-progress."

satirizes her own lyrical vein (*WD,* p. 104). Sometimes the self-satire is the quick and obvious joke that insiders can enjoy, as in Woolf's good-humored parody of the techniques perfected in *To the Lighthouse.* Her lyrical treatment of time in the much criticized "Time Passes" section of that novel is comically rendered in the biographer's feeling that the passage of the seasons could best be indicated by the simple statement "Time Passed" with the "exact amount . . . indicated in brackets" (p. 98). The long excursus on "the seamstress" Memory (pp. 79-80) is a more considered comic look at the associationalism endemic to British and Woolfian fictional psychology. And there is the more searching satire on Woolf's own stylistic mannerisms in which Orlando, as a poet communing with her deity, struggles to overcome the temptations lurking in the poet's paradise, of which the termination "-ing" is said to be Devil himself (p. 173). Woolf's own fondness for the present participle as a verbal artifice to prolong the lyricism of the present moment had bedevilled her prose and would bedevil her prose until *Between the Acts,* her most mature work, a work whose terse, quasi-allegorical style is prefigured in *Orlando.* Woolf's own sense of "period" in the shorter time encompassed by her own literary labors to date is synchronized with the consideration of the larger historical periods through which Orlando travels.

By viewing her own stylistic development in the perspective of larger historical periods, Woolf rescues *Orlando* from the danger often incurred by fictions advertising themselves as "works-in-progress"—the danger that with each new development in style or artistic technique the writer must unwrite what has been written earlier. Orlando's work on "The Oak Tree" is often threatened by the prospect that "in the process of writing the poem would be completely unwritten":

> For it is for the historian of letters to remark that he had changed his style amazingly. His floridity was chastened; his abundance curbed; the age of prose was congealing those warm fountains. [p. 113]

Social criticism, literary criticism, and self-criticism coincide in the age of prose, providing Orlando with a standard of excellence and rescuing her from the endless self-editing and self-censoring that threaten the completion of her art. That is why only the works of Pope, Addison, and Swift, besides Vita Sackville-West's own poetry and, of course, Shakespeare, are directly quoted. Dr. Johnson, "the great rolling shadow" from whom "there rolled out the most magnificent phrases that have ever left human lips" (p. 223), is observed from afar, proving perhaps too formidable an example to disparage, a cynosure too venerable to approach. And the influence of Defoe, Sir Thomas Browne, Sterne, Sir Walter Scott, Lord Macaulay, Emily Brontë, De Quincey, Walter Pater, and the illustrious dead of British literature acknowledged by Woolf in her preface to *Orlando* are veiled in extended parodies, much in the manner of "The Oxen in the Sun" chapter of *Ulysses.* The great masters of the eighteenth century are directly quoted because it is they who instruct Orlando in the prosaic potentials of poetry and the poetic properties of prose. It is from them that she learns "the most important part of style, which is the natural run of the voice in speaking" (pp. 211–12). For Woolf, the genius of the age of prose lay in perfecting a naturalistic style in which "every secret of a writer's soul, every experience of his life, every quality of his mind is written large in his works" (p. 209). The Augustan style simultaneously masks and expresses the poetic personality, as Pope's *Rape of the Lock,* Addison's *Spectator* essays, and Swift's *Gulliver's Travels* testify. Their satiric, observant, or violent "wit" is perfectly representative of their idiosyncratic characters: how Pope's "hand trembled, how he loved, how he lied, how he suffered" (p. 209); how Addison, "every ripple and curve of his wit" exposed, "would marry a Countess and die very respectably in the end" (p. 210); how Swift, a violent man, is "so coarse and yet so clean; so brutal, yet so kind; scorns the whole world, yet talks baby language to a girl, and will die, can we doubt it, in a madhouse" (p. 211). It is to such a level of wit that Woolf's own comedy aspires and finally attains. The goal of Orlando's quest—a serviceable and expressive style—comes at the midpoint of her travels, providing both the historical and stylistic fulcrum for the book, just as the sexual metamorphosis in the third chapter provides the episodic fulcrum of the narrative. Both the knowledge of style and the knowledge of sex are conjugated roughly *in medias res,* which explains why after the eighteenth century Orlando's adventures become less fantastic and picaresque, and to some critics less comically energetic. For it is at the midpoint of her literary career that Orlando's quest begins in earnest. At thirty, the licensed enthusiasms of youth must either submit to the disciplines of an authentic literary vocation or deteriorate into precious dilettantism.

Embarrassed Figurations: The Progress of Orlando

Orlando's poetic quest begins, conventionally enough, on the threshold of manhood and terminates, narratively, if not psychologically, with the birth of a child, metaphorically linked to the delivery of her manuscript after a long period of gestation. These events mark the natural milestones of Orlando's life, the only events that indicate her subservience to biological necessity. Immortal he and she may be, but unnatural she is not. In fact, Orlando's attachment to Nature, the "English disease," remains constant throughout her transformations and evolutions. Natural desire, indeed, seems to be the energy that sustains her and accounts for her vitality and endurance. The erotic energy unleashed in *Orlando* cannot be simply explained by biographic fidelity to Woolf's original subject. Vita Sackville-West's sex life is certainly intriguing, but it does not fully account for the sexual lyricism and license Woolf enjoys in *Orlando.* "What is Love?" is the "first question" (p. 100) posed in *Orlando,* a question that would "hustle Books or Metaphors or What one lives for into the margin, there to wait till they saw their chance to rush into the field again." Love is the text of *Orlando;* the biographer's thoughts on books, metaphors, and what one lives for glosses on that text. The representation of love necessarily entails, as Roland Barthes has argued, "an embarrassed figuration, encumbered with other meanings than that of desire: a space of alibis (reality, morality, likelihood, readability, truth)."[20] Orlando exposes the alibi when he discredits his own figures for love as manifestly untruthful (p. 101). Nature and letters, as the biographer earlier observed, seem to have a natural antipathy (p. 17), an antipathy that embarrasses the fledgling poet in love:

> "The sky is blue," he said, "the grass is green." Looking up, he saw that, on the contrary, the sky is like the veils which a thousand Madonnas have let fall from their hair; and the grass fleets and darkens like a flight of girls fleeing the embraces of hairy satyrs from enchanted woods. "Upon my word," he said . . . , "I don't see that one's more true than another. Both are utterly false." And he despaired of being able to solve the problem of what poetry is and what truth is and fell into a deep dejection. [p. 102]

Orlando's embarrassment—and poetic dejection—in his own figurations comes because he cannot transform the violence of his desires into the tranquillity of art, an embarrassment of style. Nor can he accept the necessary sublimations of desire into poetic figure—madonnas with veils in their hair. Only at the end of the quest does Orlando comprehend the subtle relationship between desire and its artifices when she gazes at the antique tapestry depicting the legend of Daphne and Apollo, the god of poetry in pursuit, the maiden fleeing from his embraces, the eternal round of poetry and desire (p. 317).

For Woolf true poetry never falsifies the terror of erotic desire nor the Muse's terrible inspirations. But true poetry

---

20. Roland Barthes, *The Pleasures of the Text,* tr. Richard Wilbur (New York: Hill and Wang, 1973), p. 56.

also overcomes those terrors in its own fine discriminations
between the double faces of love:

> For Love . . . has two faces; one white, the other black;
> two bodies; one smooth, the other hairy. It has two
> hands, two feet, two tails, two, indeed, of every member
> and each one is the exact opposite of the other. Yet, so
> strictly are they joined together that you cannot separate
> them. [p. 117]

Orlando's impulse is to follow the white form of Love, but avert
his glance and flee from its black face. He has still to learn that
Lust, the vulture, attends Love, the bird of Paradise, both of
which conjoin in the triumph of natural desire—the wild goose
released at the book's end.

The triumph of love, however, is that it takes a human
shape, such is its pride (p. 161), the pride of figuration. That
is why Orlando can equate the betrayal of Sasha and the
treachery of Greene, for both personify for him the beloved
figure of the Muse. And it is precisely his failure to discriminate between the objects of his passion and the sources of his
poetic inspiration that dooms him to early disappointment and
despair. His demand for a Muse as a real presence, be it Sasha
or Greene, betrays Orlando's jejune literalism, a literalism that
does not encumber the imaginings of the mature Orlando who
accepts the artifice of the Muse as a purely metaphoric phenomenon. She accepts the necessary displacements of desire,
whereas the young, male Orlando insists on the coincidence of
the real and the phantom, love and its images. It is, after all,
a childish confusion, this conflation of the imaginary and the
real, this blending of the objective and subjective, this literalization of figure.

Orlando's sentimental and aesthetic education is thus
effected by a progress through the embarrassed figurations of
love, of which Sasha is both origin and end. She is Orlando's
first and abiding love, his comic Muse. Like the love she inspires, she has a double nature. She is faithless, a devil, an

adulteress and deceiver. But she is also the green flame hidden in the emerald, or the sun prisoned in a hill (p. 47), whose fitful, evanescent light Orlando must pursue. In a playful allegorical scene, Orlando abandons the Lady Euphrosyne for the tempestuous, elusive Sasha, the calmer joys of temperance and respectability for the ecstasies of importunate, perhaps unattainable desire. Significantly their relationship begins with a laugh, a joke at the expense of the manners of the Court. Sasha's satires at first discompose Orlando, but "they were put with such archness and drollery that he could not help but laugh" (p. 41). Sasha's arch and droll wit redeems her caricatures from censure. Woolf's own strategy in *Orlando* depends on maintaining that same tone, inducing her readers to laugh in spite of themselves, implicating them, as Sasha implicates Orlando, in the disparagements of her satire.

Woolf, of course, is in full control of her satiric Muse; Orlando is not. His erotic and poetic transports over Sasha, transports rooted in the anarchy of his blind passion for her, are involuntary, treading the comic edge of pleasure and pain. He pursues his Muse, "vowing that he would chase the flame, dive for the gem, and so on and so on, the words coming on the pants of his breath with the passion of a poet whose poetry is half pressed out of him by pain" (p. 47). The passion for poetry, like the passion of love, comes in quick breaths, a spasmodic, if authentic form of inspiration. Orlando's love for Sasha inspires a riot of "metaphors of the most extreme and extravagant [that] twined and twisted in his mind" (p. 37), heralding the presence of a genuine, but as yet undisciplined poetic gift. But the body of the beloved proves too volatile and corruptible to be a permanent source of inspiration. Thus on the twelfth stroke of midnight, the witching hour when the spellbound Orlando seeks to possess the Muse who enchants him, he awaits her coming in vain. It is only at the end of *Orlando*, again at the stroke of midnight, that the epicene Sasha finally comes, transfigured into her comic double, the androgynous Shel, from whose head flies the wild goose. The phantom husband replaces the actual husband and, paradoxically, becomes more faithful. Concomitantly, the sexual tragedy (the betrayal of Sasha) modulates into a sexual comedy in which the violence of desire is comically contained and fulfilled.

The trauma of disillusionment in love, necessary for Orlando's development, is severe, but not fatal nor, finally, incapacitating. *Orlando* never honors, as do many of Woolf's novels, the potential tragedy of disenchantment. Woolf's comic art in *Orlando* always recovers from its skirmishes with a harsh and demoralizing reality, much as Cervantes's art continually provides new sources of enchantment for Don Quixote's inspired madness. The recurrent symbols for Orlando's recuperative power are the trancelike sleeps that function as intervals of convalescence between the death of one illusion and the birth of another. Though the length of Orlando's sleeps are unnatural, their purpose is not. As his biographer speculates:

Are they remedial measures—trances in which the most galling memories, events that seem likely to cripple life for ever, are brushed with a dark wing which rubs their harshness off and gilds them, even the ugliest, and basest, with a lustre, an incandescence? Has the finger of death to be laid on the tumult of life from time to time lest it rend us asunder? . . . And then what strange powers are these that penetrate our most secret ways and change our most treasured possessions without our willing it? [pp. 67-68]

Sleep is Nature's art, her means of restoring beauty to the world. Like passion, sleep challenges the autonomy of the mind, penetrating our most secret desires and transforming our most treasured possessions without our consent.

This submission to Nature's strange powers of renovation, Johnson argued in *The Idler,* is the "one common wish" of humanity, collectively imploring "from nature's hand the

nectar of oblivion."[21] But the more the mind gains in temporary self-forgetfulness the more it loses its individuality: "And
the mind which, from time to time, sunk gladly into insensibility, had made no very near approaches to the felicity of the
supreme and self-sufficient nature." Orlando's insensibility
during his long trancelike sleeps is a sign of his dependence on
nature as a restorative power and as such accounts for his
extreme "infelicity" in the early portions of his life, an infelicity betrayed by his temperamental disposition to melancholy and thoughts of death. His sleeps are literal moments of
oblivion in the narrative, moments in which he dreams—and
imagines—nothing. The trances of Orlando after his metamorphosis, however, are of a different order. They are the sleep
Johnson calls "semi-slumbers," sleeps in which "it is easy . . .
to collect all the possibilities of happiness, to alter the course
of the sun, to bring back the past, and anticipate the future,
to unite all the beauties of all seasons, and all the blessings of
all climates, to receive and bestow felicity, and forget that
misery is the lot of man."[22] Woolf's *Orlando* eventually realizes all these possibilities of happiness—with consummate ease.
Orlando is that "voluntary dream, a temporary recession from
the realities of life to airy fictions; and habitual subjection of
reason to fancy"[23] of which Johnson speaks. Thus the mature
Orlando's felicity contrasts sharply with the melancholy of her
youthful self, her ecstasies with his despairs. Her semi-slumbers
are never retreats into the oblivion of unconscious, involuntary
life, but a Keatsean adventure in negative capability in which
the misery of the human lot is forgotten, and her awareness
heightened and enhanced by the incandescent, lustrous beauty
of the world.

After her metamorphosis, Orlando's musings always follow
a Keatsean progression: "She began to think, was Nature

21. Samuel Johnson, "Idler #32, *The Idler and The Adventurer,* ed. W. J. Bate,
John M. Bullitt, L. F. Powell (New Haven: Yale University Press, 1970), p. 100.
22. Johnson, "Idler #32," p. 101.
23. Ibid.

beautiful or cruel; and then she asked herself what this beauty was; whether it was in things themselves, or only in herself; so she went on to the nature of reality, which led her to truth, which in its turn, led to Love, Friendship, Poetry . . ." (p. 145). In tracing the Keatsean meditative progress from Nature to Beauty to Love, Friendship, and Poetry, Orlando converts and confesses to the Keatsean faith that is "certain of nothing but of the holiness of the Heart's affections and the truth of the Imagination."[24] It is a faith best articulated in the great "Ode on a Grecian Urn" to which Orlando alludes in describing her passion for Sasha: "and if there is anything in what the poet says about truth and beauty, this affection gained in beauty what it lost in falsity" (p. 161). Orlando's renewed faith in the authenticity of the imagination is evidenced in the recovery and recognition of "Sasha the lost": "At last, she cried, she knew Sasha as she was" (p. 161). This Keatsean act of projection is at the heart of Woolf's aesthetics. Her sublimities are never egotistical, Wordsworthian excurses into a nature that reflects the agitations—or tranquillities—of her own mind. Woolf endorses the selflessness of Keatsean poetics that believes men of genius "have not any individuality, any determined character."[25] Women, as Pope had argued, have no characters at all, a sentiment Woolf deliberately distorts in *Orlando* in order to suggest that the "characterless" poetic stance defined by Keats may be naturally and primarily female in its values and techniques. The "Humility and capability of submission"[26] intrinsic to the Keatsean poetic stance has been culturally and biologically associated with women. The Keatsean question Orlando asks—"Which is the greater ecstasy? the man's or the woman's?"[27]—is resolved in favor of

24. John Keats, *The Letters of John Keats,* ed. Hyder Edward Rollins (Cambridge, Mass.: Harvard University Press, 1958), vol. 1, p. 184.
25. Ibid.
26. Ibid.
27. The question ultimately refers to the Tireseian riddle concerning the "secrets of Hera," secrets only revealed to the prophetic seer, who, of course, pays dearly for his knowledge.

feminine rapture: "For nothing . . . is more heavenly than to resist and to yield; to yield and to resist. Surely it throws the spirit into such a rapture than nothing else can" (p. 155). The capability for imaginative receptivity can only be preserved by the anonymity of the poetic speaker, a notion later to be expanded in *The Waves.*

The discovery of the aesthetic of anonymity, which follows from the recognition of Sasha as she really was, not as Orlando desired her to be, marks a major stage in Orlando's aesthetic education. Her initiation into the Keatsean mysteries of imagination is psychologically prepared for in the Nick Greene episode that comprises Orlando's most systematic attempt to study literature. Greene had replaced Sasha as the figure of the "Muse in person" (p. 103) and like Sasha, he had proved treacherous. The portrait of Greene, based partially on Edmund Gosse,[28] is exploited for its full caricature value. Greene's self-serving and self-glorifying aesthetic is ridiculed in his Dickensian repetition of "Le Gloire" (le Glawr), an eccentric, Anglicized pronunciation that emphasizes his parochial sense of literary worth. "Glawr" is a precise, if vulgarized expression for Greene's reactionary, smug aesthetic. His notion of the artist as a hero inspired by a "divine ambition" appeals to the young Orlando who, like Quixote, has been schooled, if not maddened, by the legacy of chivalry and the literature of epic and romance. Orlando's tendency to idealize men of letters as models of moral as well as literary excellence leads him to venerate both Greene and his art. Only Orlando's later encounter with the greater poet, Alexander Pope, effectively checks this idealizing compulsion. In Woolf's unsentimental caricature of the poet, Pope's physical deformity is emphasized as an emblem of his wretchedness: "Deformed and weakly, there is nothing to venerate in you, much to pity, most to despise" (p. 206). Yet Orlando can and does distinguish between the poet's ignoble and pitiable body and his

28. Quentin Bell, *Virginia Woolf: A Biography,* p. 132n.

noble brow that houses a wealth of wit, wisdom, and truth. To divorce the artificer from the artifact, the poet from his personality is part of Woolf's comic good sense in *Orlando,* another of her fine discriminations between the double faces of love.

Greene personifies, then, the aesthetic of personal Glawr; Pope personifies the untenability and unattractiveness of such an aesthetic. Poetry may be the witch, but the desire for personal fame is the strumpet in Woolf's allegory of the Muses (p. 81). Orlando's disenchantment with the glory-seeking Greene leads him to adopt a self-suppressing and self-disguising aesthetic whose great model is, of course, Shakespeare. Thus the caricature value of Greene's aesthetic is that it generates an antithetical value, the "value of obscurity and the delight of having no name" (p. 104). Now "careless of glory," Orlando meditates on

> how obscurity rids the mind of the irk of envy and spite; how it sets running in the veins the free waters of generosity and magnanimity; and allows giving and taking without thanks offered or praise given; which must have been the way of all great poets . . . for, he thought, Shakespeare must have written like that, and the church builders built like that, anonymously, needing no thanking or naming. . . . [p. 105]

The aesthetic whose ideal is the anonymous work of creation is rooted in a psychological paradox. Only a selfless mind, freed from the petulant claims of the ego with its envies and spites, from the distractions of sex, from the cares of fame and the impulses toward anger and self-justification, manages to express itself and the singularity of its vision fully. The emblem of such anonymous yet self-substantiating creation is Orlando's estate, dating from the chivalric age and embodying the Medieval aesthetic of anonymity:

> Not one of these Richards, Johns, Annes, Elizabeths has left a token of himself behind him, yet all, working

together with their spades and their needles, their love-
making and their child-bearing, have left this.

Never had the house looked more noble and humane.
[p. 106]

The nobility and humanity of this anonymous creation contrasts with Greene's self-promoting, ambitious aesthetic. Yet
Greene's theorizing is distinguished from Greene's poetical
practice—with rewarding results. Through Greene, Orlando
learns "the power of mimicry which [brings] the dead to life"
(p. 91). The power of mimicry explains why Greene is the
only character in *Orlando* who survives, like the eponymous
hero, from Elizabethan into modern times. Woolf's own
generosity is evidenced in this distinction between the gift and
the giver. The accommodation of Greene, "that querulous
voice" (p. 94), into the narrative voice results in a more
spirited and focused satire on literary and social manners.
Greene's contribution to the narrative is to energize and expand the comic consciousness of what had been, before his
arrival, an essentially frivolous fantasy. Through Greene's
negative example, the comic biography becomes more responsible to its own historicity and conscious of its status as
satiric fiction.

"Amor Vincit Omnia"

Greene's presence in *Orlando* actuates the satiric potential
of *Orlando* as comic biography and literary history. His
"character" is the vehicle by which the fantastic and absurd
elements treated in the narrative are gradually domesticated as
aspects of the familiar historical world. From the picaresque
and historical romance, the forms Woolf most closely mimics
in her representation of the Elizabethan age, *Orlando* evolves
into a comedy of manners that reflects the literary forms and
cultural concerns dominant from Restoration society to the

reign of Queen Anne. Woolf's recreation of eighteenth century society focuses on the historical change of consciousness reflected in an age increasingly preoccupied with the relationship of the sexes and the role of wit in society and literature. In what Lamb called the "artificial comedy" of "the age of Reason," the drawing room becomes the realm of enchantment and the hostess the "modern Sibyl" (p. 199). Society becomes an art responsible for generating the illusion of community, of happiness, of life itself. And London, the city of Congreve, Addison, Swift, Pope, Boswell, and Johnson, the city of coffee houses and salons, replaces the mysterious and exotic East as enchanted, poetic ground. Orlando, who had sought romance in Turkey and in gypsy camps, finds a more subtle romance in London society, which explains why she is never tempted to wander from her native ground again. When she is compelled to seek "life and a lover" it is to London, not to foreign lands, that she directs her quest.

As the eighteenth century draws to a close, the narrative style modulates into a Dickensian tenor that signals the transformation of London, the city of light, into London, the city of mystery and dark designs. Woolf's satire on Victorian manners and style is the most savage in *Orlando,* her most immoderate assault on the extreme conventionality Victorian society tried to impose on its own "undistinguished fecundity" (p. 231). Woolf's analysis of the Victorian temper is one of her most impassioned satires on cultural repression: "Love, birth, and death were all swaddled in a variety of fine phrases. The sexes drew further and further apart. No open conversation was tolerated. Evasions and concealments were sedulously practised on both sides" (p. 229).

Orlando's own revolt against the spirit of the age is dramatized in a scene in which she protests against the Victorian "discovery" of marriage, whose creed of the "indissolubility of bodies" is repugnant to her sense of decency and sanitation (p. 242). Her internal resistance to the creed of marriage is histrionically played out in a tableau that echoes Catherine Earnshaw's mad scene in *Wuthering Heights:*

> "I have found my mate," she murmured. "It is the moor. I am nature's bride," she whispered, giving herself in rapture to the cold embraces of the grass as she lay folded in her cloak in the hollow by the pool. "Here will I lie. (A feather fell upon her brow.) I have found a greener laurel than the bay. My forehead will be cool always. These are wild birds' feathers—the owls, the nightjars. I shall dream wild dreams." [p. 248]

To be nature's bride is the radical solution espoused by the Romantic and solitary imagination. To be wed and accept marriage as the final feminine destiny is the categorical imperative of Victorian society. Orlando's dilemma is emblematic of an authentic cultural impasse generated by the contradictions inherent in the spirit of the nineteenth century, an impasse she circumvents through her marriage to the androgynous Shel. Their resolve to marry is comically effected through Orlando's recitation of Shelley's "Ode to the West Wind," whose famous line "Be thou me" Orlando seems to have taken literally. Shelley's metaphoric wind materializes in the pages of *Orlando,* pursuing and leading Orlando and Shel to the Chapel where their marriage rites will be solemnized. There amidst all the confusion and movement of a resurgent and outraged nature, they recite their vows, although a clap of thunder obliterates the word "Obey" and obscures the passing of the ring from hand to hand (p. 262). Always suspicious of legalism, Orlando submits to a marriage that is more mystic than legal, more poetic than conventional. But her marriage does climax her struggles with the repressive spirit of the Victorian age, the most enervating and demoralizing period of her long historical life (p. 245).

It is only in the modern world that the romantic Orlando finds a serviceable and congenial style. *Orlando*'s comic expanses ultimately congeal in the form of the psychological narrative, a formal change symbolized by Orlando's retreat indoors after her marriage (p. 263). This introversion of the narrative relocates the phantasmagoric and the marvellous within the mind itself, Orlando's mind, the mind of a woman and a poet. Hers is a mind determined to write of love in her own way. Such determination still constitutes something of a transgression against the dictates of the spirit of the age, but Orlando, now mature, artfully dissembles her intentions by propitiating the jealous guardians of art:

Orlando now performed in spirit (for all this took place in spirit) a deep obeisance to the spirit of her age, such as —to compare great things with small—a traveller, conscious that he has a bundle of cigars in the corner of his suitcase, makes to the customs officer who has obligingly made a scribble of white chalk on the lid. For she was extremely doubtful whether, if the spirit had examined the contents of her mind carefully, it would not have found something highly contraband for which she would have had to pay the full fine. She had only escaped by the skin of her teeth. She had just managed, by some dexterous deference to the spirit of the age, by putting on a ring and finding a man on a moor, by loving nature and being no satirist, cynic, or psychologist—any one of which goods would have been discovered at once—to pass its examination successfully. [pp. 265-66]

By comparing great things to small, that is, by successfully caricaturing the transactions between a woman writer and the spirit of the age, Woolf disguises the radically contraband nature of her art. Her stratagem is culturally regarded as "feminine," an act of "dexterous deference" no male writer would feel compelled or even know how to perform. Orlando's own induction into the "sacred fraternity" of artists is thus negotiated by a comic sleight of hand, a feminine wile that deceives the guardians of "customs" by feigning conformity and by masking the satirical, cynical, and psychological urges in her art.

Through such dissimulation, Orlando not only passes the examination or trial preparatory to her poetic initiation, she also gains, "by the skin of her teeth" (a tried and true formula in the timing of comic denouements), an assured independence: "Orlando had so ordered it that she was in an extremely happy position; she need neither fight her age, nor submit to it; she was of it, yet remained herself. Now, therefore, she could write, and write she did" (p. 266). Orlando's happiness is self-willed and self-ordained, as if by imaginative fiat. She authorizes her own arrangement with the spirit of the age, no longer dependent on the praise and blame of the times. Freed from the tyrannies of conventionality in sex, social mores, and literary manners, she can write without distractions.

And she can write and behave according to the dictates of her singular feminine consciousness, much to the biographer's consternation. "Life, it has been agreed by everyone whose opinion is worth consulting, is the only fit subject for novelist or biographer" (p. 267), but Orlando spends her time thinking and imagining, and, as her biographer despairingly remarks, "Thought and life are as the poles asunder" (p. 267). Orlando simply refuses to conform to the canons of mimetic fiction, at least as that canon has been defined by male novelists. Nor will Orlando oblige her biographer by thinking of love in the conventional sense, an acceptable substitute for action in fictions centering on women. Vainly the biographer hopes that Orlando will turn her thoughts to a man, even if those thoughts are of a Laurentian gamekeeper:

Surely, since she is a woman, and a beautiful woman, and a woman in the prime of life, she will soon give over this pretence of writing and thinking and begin to think, at least of a gamekeeper (and as long as she thinks of a man, nobody objects to a woman thinking). And then she will

> write him a little note (and as long as she writes little
> notes nobody objects to a woman writing either) and
> make an assignation for Sunday dusk . . . [p. 268]

Orlando is no Lady Chatterley and her acts of love bear little
resemblance to love as the male novelists define it ("and who,
after all," the narrator slyly remarks, "speak with greater
authority?"): "Love is slipping off one's petticoat and—But we
all know what love is. Did Orlando do that? Truth compels us
to say no, she did not" (p. 269). What male novelists have proclaimed "the very stuff of life and the only possible subject
of fiction" is not the stuff of Orlando's imaginings. When her
biographer asks what life is to such a woman, he is only
greeted with the indifferent, perhaps derisive "tee hee, haw
haw, Laughter, Laughter!" (p. 271), the wild nonsense of
nature's brute, if not totally inarticulate creatures. And when
Orlando later laughs at the growing fame of "The Oak Tree"
the biographer is completely exasperated:

> we must here snatch time to remark how discomposing it
> is for her biographer that this culmination and peroration
> should be dashed from us on a laugh casually like this;
> but the truth is that when we write of a woman, every-
> thing is out of place . . . the accent never falls where it
> does with a man. [p. 312]

There is much casual laughter in the last pages of *Orlando,*
and there is also the laughter of mania, the great pathological
correlate of the comic.[29] Orlando's untimely, indecorous, and
often irrational fits of laughter, so disconcerting to her biographer, suggests that the object of Woolf's extended joke on
life and art is to effect a permanent transformation of the
creative ego. From the didactic impulses of satire, *Orlando*
turns towards a more aesthetic perspective on comedy that
treats the ego as a work of art. Bergson, in his essay "On

---

29. Kris, *Psychoanalytic Explorations in Art,* p. 186.

Laughter," noted this double function of comic art. Bergson argues that

> [though laughter] does not belong to the province of esthetics alone, unconsciously (and even immorally in many particular instances) it pursues a utilitarian aim of general improvement. And yet there is something esthetic about it, since the comic comes into being just when society and the individual, freed from the worry of self-preservation, begin to regard themselves as works of art.[30]

As satiric fiction, *Orlando* pursues the utilitarian aim of general improvement. As modern psychological fiction, *Orlando* describes the postromantic quest for self-integration, allegorized in an immensely playful and amusing psychomachia in which the multiple selves composing the modern ego, each with "attachments elsewhere, sympathies, little constitutions and rights of their own" (p. 308) compete for psychic dominance. The resulting dumb show dramatizes the gestures of these selves trying to communicate with and invoke "this Orlando, what is called, rightly or wrongly, a single self, a real self" (p. 314).

The art of life in *Orlando* is thus of the same order as the art unconsciously created by Mrs. Ramsay in *To the Lighthouse*—the synchronization of time as a humanized form of eternity. Nothing more quickly disorders the mechanism of chronological time, observes the narrator, than contact with any of the arts (p. 306). The comic intent of Orlando is "to synchronise the sixty or seventy different times which beat simultaneously in every normal human system so that when eleven strikes, all the rest chime in unison, and the present is neither a violent disruption nor completely forgotten in the past" (p. 305). The aesthetic of laughter, with its broad

30. Henri Bergson, "On Laughter," in *Comedy* (Garden City, New York: Doubleday Anchor, 1965), p. 73.

encompassing powers, unites past and present, making them "one and entire" and presenting "a larger surface to the shock of time" (p. 320).

But the real triumph of comedy, like the authentic triumph of love, is in generating the urge to futurity. As Orlando travels along the Old Kent Road on Thursday, the eleventh of October, 1928, she searches among its crowded streets for portents of her own future. She sees over a porch an incomplete legend that could serve as an epigraph for her own comic quest: "Amor Vin—" (p. 307). But absorbed as she is in the immediate present, "nothing could be seen whole or read from start to finish" (p. 307). Only imagination can extrapolate from the labor of the present a sign of the fruition to come: *Amor Vincit Omnia.* The legend is completed and Orlando's quest fulfilled on the banks of the Serpentine as she watches a toy boat "climbing through the white arch of a thousand deaths" (p. 322). An object for child's play becomes an object of cosmic play. Orlando's imagination participates in this fantastic enlargement of reality. The toy boat becomes her husband's brig, sailing on the Atlantic, and her mind traces and participates in its comic ascent:

> Up, it went, and up and up. The white arch of a thousand deaths rose before it. Oh rash, oh ridiculous man, always sailing, so uselessly, round Cape Horn in the teeth of a gale! But the brig was through the arch and out on the other side; it was safe at last!
> "Ecstasy!" she cried, "ecstasy!" [p. 327]

Orlando's ecstasy represents the last marvellous transformation in *Orlando,* the transfiguration of the comic, in all its manic, ridiculous, and often useless inventiveness, into the sublime. As Kris writes, "we must look to the sublime for the experience which corresponds in normal life to ecstasy": "This variety of the comic is latest in developing in the course of a man's life; it passes as a sign of emotional maturity and is less dependent on restricted social and temporal norms than other forms of the comic."[31] Woolf's sublimities, however, are not to be understood solely in the tradition of Freud. Clearly her master is Laurence Sterne, whose *Tristram Shandy* also elevates the comic into the upper regions of the sublime. Woolf sees *Tristram Shandy* as a book

> in which all the usual conventions are consumed and yet no ruin or catastrophe comes to pass; the whole subsists complete by itself, like a house which is miraculously habitable without the help of walls, staircases or partitions. . . . For Sterne by the beauty of his style has let us pass beyond the range of personality into a world which is not altogether the world of fiction. It is above.[32]

Orlando, too, is such a book, just as its wild goose springing, like a burgeoning Athena, from the head of Shel in a moment of comic theophany, is as much a cock and bull story as that ending *Tristram Shandy*—and one of the best ever heard.

So it is to Sterne, the master of comic sublimities, that Woolf turns when assessing the centrality of fantasy in the tradition of the novel. In "Phases of Fiction," another essay written contemporaneously with *Orlando* and reflecting its literary concerns, Woolf locates the "Satirists and Fantastics" between "The Psychologists" and "Poets" of the tradition, thus canonizing, however eccentrically, the phases of her own literary career. Between the psychological romance of *To the Lighthouse* and the poetic lyricism of *The Waves* comes

31. Kris, *Psychoanalytic Explorations in Art,* p. 187.

32. "Phases of Fiction," *Collected Essays,* vol. 2, p. 93. John Graham explores the relation between *Orlando* and *Tristram Shandy* in a slightly different context in his "The 'Caricature Value' of Parody and Fantasy in *Orlando*," p. 116. Tracing a more general line of descent and affiliation, Carl Woodring argues that Woolf "says over and over that the history of the novel carries forward no external rules. She read the experimenters, but she was learning from Scott and the Brontës; as a novelist, she was first freed by Sterne." Carl Woodring, *Virginia Woolf* (New York: Columbia University Press, 1966), pp. 4-5.

Orlando. In the same essay Woolf offers her own predictions
for the novel of the future, a fiction that will supersede the
willful, playful, often comically regressive, but finally exuber-
ant fantasies of the past. It will be a poetic novel in the
manner charted by James and Proust, comedians of culture
in their own right, which will "reveal and relate finer threads
of feeling, stranger and more obscure imaginations."[33] Such,
of course, would be the achievement of *The Waves,* in which
Woolf expressed and further refined her strange and obscure
imagination.

33. "Phases of Fiction," p. 102.

5

The Waves

THE EPIC OF "ANON"

"Strange Communications"

The Waves, that "abstract mystical eyeless book"[1] that stands
at the center of the Woolf canon has not, apparently, despite
its highly enigmatic form and baroque style, blinded or confused even the most pragmatic critics of the plain style to its
concrete and visible virtues. Near unanimity supports Leonard
Woolf's contention that *The Waves* is Virginia Woolf's masterpiece.[2] And surely masterpieces were on Woolf's mind in those
years between 1926, when *To the Lighthouse* was completed,
and 1931, when *The Waves* was published. "What has praise
and fame to do with poetry?" Orlando might ask, yet the fact
remains that the unassuming authoress who chose to project
herself, in Lily Briscoe, as a skittish spinster who felt her
paintings were doomed to be hung in attics, must have yearned,
indeed she did yearn, for public praise commensurate to her
own valuations of her literary worth. In fact, *Orlando,* written
in the flush of *To the Lighthouse*'s success, betrays a mind
growing in confidence and ambition. Lily Briscoe's minor
productions, "matches struck suddenly in the dark," yield to
Orlando's epic production, "The Oak Tree," a manuscript
"sea-stained, blood-stained, travel-stained" (*Orlando,* p. 236).

---

1. *WD,* p. 134.
2. " 'It is a masterpiece,' said L., coming out to my lodge this morning. 'And
the best of your books.' " *WD,* p. 168.

As a poem that takes its coloring and themes from the "big world," "The Oak Tree" lies beyond the horizon sketched by Lily Briscoe, firmly planted and perennially fixed on the shore of the carefully limited "little world" of feminine domesticity. The imaginative daring of *Orlando* is in its expansiveness, its extension of the female experience through times and across spaces that Lily Briscoe, gathering her skirts to avoid the oncoming waves, presumably had neither the occasion nor the talents to explore. In *To the Lighthouse* only males are the sailors and adventurers into the wider world, but in *Orlando,* Virginia Woolf allows herself to get her feet wet. Minor feminine talents reach the age of majority in *Orlando,* who, after all, is only four hundred years old.

Orlando reflects the growing feminist concerns that were to occupy Virginia Woolf's political and literary thought for the remainder of her career. It can be read as a fanciful vindication of the rights of literary women. But it remained for *A Room of One's Own* to convert fancy into dogmatic prescription. If women were to become their own masters, they must accept the burden of writing masterpieces, and, Virginia Woolf counsels, accept their place and adjust their vision to the perspectives of the wider world: "For masterpieces are not single and solitary births; they are the outcome of many years of thinking in common, of thinking by the body of the people, so that the experience of the mass is behind the single voice" (*Room,* pp. 68–69). But out of whose body does such masterful thinking emerge, and whose voice speaks with authority about the experience of the masses? The ideology implicit in this statement is not exclusively feminist, but humanistic, an expression of Woolf's perennial optimism in the "common life which is the real life," the life that men and women writers struggle equally to communicate.

Such optimism was not to be sustained. "The words of authority are corrupted by those who speak them"[3] as Neville,

---

3. Virginia Woolf, *The Waves,* (New York: Harcourt Brace Jovanovich, 1959), p. 198. All subsequent references will be to this edition of *The Waves,* which is bound with *Jacob's Room* and constitutes pp. 179–383 in this binding.

the stern classicist of *The Waves,* admonishes. More importantly, in Woolf's own attempted masterpiece, it is the "strange communications" of the visionary Rhoda that take precedence over the common and intelligible communications of the masses. Yet one more glaring anomaly between prescription and performance presents itself in *The Waves:* with the exception of the prefaces that introduce the main body of the narrative, there is no single voice, but six voices competing for authority, and if one voice, Bernard's, speaks last and speaks longest, what is to be made of Percival, the putative hero of the novel who does not speak at all? Strange communications indeed.

Jean Guiguet, one of the earliest and best of Woolf's French critics, has persuasively argued that the kind of thinking embodied in *The Waves* does not derive from a common experience, but from a uniquely autobiographical impulse. Guiguet observes that Woolf initially designated the form of the novel as "autobiography," which, as Guiguet argues, indicates that the novel's six speakers "are not six voices in search of characters, but a single being in search of voices."[4] The anonymity of this single thinker searching for speech or speakers, however, belies the quest for personality that motivates conventional autobiographical narratives. "But who is she?" Virginia Woolf herself enquired, this thinker and creator of masterpieces?

> I am very anxious that she should have no name. I don't want a Lavinia or a Penelope: I want "she." But that becomes arty, Liberty greenery yallery somehow: symbolic in loose robes. [*WD,* p. 140]

The allusion to Lavinia and Penelope, respective heroines of the two great epics of domestication in the tradition, confirms Woolf's growing desire to engage subjects of great, one might even venture, epic amplitude. Perhaps Woolf entertained

4. Jean Guiguet, *Virginia Woolf and Her Works* (London: Hogarth Press, 1965), p. 285.

in her original plan for *The Waves* a feminization of the epic
on the order suggested by Samuel Butler, an author she admired, who must have enchanted Woolf with his theory of an
"authoress" of *The Odyssey*.

But a more inveterate habit competes with Woolf's desire
to invoke a masterful female presence as the controlling voice
of *The Waves*—the habit of dissimulation. It is such a habit
that compels her to drape her epic speaker in the loose and
arty robes of a symbolic "she," a narrative speaker not yet
desexed, but symbolically denatured. Nevertheless, the narrating presence, however slack or modish the artifice meant to
conceal her identity, does establish her authority in the opening panel of *The Waves* where the mythopoeic figure dividing
light from darkness in imitation of the primal, traditionally
male act of genesis, is transfigured into Eos (Aurora in the
Roman pantheon), the goddess of dawn. Woolf invokes a
solar myth whose origins are more archaic than that of the
classical Apollonian tradition or the kindred Christian myth of
the God of Light. Her account of the creative division of
chaos, the separation of light from darkness, day from night,
is essentially Pelasgian, a reversion to pre-Hellenic cosmolo-
gies that recognized only a matriarchal earth-goddess and her
priestesses.[5] Woolf's radical adoption of such an archaic and
primordial myth permits her to refeminize the nominally
masculine sun, making clarity and clarification a female power:

Gradually the dark bar on the horizon became clear as if
the sediment in an old wine-bottle had sunk and left the

5. See Robert Graves, *The Greek Myths* (Baltimore: Penguin Books, 1972),
especially the "Introduction" and notes and commentary on the Pelasgian creation
myth (pp. 27–30) and J. J. Bachofen, *Myth, Religion and Mother Right* (Princeton:
Princeton University Press, 1967), especially Joseph Campbell's introduction to
Bachofen's selected writings (pp. xlvi–xlix) and Bachofen's own essays on "Mother
Right." Jane Marcus's recent work on Woolf's indebtedness to the work of the
classicist, Jane Harrison, is particularly illuminating on this issue, although Marcus has
mainly confined her source studies to *The Years*, which she considers to be Woolf's
"female epic." See especially, Jane Marcus, "Pargetting 'The Pargiters': Notes of an
Apprentice Plasterer," Bulletin of New York City Public Library, vol. 80 (Spring
1977): pp. 416–35.

> *glass green. Behind it, too, the sky cleared as if the white*
> *sediment there had sunk, or as if the arm of a woman*
> *couched beneath the horizon had raised a lamp and flat*
> *bars of white, green and yellow, spread across the sky like*
> *the blades of a fan. . . . The surface of the sea slowly*
> *became transparent and lay rippling and sparkling until*
> *the dark stripes were almost rubbed out. Slowly the arm*
> *that held the lamp raised it higher and then higher until*
> *a broad flame became visible.* [p. 179]

The light that renders the world transparent is an objectifying medium distinctly, if languorously, feminine. It is a light rising higher and spreading farther as it aspires to its own liberation as a translucent visionary medium: *"The light struck upon the trees in the garden, making one leaf transparent and then another"* (p. 179).

Such transparency does not apply, however, to the goddess of dawn, nor to the incognito "She" of which she is both projection and similitude. Eos remains a veiled mythic being whose presence may be imputed, but never revealed and examined in its own right like Percival's, the masculine "Hero" of *The Waves* who invokes an alternate tradition. The veiling of voice and the veiling of power is a primary strategy in *The Waves*. Veils abound in the novel, initially as descriptive metaphors, finally as a narrative technique. The use of the veil as both a descriptive and prescriptive metaphor is first introduced by the thin veil of white water that the first wave breaking in the novel spreads across the sands, a veil that suggests that the initiatory movement in *The Waves* is simultaneously a movement to conceal, to cover over. The novel's inaugural act is equally an act of dissimulation, a veiling not only of the sands, but of the female divinity whose power it is to authorize, as Mrs. Ramsay once authorized, that the bare and sterile grounds of life be draped, as the boar's skull was draped in *To the Lighthouse* and as the deserted beach in *The Waves* is draped, by a protective covering. The veil masks the narrator whose power and whose voice will control the ensuing narrative. If

Eos is a minor divinity displaced by the major, if belated, male divinities in the Olympian pantheon, then the veil may be seen as a protective covering adopted to disguise her subversive and rebellious desire: to rise higher and higher, to supplant the male "sun"—Apollo or Christ, the speaker of oracles in the classical tradition, The Word made flesh in the Christian tradition. If this presumptive female act is at the heart of *The Waves*—and the novel's obsession with creation and the conditions of creation suggest that it is—then Eos becomes a figure of the veiled prophetess reclaiming her original, but now disputed or denied role in the Creation or in the interpretation of creation. Her veil is both a covering and a mantle of investiture proper to oracular or prophetic figures. Veils, that is, are not just metaphors in the novel's imagistic texture; they are narrative garments, strategies, and ploys that permit the "She" behind *The Waves* to speak—and to speak authoritatively. Since "She" has no transparent identity, the words of authority cannot be discredited by she who speaks them. Woolf's dissimulation is the dissimulation of the chaste and pure speaker who conceals herself behind a veil of anonymity in order to speak the truth. This strategy extends and deepens our sense of the traditional anonymity adopted by omniscient narrators (as in the novels of Jane Austen or Henry James), and redefines it as a peculiarly feminine guise, while at the same time not so modestly claiming omniscience—traditionally the attribute of male gods—as within a woman's power as well.

This strategy is not new to Woolf, but readapted and reinterpreted after many years of "thinking in common". The decorum of the veil alludes to St. Paul's pronouncements that a woman must be veiled when she prays or prophesies, a tradition of which Virginia Woolf was only too much aware and which she was to examine and repudiate, with her customary wit, in *Three Guineas*.[6] Anonymity may be the narrative strategy adopted to avoid public shame, for "any woman,"

6. Virginia Woolf, *Three Guineas* (New York: Harcourt, Brace and World, 1966), pp. 166–67.

warns St. Paul, "who prays or prophesies with her head un-
veiled dishonors her head" (1 Cor. 11:5). Later St. Paul attempts to withdraw even this privilege from the woman minis-
trant: "For they [women] are not permitted to speak, but
should be subordinate, as even the law says. If there is anything they desire to know, let them ask their husbands at
home. For it is shameful for a woman to speak in church. What!
Did the word of God originate with you, or are you the only
ones it has reached?" (1 Cor. 14:34–36). Woolf harbored no
desire to speak in churches, although she was to make their
interiors, especially the interior of St. Paul's, the scene of her
more biting satires on religious hypocrisy. But she is seriously
concerned with Paul's charge that the "word" did not originate in or with women. Paul's pronouncement that "all things
should be done decently and in order" (1 Cor. 14:40) is invoked, of course, ironically. The narrative voice of *The Waves*
assumes the Pauline veil of decency not so that the truth will
be concealed or her power chastised, but so that the veil necessary to the truth, the feminine truth, can be pierced and
Truth revealed.

Woolf's double and dissimulating habit of irony also oper-
ates in Percival's name, a name that denotes in its original
French, to pierce the veil (perce-voile).[7] The truth that Percival
covers but that Woolf herself discovers in the private discourse
of her diary rather than in the public discourse of her novel is
the original source of *The Waves*—Woolf's private memory and
love of her late brother, Thoby Stephen:

> Here in the few minutes that remain, I must record,
> heaven be praised, the end of *The Waves*. I wrote the
> words O Death fifteen minutes ago, having reeled across
> the last ten pages with some moments of such intensity

7. See Urban T. Holmes and Sister M. Amelia Klenke, O. P., *Chrétien, Troyes,
and the Grail* (Chapel Hill: University of North Carolina Press, 1959), p. 82, for a
discussion on Percival's name and its symbolic resonances.

and intoxication that I seemed only to stumble after my own voice, or almost, after some sort of speaker (as when I was mad) I was almost afraid, remembering the voices that used to fly ahead. Anyhow, it is done; and I have been sitting these 15 minutes in a state of glory, and calm, and some tears, thinking of Thoby and if I could write Julian Thoby Stephen 1881–1906 on the first page. I suppose not. [*WD,* p. 165]

"I suppose not"—the veiling of personality and feeling is a decorum never violated.

Percival, then, is an inspired name for the hero of a narrative concerned with the powers of dissimulation and obsessed with the recovery of a departed past. He is the central quest figure in a cycle of romances centered in the legend of the Holy Grail whose possession restores the possessor to spiritual wholeness. Yet this seeker of insight is plagued by blindness, this quester for the incorruptible truth revealed by Christ, the eternal Word incarnated in the perishable Flesh, fails because of his silence, his repeated failure to ask the Grail questions. Blindness, incommunicability, a fatal silence, and the mutability of all-too-human words—these are the problems inherited by *The Waves.* Its hero stands as a duplicitous embodiment of that power of momentary and revelatory exaltation in which "the shattered mind is pieced together by some sudden perception" (p. 201). "To bring back exaltation and Percival" (p. 360)—that, as Bernard states, is the project of *The Waves,* a project that records its sources both in an elegiac impulse to commemorate Thoby Stephen and the impulse of romance whose legacy Woolf attempts to revive.

But Percival, like Thoby, may be an irrecoverable presence. If he is to be invoked, he can only be invoked as one invokes a shade or a muse, another mode of "strange communication" common to prophetic voices. Bernard, again, suggests the difficulty of such dialogue between the living and their attendant ghosts:

"I ask, if I shall never see you [Percival] again and fix
my eyes on that solidity, what form will our communication take? You have gone across the court, further and
further, drawing finer and finer the thread between us.
But you exist somewhere. Something of you remains.
A judge. That is, if I discover a new vein in myself I shall
submit it to you privately. I shall ask, 'What is your
verdict?' You shall remain the arbiter." [p. 283]

Percival need not speak; he need only exist as a silent standard
of judgment; indeed he represents the terms of judgment to
which the poetic "novelist" Bernard submits. One of those
terms of judgment is exaltation, that flight of emotion through
which the self arrives at the zenith of its experience on that
"curve of being" traced by the waves. Exaltation is both the
midpoint and apex of the visionary life, a life that can only be
judged by the midpoint and apex of *The Waves*—Percival's
death, his "fall" in India. Percival represents that absence that
defines and measures the fullness of the present, a contradiction succinctly condensed in Bernard's phrase "exaltation and
Percival," a phrase that substantively links the noun of ascent
with the name of the hero who falls. This paradox of a rise
that is simultaneously a fall, a fall from joy, just as a leaf falls
from joy (p. 230), is sustained throughout the novel. Percival
is not the force of life, but the finality of death that measures
"this interminable life." Percival stands for that exaltation that
is also a penetration, a piercing of the veil of life that discloses
death, silence, and nothingness: "'About him'" Bernard
laments, "'my feeling was: he sat there in the centre. Now
I go to that spot no longer. The place is empty.'" (p. 282).
    Percival, then, is that monitory absence that reminds us
that death exerts its claims even in the fullness of life. Yet
the hero who pierces the veil of life cannot relate what is disclosed to him. Percival becomes that absurd and pathetic
figure, a mute seer. Like the oracles displaced by the coming
of Christ and the new dispensation, Percival is an archaic voice

silenced by a new oracular presence that fulfills even as it terminates the prophecies of an earlier age. His mode of exaltation, as Bernard rightly guesses, is over, for always "there will be new things" (p. 283). Chaos and incommunicability replace order and dialogue. This is "more truly death than the death of friends, than the death of youth," says Bernard, "this nothingness" in which "no fin breaks the waste of this immeasurable sea" (p. 374).

The fin that promises the eye relief from the spectacle of the watery wastes is a concrete image of resurgent life and a renascent visionary power, an emblem of that elevation above the wastes that is simultaneously a penetration of the wastes. The fin replaces Percival, whose day is over, as a sign of election, a sign that saves the seer from despair by providing a point of reference on the horizon, a vantage point by which to measure the immeasurable. It is in just such an image that Woolf records the origin of the novel. In the same diary entry in which Woolf expresses her wish to dedicate the novel to Thoby, she writes in another mood of exaltation:

> How physical the sense of triumph and relief is! Whether good or bad, it's done; and, as I certainly felt at the end, not merely finished, but rounded off, completed, the thing stated—how hastily, how fragmentarily I know; but I mean that I have netted that fin in the waste of water which appeared to me over the marshes out of my window at Rodmell when I was coming to an end of *To the Lighthouse*. [*WD*, p. 165]

The netted fin, like the lighthouse, is a symbol of a stabilizing power in the fluidity of an immeasurable sea. As a symbolic object, however, the fin stands in inverse relation to the lighthouse. The lighthouse is a stable, monitory object that wards off danger,[8] yet it is not subject to the disasters it is designed

8. See Geoffrey Hartman's "Virginia's Web" in *Beyond Formalism*, (New Haven: Yale University Press, 1970), p. 73.

to prevent. The fin emerges out of the elemental chaos that is its natural habitat. The first significant symbolic identification of the fin is with a porpoise (p. 307), a creature traditionally associated with the journey of the newly dead through the watery wastes to that other world where they shall gain a new mode of existence.[9] The resulting difference between the lighthouse and the fin as symbols of transcendence is one of formal configuration and imaginative stance. The lighthouse displays the phallic contours redolent of "the bald, the separate identity" (p. 306) characteristic of the masculine consciousness and is thus allied to the male's tragic estrangement from nature. The fin is not described by its definite shape, but by its movements, whose "feminine" turns, "unattached to any line of reason" (p. 307), is allied to the comic rhythm that imitates nature's own cycles of generation. The fin becomes a symbol that comments on its own symbolic nature as a medium in which the mutable constantly transforms itself into ever finer emblems of permanence. Thus Bernard conscientiously writes in his notebook "Fin in a waste of waters," only to observe that the fin that symbolically attached itself to a porpoise transfers its meaning to still another object, this time a pretty woman entering the restaurant where Bernard is dining: "Look where she comes against a waste of waters" (p. 307). Patrolling the wastes is a female presence, not, as in *To the Lighthouse,* the master mariners of the Victorian age. The portentous appearance of the woman foretells a new freedom and power in Woolf's fiction, suggesting that the importance of the recurring fin symbolism in *The Waves* may be in expressing the revisionist impulse always operating in Woolf's formal experimentations.

To the Lighthouse observed a tripartite structure, "The Window," "Time Passes" and "The Lighthouse," a structure in

9. Yeats draws on this tradition in "Byzantium," a poem also exploring the antithetical relation between the artifice of eternity and the mutability of the seas of generation.

which the two outward, inherently stabilizing panels had their continuity interrupted, their light eclipsed, and their values subverted by the middle panel, the empty center of the novel. The window as the symbolic medium that reflects or refracts light, the lighthouse as the symbolic medium that casts light, stood, then, in proper antithetical relation to each other, a relation opposed and threatened by the silence and darkness that characterized the "Time Passes" section. *The Waves* may be an extrapolation of that middle section, suggesting a revisionist reading of Lily's confidence that "Yes, I have had my vision." Both novels center in the memory of a primal garden of childhood, the Isles of Skye in *To the Lighthouse,* the mythical "Elvedon," to which the childhood memory of *The Waves* repeatedly returns and refers. At the center of the first garden is a mother reading to her son, Mrs. Ramsay and her son James, a primal relationship defined and bounded. At the center of Elvedon is a lady *writing.* The woman is no longer a transmitter, but an interpreter of reality. Women will always be revered in Woolf's fiction as mothers, but *The Waves* extends Woolf's sense of feminine creativity, an extension that necessitates broadening the area of female communications. No longer is the primal feminine relationship confined to the dialogue between mother and child, private voice addressing a private listener in the intimacy of domestic life. Now the feminine voice addresses a wider audience.

The visionary power represented in both women is, of course, the same—the power of dreams. Dreams are the mode of representation favored by, though not confined to, the feminine imagination. Mrs. Ramsay, Lily Briscoe, Cam, Rhoda, and finally the anonymous narrator of *The Waves* collectively compose Woolf's portrait of the artist, the artist "in whose mind dreams have power" (p. 221). Like Bernard, that novelist with the "sensibility" of a woman, the feminine artist inhabits "the sunless territory of non-identity. A strange land" (p. 255), the land of dreamers. Such territory, the dreamscapes of the mind, constitutes the narrative terrain of *The Waves,* from Louis's dream of women passing with red pitchers to the Nile (p. 182) to Rhoda's dream of "marble columns and pools on the other side of the world where the swallow dips her wings" (p. 248) to Bernard's "world seen without a self" (p. 376).

In dreams, then, there is no self, only the projection of the self—Percival, the hero, the idealized figure of human desire. On him are projected all the private longings of the characters in the novel, but, as in dreams, such projections are not unaccompanied by secret feelings of resentment, envy, and, occasionally, scorn. The ambivalence latent in the dream work of the novel reveals itself in the absurd death of the glorious hero, Percival's ignominious fall in India. Percival's demise combines bathos and pathos. His burlesque fall functions as a criticism of the pretensions of imperial Britannia, that messianic empire of light enforcing its values and its manners on the darker races. Yet if Percival as a public symbol is subject to satiric criticism, Percival as a private symbol is the emblem of personal grief, his death recalling the pathos of a hero dying young, the great theme of heroic elegy.

Woolf's ambivalent treatment of Percival constitutes yet another mode of narrative dissimulation. Percival may represent, that is, only the manifest, not the latent content of the dream desire. For example, in a dream interpretation that also centers in the memory of a loved figure of authority, Freud reports a dream of his dead father in which his father is represented in a manifestly absurd situation, an absurdity, Freud explains, that initially would seem to indicate "the presence in the dream-thoughts of a particularly embittered and passionate polemic."[10] But Freud argues that the polemic surface of the dream merely worked to disguise the true subject of his dream:

10. Sigmund Freud, *The Interpretation of Dreams,* in *Standard Edition,* vol. 5, p. 436.

My father was made into a man of straw, in order to
screen someone else; and the dream was allowed to
handle in this undisguised way a figure who was as a rule
treated as sacred, because at the same time I knew with
certainty that it was not he who was really meant.[11]

One may apply Freud's theory that dreams invariably
disguise or distort their true subjects to Woolf's seemingly
"absurd" treatment of Percival, a figure who as a rule is
treated as sacred. Percival may be provisionally regarded as
a decoy figure whose function it is to divert attention from the
novel's real center, the "She" not the "He" who successfully
pierces the veil. Displacement and dissimulation are necessary
to avoid all those censors of private feminine dreams, in this
case, the loud clammering world ever insisting that "women
can't paint, women can't write" or to comply with the Pauline
pronouncement that women, to avoid censure, must veil themselves. The analogy between dream-censorship and the repressive forces at work in social and public life is one constantly
used by Freud to explain the indirection and distortion common to dream formation. As Freud writes: "In social life,
which has provided us with our familiar analogy with the
dream-censorship, we also make use of the suppression and
reversal of affect, *principally for purposes of dissimulation*"
(emphasis mine).[12]

The suppression of the true subject of the novel and the
reversal of affect that surrounds Percival's death may, then,
be yet another Woolfian effort at dissimulation. To paraphrase Freud, even though it is a "He" or Percival who seems
to occupy the novel's empty center, even though it is Percival
from whom the reader expects the final unveiling, "it is not he
who was really meant." The disguised presence and subject
of the novel, a presence distorted and concealed in the dream

11. Ibid.
12. Ibid., p. 471.

work of the novel, is the "real novelist"—Virginia Woolf, the woman writing in the seclusion of Rodmell-Elvedon. Bernard, near the conclusion of his "summing-up" that purports to be a full statement—or exposure—of the meaning latent, distorted, displaced, condensed, and symbolized in the novel, raises his old objection to those feminine presences allied to nature and the dreaming feminine will. He recalls a visit to Susan, another female working out her destiny in a secluded garden, another female who took the veil and left the world, and in so doing, refused Percival's offer of love. "She who had refused Percival lent herself to this, to this covering over" (p. 363), Bernard criticizes, lamenting the missed marriage between the maternal, generative power of the eternal feminine embodied in Susan and the heroic, executive, and judicial powers embodied in Percival, the hero who could have "saved" India. Through choice and through blind chance respectively, both Susan and Percival submit to the stupidity of nature, one by covering over, the other by being covered over (Percival in the tomb).

Bernard contrasts this double image of insensible surrender with "the old image" retrieved from childhood, a memory of gardeners sweeping and a lady writing:

> "Sitting down on a bank to wait for my train I thought then how we surrender, how we submit to the stupidity of nature. Woods covered in thick green leafage lay in front of me. And by some flick of a scent or a sound on a nerve, the old image—the gardeners sweeping, the lady writing—returned. I saw the figures beneath the beech trees at Elvedon. The gardeners swept; the lady at the table sat writing." [p. 363]

Bernard constantly refers to this "old image" at those moments when the fluidity and insensibility of nature threaten to overwhelm that fixity of vision by which the mind pictures to itself a world immune from change. Perplexed by the "mystery of things" (p. 379), Bernard reverts to this image to oppose nature's mystery with the imagination's own "strange" powers:

> Down below, through the depths of the leaves, the gardeners swept the lawn with great brooms. The lady sat writing. Transfixed, stopped dead, I thought, "I cannot interfere with a single stroke of those brooms. They sweep and they sweep. Nor with the fixity of that woman writing." It is strange that one cannot stop gardeners sweeping nor dislodge a woman. . . . [p. 343]

Neither nature nor the doubts of a skeptical world can interfere with the fixity of that lady writing in her garden. The garden setting provided for the image recalls more Edenic times, but the roles of women and men assigned in Edenic times are reversed and exchanged. Men are now the gardeners, reducing to order the mindless fecundity of nature, and it is the woman who possesses the power of naming, who challenges the strangeness of nature with her own "strange" powers of communication and concentration. Such is the self-generated and self-authenticating power Woolf sought and found in writing *The Waves.* Nor will, one suspects, that authority ever be seriously challenged again, nor will that lady writing be easily dislodged.

The Waves, then, completes and fulfills the quest for artistic autonomy begun in *To the Lighthouse* with the laying to rest of ancestral ghosts. *To the Lighthouse* represented a displaced version of the incarnation of the poetic voice that confirmed the authenticity of a female visionary presence through an elaborate family ritual of literary investiture. *The Waves* terminates the era of female regency, an era in which men rule the literary world while minor feminine talents mature and await the age of majority.

Such displacements of literary intentions are not merely evasions. They are the proper mode of representation in dreams, as Freud has taught us. Moreover, no other form of

representation could serve Woolf's ambitions and visions so well.
Dreams, too, are modes for those "strange communications" of
the private and inspired self, and yet, dreams are also the most
archaic and continuous mode of thinking "common to all men."

The Myth of the Body

The Waves, then, presents a displaced creation myth rendered
in distinctly feminine terms and expressing peculiarly feminine
ambitions. It describes the formation of a subjectivity which,
although common to all minds, finds its representative voice in
the female "She" who reflexively comes to know and identify
herself. Percival, the reputed hero of the novel, is denied a
speaking voice for reasons more substantive than mere feminine whimsy. He represents in the novel a privileged masculine
tradition that envisions no ultimate *external* obstacle to the
romantic project of self-integration. He embodies an earlier
revered, but now anachronistic "myth of the body,"[13] as
Woolf designates the tradition in an essay on Spenser. The
male quest hero experiences no radical and unsurmountable
opposition between public and private roles, between the
active and contemplative life, between body and mind, between knowing and loving, whereas it is precisely such a disjunction between private and public life, Woolf argues in the
polemical sections of *A Room of One's Own,* that has traditionally divided the social and historical "being" assigned and
reserved for women.

Yet by one of those peculiar turns of fortune that always
fascinated Woolf as a novelist and as a social and literary
critic, it is precisely the collective history of women that
makes them selectively adapted to the "modern" sensibility, a
sensibility for which, to use Woolf's own suggestive analysis,

Feelings which used to come single and separate do so no
longer. Beauty is part ugliness; amusement part disgust;

13. "The Faery Queen," *Collected Essays,* vol. 1, p. 16.

> pleasure part pain. Emotions which used to enter the
> mind whole are now broken up on the threshold.[14]

The modern mind no longer receives nor contains its emotional impressions as single, separate, yet unified wholes. It is
precisely such a mind, divided and at odds with itself, that
The Waves represents in its six speaking voices. Neville, Jinny,
Susan, Bernard, Louis, Rhoda—these fragmentary "beings"
are merely aspects of "the body of the complete human being
whom we have failed to be, but at the same time, cannot
forget" (p. 369). Their nascent modern consciousness of
disassociation frustrates the search for "one life" that is the
novel's stated desire. As Bernard says:

> When I meet an unknown person, and try to break off,
> here at this table, what I call "my life," it is not one
> life that I look back upon; I am not one person; I am
> many people; I do not altogether know who I am—Jinny,
> Neville, Rhoda, or Louis: or how to distinguish my life
> from theirs. [p. 368]

Self-definition is the central problem in *The Waves*. Each
speaking voice is not a "character" in the traditional novelistic sense, a figure with a unique moral life and a distinct
moral destiny. Rather each voice laments its own condition as
a threshold being, a being whose love, like Neville's, is partly
beautiful, partly ugly, inspiring pity as well as revulsion; whose
joys, like Jinny's in her ecstatic love affair with the body, inspire both amusement and disgust; whose happiness, like
Susan's, is part pleasure and part pain ("I hate and I love");
whose life is "accented," like Louis's, by social forces and acci-
dents of birth beyond its control; or whose visionary power,
like Rhoda's, causes as much anxiety as ecstasy. Even taken
collectively, these six characters in search of an author to
integrate their personalities and substantiate their vague
identities do not compose a satisfactory whole: "We are

14. "The Narrow Bridge of Art," *Collected Essays,* vol. 2, p. 222.

edged with mist. We make an unsubstantial territory" (p. 185). Neville echoes Bernard's despair in a still more desperate register: "But without Percival there is no solidity. We are silhouettes, hollow phantoms moving mistily without a background" (p. 259).

The plight of six characters in search of an author is secondary, however, to the plight of an author in search of a "character." Woolf, like so many modern novelists, is plagued by the modernist's apparent inability "to display a typical figure," an ability she credits Spenser, and in general all the Renaissance masters, especially Shakespeare, with possessing. On reading Spenser's *Faerie Queene,* Woolf exulted that "we feel that the whole being is drawn upon, not merely a separate part."[15] On reading *The Waves,* we might despair, all we feel is the struggle of a degenerating organism whose psychic and motor functions operate independently; we observe the sad spectacle of the literary "figure" trying to reassemble and reintegrate itself so as to recover "that mobility and fearlessness and simplicity" that belongs to the unified self.

The modern literary "figure" inhabits an unsubstantial territory. The literary self and its projected world are no longer polarized for tragic—or comic—confrontation, but reconverge into an undifferentiated, phantasmal shadowland, that shadowland that existed before and awaits anew the individuating power of the light. The modern self is a misty figure doomed to be reclaimed by that primordial waste of water out of which it originally emerged. Without Percival there is no solidity, no opposition to the liquidation of the human form that is "the divine specific" against nature's generalities, her "sublimities and vastitudes and water and leaves" (p. 210). The task of the creative, form-endowing consciousness is to detach itself from the liquidities of nature and project onto nature's misty background that solidity of form that assures the human figure of its intactness and its

15. "The Faery Queen," p. 16.

reality. *The Waves* formally embraces autobiography and cosmogony; it simultaneously creates and reclaims out of the primordial wastes that typical figure whose destiny mirrors the abiding reality concealed behind what breezily passes for life:

> Now is life very solid or very shifting? I am haunted by the two contradictions. This has gone on for ever; will last for ever; goes down to the bottom of the world—this moment I stand on. Also it is transitory, flying, diaphanous. I shall pass like a cloud on the waves. Perhaps it may be that though we change, one flying after another, so quick, so quick, yet we are somehow successive and continuous we human beings, and show the light through. But what is the light? [*WD,* p. 138]

Solidity and liquidity—these appear to be the fundamental categories of human existence and human thought, categories that in turn generate those fundamental contradictions explicit in Virginia Woolf's ontology: permanence and mutability, identity and selflessness, solitude and community, realism and romance, rationality and dreams, and, even more fundamentally, male and female who embody and participate in these contradictions in varying, if indeterminate degrees. Such contradictions inform that "body" of reality untransfigured by any human semblance and significance. In her darkest moments of vision, Woolf's metaphysics is indebted to Lucretius, the classical poet whose own vision of "the nature of things" depends, for all his unrelenting and uncompromising materialism, on the proposition that "there is a vacuity in things,"[16] an intangible and empty space that permits movement. For Lucretius, as for Woolf, the nature of reality is double:

> In the first place, we have found that nature is two-fold, consisting of two totally different things, matter and the space in which things happen. Hence each of these must

16. Lucretius, *On the Nature of the Universe,* tr. R. E. Latham (Baltimore: Penguin Books, 1971), p. 37.

exist by itself without admixture of the other. For where there is empty space (what we call vacuity), there matter is not; where matter exists, there cannot be a vacuum. Therefore the prime units of matter are solid and free from vacuity.[17]

Absolute solidity of substance and empty space are two of the three "everlasting objects" in the Lucretian universe.[18] Percival's "solidity" and the empty space created by his death are the two central realities in *The Waves.* Solidity is a substantive noun in the rhetoric of *The Waves,* designating that density of being that alone can protect itself from the tireless efforts of nature to "liquidate" all that man is and all that man creates. For example, in the fourth preface of the novel, when the sun, *"risen, no longer couched on a green mattress"* bares its face and looks straight over the waves, it regards, with divine indifference, a world totally devoid of shadows:

> *Everything was without shadow. A jar was so green that the eye seemed sucked up through a funnel by its intensity and stuck to it like a limpet. Then shapes took on mass and edge. Here was the boss of a chair; here the bulk of a cupboard. And as the light increased, flocks of shadow were driven before it and conglomerated and hung in many-pleated folds in the background.* [p. 251]

The individuating power of the light is the power to endow shapes with mass and edge, to *materialize* the shadowy forms that languish in nature or in the mind. Yet such a solidifying power is challenged by the equally relentless movement of the waves, moving *"in and out with the energy, the muscularity of an engine which sweeps its force out and in again"* (p. 250). Solidity—the integrity of individuated matter—and liquidity—the original amorphous state to which matter is destined to return—these terms define the world polarized for that nascent

17. Ibid., p. 120.
18. Ibid.

subjectivity, that "She" in pursuit of an original form of being that shows the light through.

But what is the light, as Woolf herself wondered? It is clear that the light which is the master-light of all our seeing illuminates a world of startling contrasts, a world of shadowy backgrounds as well as substances. And if that light reveals to the visionary a "world immune from change," that world is finally humanized by the presence of two figures "without features robed in beauty, doomed yet eternal" (p. 365). In Woolf's heaven, there may be no marriages or giving in marriage, but there is that eternal dialogue of "what he said and she said" out of which the elected seer can "make poetry" (p. 314).

This poetic dialogue constitutes Woolf's own version of a "myth of the body" whose proper symbol is the androgyne. In the androgynous poetic body, male and female speak from a "centre of some different order and system of life," as Woolf explains her myth of androgyny in *A Room of One's Own* (*Room*, p. 90). This dialogue between what he said and what she said encourages "such a natural difference of opinion" that the mind is charged with "some stimulus, some renewal of creative power which is in the gift only of the opposite sex to bestow" (*Room*, p. 90). The "normal and comfortable state of being," Woolf surmises, is "that when the two live together, spiritually cooperating." And, she concludes, "Perhaps a mind that is purely masculine cannot create, any more than a mind that is purely feminine" (*Room*, p. 102). Both Bernard, the "androgynous" novelist who possesses "the logical sobriety of a man" that is "joined to the sensibility of a woman" (p. 227), and the "mind" expressing itself through *The Waves* appear to verify this proposition. Yet the novel itself seems to focus on the purely masculine and purely feminine minds of "characters" who are incapable of achieving such normalcy and comfort. The primal "He" of *The Waves*—Percival—and the primal "She" in *The Waves*—Susan—represent a marriage of opposites that fails to be consummated. Both confuse the integrity of their sexual natures with that purity of being that is the goal of desire for the novel's "authentics" (p. 255), Louis and Rhoda, the novel's actual lovers. Susan and Percival, each speaking from the center of a different system and order of life are, in the parlance of conventional romances, "meant for each other." But *The Waves* is not a conventional romance. Susan and Percival are not disposed toward spiritual cooperation and sexual union. The only common life they share is rooted in a contradiction: both "have been born without a destiny" (p. 315). Their lives, like their dialogues, lack a moment of consummation, a disaster for the imagination. In their failed communication Woolf centers her most profound meditation on the nature of sexual destiny and the sexual imagination. In *The Waves* what he said and what she said does not always issue in poetry, but, as the love story of Percival and Susan indicates, in rejection, estrangement and death.

At the heart of Susan's and Percival's relationship, at the heart of all Woolf's novels, lies a pure negativity. Percival's solidity is the solidity emanating from that complex force of masculinity that has subjugated the world and has led man from the state of nature to the state of culture. Percival embodies the Roman *virtus,* that virile and potent maleness that posits a "world that our own force can subjugate and make part of the illumined and everlasting road" (p. 277). He represents Woolf's respectful but ironic homage to classical man, *homo faber,* who projected onto the world his illusions of linearity, of clarity, of a permanence that triumphs over time, of a centrality that accumulates all things to itself. All roads do in fact lead to Rome and to Percival "who is allied with the Latin phrases on the memorial brasses" (p. 199). In describing him during the "summing up" of *The Waves,* Bernard remembers Percival's "magnificent equanimity (Latin words come naturally) that was to preserve him from so many meannesses and humiliations" (p. 344). Latin words *do* come naturally to Percival, though they do not come *from* him naturally. In "applying the standards of the West" to the "Oriental problem" he uses "the violent language that is

natural to him" (p. 269). Yet his exploits inspire a more measured and civilized style. As one in a long line of founders in
the Western tradition, Percival recalls "the exactitude of the
Latin language, . . . the sonorous hexameters of Virgil, of
Lucretius; [the] chant with a passion that is never obscure or
formless[,] the loves of Catullus" (p. 196). Percival is part of
the "big book" that chronicles the masculine adventure, annals
filled with "tremendous and sonorous words" (p. 196). He
embodies the masculine "high style" whose Latinate cadences
and sonorities no woman, as Woolf observed, can or should
imitate,[19] but neither is he the high style that should be
destroyed.

But destroyed that style has been, as destroyed it had to be.
Bernard, too, has a Roman vision in the novel in which he contemplates, in a scene loosely echoing Dorothea Brooke's
Roman vision in George Eliot's *Middlemarch,* the grandeur
that was Rome. As he watches a Roman street scene, a woman
enters, and Bernard, like Dorothea as she gazes on "ruins and
basilicas, palaces and colossi, set in the midst of a sordid
present,"[20] hears the accent of catastrophe, a "fatal sound of
ruining worlds and waters falling to destruction" (p. 307). Out
of this catastrophe Bernard conceives of a new chapter for his
novel, whose subject will be "the formation of this new, this
unknown, strange, altogether unidentified and terrifying
experience—the new drop—which is about to shape itself"
(p. 307). Bernard does not simply describe the beginning of
a new era, the new world of modernism struggling to be born
out of the ruins of the old; he also identifies both the source
and the agent of catastrophic change: "Look where she comes
against the waste of waters" (p. 307).

At this point in the narrative what he, Bernard, said, is followed by what she, Susan, said. Susan resumes the dialogue
with her answering celebration of the feminine work, the work

19. *Room,* p. 79.
20. George Eliot, *Middlemarch* (Boston: Houghton Mifflin Co., 1968), p. 143.

of her "laboriously gathered, relentlessly pressed-down life" (p. 308). Her peaceful and productive years, unlike Percival's, are rewarded by security, familiar surroundings, and possessions, although she also voices some discontent with her feminine powers: "I am sick of the body, I am sick of my own craft, industry and cunning, of the unscrupulous ways of the mother who protects, who collects under her jealous eyes at one long table her own children, always her own" (pp. 308-09). Susan, the ancient "She" who "first became wholly woman, *purely* feminine" (p. 348, emphasis mine), challenges Percival's solidity with her own "hardness" (p. 325). She, too, has "seen life in blocks, substantial, huge; its battlements and towers, factories and gasometers" (p. 325), but her vision remains resolutely conservative. Her monuments testify to the essentially feminine project of reducing nature to "a dwelling place made from time immemorial after an hereditary pattern" (p. 325). Nor does she, like Percival, wish to tamper with those hereditary patterns transmitted from generation to generation. Susan registers the eternal ambivalence indigenous to a feminized nature, an ambivalence toward man and toward the work of man that expresses itself through the words of Catullus: I hate, I love, *odi et amo.* She incarnates the powers of a jealous nature, a nature possessed by and possessing man, a nature which counters the productivity of man with her own transcendent egoisms: "I think I am the field, I am the barn, I am the trees; mine are the flocks of birds, and this young hare who leaps, at the last moment when I step almost on him. Mine is the heron that stretches its vast wings lazily; and the cow that creaks as it pushes one foot before another, munching; . . . the silence and the bell; the call of the man fetching cart-horses from the fields—all are mine" (p. 242). Susan's integrity is the integrity of that voracious nature that "cannot be divided, or kept apart" (p. 242).

Yet if she battles and hates the intrusions of the male will into her domain, she also loves and nurtures those of her sons who will, in their maturity, learn to oppose her: "Sleep,

sleep, I croon, whether it is summer or winter, May or November. Sleep I sing—" (p. 294). Sleep I sing—Susan is the muse of an epic Nature, singing nature's lullaby. Yet her crooning, pacific voice disguises "some wilder, darker violence, so that I would fell down with one blow any intruder, any snatcher, who should break into this room and wake the sleeper" (p. 294). Susan's "art," like Mrs. Ramsay's, whose tyranny she refines and sublimates, is rooted in the female power of dissimulation in its most radical form. She desires, like Mrs. Ramsay, that "sleep (fall) like a blanket of down and cover these weak limbs"; she demands, as does Mrs. Ramsay when she wraps her shawl over the boar's skull in her children's bedroom, "that life sheathe its claws" (p. 295) in the presence of innocent life. Yet out of Susan's cradle, protected and shielded from all that endangers the dreaming will, will emerge a new Percival, the child, Susan dreams, who "shall see India. He will come home, bringing me trophies to be laid at my feet. He will increase my possessions" (p. 295). For Susan, the pageantry of the ages and the victories of the imperial male will serve to expound her glories, for she never doubts who shall be the victor in the primordial, hereditary, and continuing war between "He" and "She," between culture and nature. Her will to reclaim all the artifacts of man's material culture remains indomitable: "I would bury the red tiles and the oil portraits of old men—benefactors, founders of schools" (p. 205). Susan would "bury it all."

Incarnating as she does the "bestial and beautiful passion of maternity" (p. 267), the primordial power of generation, she, like Percival, was born to be adored of poets since, as Bernard notes,

> poets require safety; some one who sits sewing, who says, 'I hate, I love,' who is neither comfortable nor prosperous, but has some quality in accordance with the high but unemphatic beauty of pure style which those who create poetry so particularly admire. [p. 348]

The purity of the feminine style is not radically different in *substance* from the purity of the masculine style. Both styles are founded in an unadulterated conventionality. Percival is conventional. He is a hero (p. 260). Susan is conventional. She is the archetypal Earth-Mother whose amoral divinity is never compromised or qualified by any mediating moral individuality. Susan exists, as Percival exists, as a background to be projected upon, a substance to be shaped by an individuating imagination. And like Percival, Susan may inspire, but she can never create her own poetry. Instead Susan buries her images in fetichistic rites, consigning to oblivion all that she hates and all that she loves.

Susan and Percival are without a destiny in the modern world, a world in which time has given, as Bernard says, the arrangement a shake, a world in which the old balances between classical man, *homo faber,* and classical woman, *Magna Mater,* have broken down. The classical myth of the body is superseded in modern times by a grimmer myth—the mythos of *sparagmos,* the dismemberment of the heroic body, the death of Percival. As Northrop Frye has argued, the mythos of *sparagmos* is generated by "the sense that heroism and effective action are absent, disorganized or foredoomed to defeat, and that confusion and anarchy reign over the world."[21] In *The Waves, sparagmos* is invoked as a trope of disorganization. The speakers in the novel are haunted by a sense that their experiences are "single experiences" (p. 260) that cannot be shared, communicated, or assimilated into the "common body" of mankind. Like mortified limbs, the speakers in *The Waves* are cut off from that "body of reality" that alone signifies endurance, meaning, and life. Their consciousness of disseverment induces a trauma that psychologically duplicates that original, biological separation from the parent body by which life itself begins. Consciousness of

21. Northrop Frye, *Anatomy of Criticism* (Princeton: Princeton University Press, 1968), p. 192.

the world, emergence into the world of reality, constitutes, as Bernard says, "a second severance from the body of our mother" (p. 261). Light may dawn in the mind, but to the newly born the world itself appears stubbornly opaque, its principles of order and organization dimly lit and imperfectly articulated. The modernist's dream of life resembles a Lucretian nightmare in which the vulnerable and isolated "I," the fragile identity to which one clings for dear life, is reduced to a free-wheeling atom racing through tracks of infinite space, longing to be relieved, as Rhoda longs to be relieved, "of hard contacts and collisions" (p. 193). "Oh to awake from dreaming!" Rhoda cries, who looks at the world through a glass, darkly.

But how does one wake from the dream? One may, like Lucretius, write "the big book," a *de rerum natura* in which the mystery of things is revealed. But without Percival, such a heroic enterprise proves impossible, for the energies of heroism are disorganized. The death of Percival—this, as Bernard complains, is "the penalty of living in an old civilisation with a notebook" (p. 304). Instead of a big book, the canonical text of the ancients, the moderns invariably express themselves in isolated notations. Or so it strikes a contemporary: "Much of what is best in contemporary work has the appearance of being noted under pressure, taken down in a bleak shorthand which preserves with astonishing brilliance the movements and expression of the figures as they pass across the screen."[22] But, as Woolf concludes in "How it Strikes a Contemporary," "the flash is soon over, and there remains with us a profound dissatisfaction."[23] Unlike the ancients, the moderns are incapable, it seems, of "that complete statement which is literature."[24]

22. Virginia Woolf, "How It Strikes a Contemporary," *Collected Essays,* vol. 2, p. 158.
23. Ibid., p. 158.
24. Ibid., p. 159.

Yet what exerts the pressure on the modern consciousness, and to what extent is that pressure "new"? Bernard notes:

> "And time . . . lets fall its drop. The drop that has formed on the roof of the soul falls. . . . The drop fell. All through the day's work, at intervals, my mind went to an empty place, saying 'What is lost? What is over?' " [p. 303]

To console himself, to dramatize his emotion, Bernard first identifies the loss, the falling drop, with the end of youth. Reconsidering, his analysis becomes more precise:

> "This drop falling has nothing to do with losing my youth. This drop falling is time tapering to a point. Time, which is a sunny pasture covered with a dancing light, time, which is widespread as a field at midday, becomes pendent. Time tapers to a point." [p. 304]

Bernard's imagery is muted, but undeniably apocalyptic in its resonances. Time becomes deformed in the modern mind. No longer linear nor widespread, time becomes dense, pendent, exerting a distinct pressure on the creative consciousness. For life, subject now to the dominion of a "new" time, is no longer susceptible, or so Bernard despairs, of "the treatment we give it when we try to tell it" (p. 362). Stories are still possible, narrative movement through time is still conceivable, but such stories and such movements no longer appear "true":

> "I have made up thousands of stories; I have filled innumerable notebooks with phrases to be used when I have found the true story, the one story to which all these phrases refer. But I have never yet found that story. And I begin to ask, Are there stories?" [pp. 305–06]

Are there stories—on that question, of course, all depends. The novelist, like Bernard, is obsessed with sequences, with stories that not only connect one event and another, one life with another, but stories whose sequences finally define a beginning and an end in imitation of that original "true" story of life and creation whose originating phrase is "Let there be light" and whose parting phrase is "It is finished." Yet the modern novelist can only note apt phrases in the margin of his mind. Never can he assemble them to make a final statement that might unveil the hidden order of things. Soon Bernard does not even trouble to finish his sentences: "Stage upon stage, and why should there be an end of stages? and where do they lead? To what conclusion?" (p. 305). Life, once released from the disciplines of a teleological narration, released, that is, from the discipline of movement initiated and sustained in pursuit of a definable end, becomes a terror for the imagination. Louis, the unhappy poet in life, begins to long for death, yet despairs of finding death or of having death find him: "Perhaps I shall never die, shall never attain even that continuity and permanence" (p. 317). Lacking a natural conclusion, life images itself forth as an uncontrollable vitality, the "great beast stamping" that frightens Louis (p. 221), the tiger about to pounce that appears to Rhoda when "An immense pressure is on me" (p. 248). Only Jinny, whose imagination emanates from her body, is equipped to live a life of indefinite extension across its own material surface. She is comfortable inhabiting a temporal world in which there would be "all one day without division" (p. 212). Jinny never seeks one story; she is content with her "hoard of life" (p. 218).

The Figures of Opposition

If there is no "story" to organize the "hoard of life" into an intelligible sequence, there is at least "the figure flashing across the sky" that can reduce that hoard to an image of totality and completeness. It is finally the figurative, not the narrative power of the novelist that Woolf appeals to in *The Waves*. When Bernard attempts at the end of the novel to sum up his vision of life, it is not life as a temporal progression. Life is apprehended as a "globe, full of figures," a world populated by the human and metaphoric "figures" of the mind.

Each figure in turn expresses, momentarily and perhaps ephemerally, its own story. In Woolf's fiction, the parts are always greater than the "whole story." There is no mathematics of being by which the novelist computes a totality. The addition, as Louis remarks, "will be complete; our total known; but it will not be enough" (p. 238). Sufficiency and comprehensiveness are inadequate measures of life. What *The Waves* forfeits in abandoning a unanimous vision, it gains in the multiplicity and diversity of its estranged figures, each projecting his various interpretations on the copious moment, the hoard of life. *The Waves* honors that "natural difference of opinion" Woolf claimed to be the stimulus of the creative life. Male and female conceive of the world as different orders because each brings to vision different desires: "Each eye makes its own contribution" (p. 262).

For Louis, whose poet is Lucretius (p. 264), there may be no certified mathematics of being, but there is the calculus of manhood, that assiduity and decision that is able "to score those lines on the map there by which the different parts of the world are laced together" (p. 291). Louis's power of figuration, his mapping of the world into unity, is rooted in a self-conscious virility which must leave its mark on all it sees. The masculine imagination is prompted and enticed by the lures of fame. As Woolf satirically comments in *A Room of One's Own,* men cannot "pass a tombstone or a signpost without feeling an irresistible desire to cut their names on it . . . in obedience to their instinct, which murmurs if it sees a fine woman go by, or even a dog, Ce chien est à moi" (*Room,* p. 52). The male instinct to leave a trace, to inscribe a mark on the material world, is indistinguishable from the territorial instinct. The masculine mind aggressively marks the boundaries of the world it inhabits, a world epitomized and comprehended in the letter "I":

> "I have signed my name already . . . twenty times. I, and
> again I, and again I. Clear, firm, unequivocal, there it

stands, my name. Clear-cut and unequivocal am I too.
Yet a vast inheritance of experience is packed in me.
I have lived thousands of years. . . . But now I am compact; now I am gathered together this fine morning."
[p. 291]

Inspired by his sense of historical mission, Louis has not
a moment to spare. For the historically responsible man,
life becomes an affair of engagement books, dates on the wall,
a punctually regulated series of appointments: "This is life;
Mr. Prentice at four; Mr. Eyres at four-thirty." For such
a man, there is no respite: "if we blink or look aside, or turn
back to finger what Plato said or remember Napoleon and
his conquests, we inflict on the world the injury of some
obliquity" (p. 292).

Only Percival can make Louis "blink" and look aside, can
make him aware "that these attempts to say, 'I am this, I am
that,' which we make, coming together, like separated parts of
one body and soul, are false. . . . From the desire to be separate we have laid stress upon our faults, and what is particular
to us. But there is a chain whirling round, round, in a steel-
blue circle beneath" (p. 270). The male need for distinctness
and separateness, at once the source of his anxiety and the
grounds of his vanity, yields, for once, to a superior and truer
desire—to join the collective body and soul of the "one life"
that courses beneath the surface of the world and its artificial
discriminations. Louis is the poet of history who still hears the
songs by the Nile, who was an Arab prince, who was a great
poet in the time of Elizabeth, who was a Duke at the court of
Louis the Fourteenth. As a poet of history, his real mission, as
dictated by Percival, is clear and unequivocal—to connect the
stage upon stage that informs the human pageant in "a steel
ring of clear poetry" (p. 264).

Yet the same image that for Louis connects and completes
the variously discriminated "times" in the ongoing common
life of all people becomes a figure of necessity for Neville, the

poet as lover. For Neville, alone gifted with the splendid clarity and remorseless honesty of intellect, indulges in no mystifications (p. 232). He alone knows how "We are doomed" (p. 281). For him the loop of time and the steel ring become a chain imposed on "the unlimited time of the mind, which stretches in a flash from Shakespeare to ourselves" (p. 366). As the poet of love, Neville, Bernard rightly claims, "changed our time" by living "by that other clock which marks the approach of a particular person" (p. 366). Neville's poetry celebrates the joys—and anxieties—that compose the lyric moment in which time is transformed through the eyes of love. Yet he is simultaneously the most conscious of mechanical time as the antagonist to the eternity love wills for itself. He alone fully comprehends the mutability of the loved one who, as a creature of time, is subject to death, the principle of division. Love, the principle of unity, must create its own images of opposition to "that immitigable tree which we cannot pass" (p. 191). Neville's private torment is thus rooted in that ancient opposition between knowing and loving, the knowledge that introduced death into the world and the loving that can redeem the darkest knowledge. Appropriately Neville transcends this self-division through poetic fable, a fable clearly echoing the myth of Eden, the paradise of pure love. In Neville's lyric adaptation of that fable, Elvedon becomes an Eden already invaded by the knowledge and presence of death —the dead man who slits his throat. And Neville himself assumes the role of Adam who has tasted the apples of "the implacable tree" of knowledge and therefore cannot "pass" the immitigable tree of life. He is the giant mourner in the novel, constantly imagining and reimagining the forms of death, sternly recalling us to the perishability of the body of love.

Jinny, on the other hand, can imagine "nothing beyond the circle cast by my body" (p. 263). She makes light of Neville's torment, moving freely past "this stricture, this rigidity, death among the apple trees":

"The torments, the divisions of your lives have been solved for me night after night, sometimes only by the touch of a finger under the tablecloth as we sat dining— so fluid has my body become, forming even at the touch of a finger into one full drop, which fills itself, which quivers, which flashes, which falls in ecstasy." [p. 329]

Jinny celebrates the carnal ecstasies of love, and so, when the drop of time falls, it merely fills her body with that fluid, Dionysian rhythm through which life endlessly recreates itself. Yet she, too, has a vision of bodies united in more permanent ways than sexual embraces. For Jinny the globe full of figures is comprehended in the figure of the dance. In her bodily imagination, men and women join bodies and are swept up in the ordered rhythms of the dance. The dance is that stylized mode through which bodies may make their own strange communications:

"We go in and out of this hesitating music. Rocks break the current of the dance; it jars, it shivers. In and out, we are swept now into this large figure; it holds us together; we cannot step outside its sinuous, its hesitating, its abrupt, its perfectly encircling walls. Our bodies, his hard, mine flowing, are pressed together within its body; it holds us together; and then lengthening out, in smooth, in sinuous folds, rolls us between it, on and on." [p. 246]

Such is Jinny's myth of the body, the dance of lovers joined in a large and perfectly encircling figure of one life, one rhythm. So complete is Jinny's figure of life that even the "hard" body of the questioning male, who, like Neville, seems fixated on the rock, the jarring note in the universal harmony, cannot perforate nor interrupt the line cast by the dancing body. The dance is an exclusively feminine figure in *The Waves,* a figure that extinguishes or transcends all the essentially masculine traces of the world, the inscribed distinctions between this and that, between he and she, between hard and soft. The dance is the feminine figure that celebrates the anonymity of bodies communicating and communing in the body's own language, the grammar of dance.

Not everyone is capable of entering this great society of bodies that in Jinny's mind forms the image of the inhabited globe. For Rhoda, all inherited figures of thought, those complex notations by which the mind reduces "this interminable life" into an ordered and stationary image of plenitude, remain a source of terror and alienation. For example, when her teacher, Miss Hudson, begins to draw "figures, six, seven, eight, and then a cross and then a line on the blackboard" (p. 188), a simple addition, Rhoda sees only figures: "The figures mean nothing now. Meaning has gone" (p. 189). As she stares at those incomprehensible, meaningless symbols, Rhoda observes that "the loop of the figure is beginning to fill with time." She commences to imitate that process in her own mind, but with terrifying results:

> "I begin to draw a figure and the world is looped in it, and I am myself outside the loop; which I now join—so— and seal up, and make entire. The world is entire, and I am outside of it, crying, 'Oh, save me, from being blown for ever outside the loop of time!'" [p. 189]

Rhoda is capable of creating an image of the world entire, but she cannot penetrate into the meaning she projects. She spends most of her life seeing or drawing figures, yet unable to read in those characters the relatedness and meaning imposed on the world.

But even Rhoda is not without her figures of opposition. She, too, can create an idiosyncratic geometry of being in which the figures of the body inhabiting space are not circular and comprehensive, but angular and austere in their configurations:

> " 'Like' and 'like' and 'like'—but what is the thing that lies beneath the semblance of the thing? Now that light-

ning has gashed the tree and the flowering branch has
fallen and Percival, by his death, has made me this gift,
let me see the thing. There is a square; there is an oblong.
The players take the square and place it upon the oblong.
They place it very accurately; they make a perfect dwell-
ing-place. Very little is left outside. The structure is now
visible; what is inchoate is here stated; we are not so
various or so mean; we have made oblongs and stood
them upon squares. This is our triumph; this is our
consolation." [p. 288]

The triumph and consolation of the mind is in its ability to
create semblances of reality, similes or metaphors—the "like"
and "like" by which the mind connects the known with the
unknown. Yet such figures of connection and similitude never
fully conceal nor eliminate that "flawless verge" (p. 379) that
exists outside any human ordering of the world. The square
may be placed on the oblong, or the oblong stood on the
square, but the two figures—or semblances—will never fully
coincide. Always something is left out, as Bernard says (p. 306).
And the design created remains fundamentally arbitrary. The
human dwelling place, with "all these callings hither and
thither, these pluckings and searchings," merely provide
a stage for "the antics of the individual" (p. 331).

Thus rather than stress this shape or that in the continuing
pageant of life, rather than continue tracing a pattern or network of semblances on the inchoate world of here and now,
Rhoda makes her own unique contribution. Outside of the
loop of time, Rhoda projects another order of existence:
"there are moments when the walls of the mind grow thin;
when nothing is unabsorbed, and I could fancy that we might
blow so vast a bubble that the sun might set and rise in it and
we might take the blue of midday and the black of midnight
and be cast off and escape from here and now" (p. 331).
Rhoda's visionary rhetoric echoes Henry James's famous
definition of romance:

The balloon of experience is in fact of course tied to the earth, and under that necessity we swing, thanks to a rope of remarkable length, in the more or less commodious car of the imagination; but it is by the rope we know where we are, and from the moment that cable is cut we are at large and unrelated: we only swing apart from the globe—though remaining as exhilarated, naturally, as we like, especially when all goes well. The art of the romancer is, "for the fun of it," insidiously to cut the cable, to cut it without our detecting him.[25]

Rhoda is the female romancer, although her art, unlike her male counterpart's, is not "for the fun of it," but is created in obedience to a law of some inner compulsion. If she seeks to escape the here and now, cutting the cable of reality, letting the "bubble" float free, it is with a singular intention: to "return to the world this beauty" (p. 214). Her art reveals the romantic aspect of things, which as James in his commodious way has said, "can reach us only through the beautiful circuit and subterfuge of our thought and our desire."[26] Rhoda's subterfuges, however, are not merely imitations of the circuitousness of desire that constitutes the beauty of romantic sublimations. For her, such subterfuges—cutting the cable without our detecting it—are a matter of necessity as well as technique. To be open and direct, to "go public" would be to expose herself to "a million arrows":

> "Scorn and ridicule pierce me. I, who could beat my breast against the storm and let the hail choke me joyfully, am pinned down here; am exposed. The tiger leaps. Tongues with their whips are upon me. . . . I must prevaricate and fence them off with lies. What amulet is there against this disaster? What face can I summon to lay cool upon this heat?" [p. 248]

25. Henry James, the "Preface" to *The American*, in *The Art of the Novel*, (New York: Charles Scribner's Sons, 1962), pp. 33-34.
26. James, *The Art of the Novel*, p. 32.

Yet no face is summoned. The female romancer must be a mistress of dissimulation, preserving her anonymity, concealing her art. Rhoda, like the narrative "She" who writes *The Waves,* represents the ultimate dissimulation, subterfuge, veiling of self: She has no face.

Rhoda's visionary romances, Jinny's stylized erotica, Susan's dark pastorals, Louis's historical romances, Neville's lyrical meditations on the limits of human love, Bernard's novelistic parables on the nature of time and story—*The Waves* reads like an anatomy of the "body" of literature in the Western tradition. Woolf's primary intention, however, is not to dissect, but to enumerate the various styles of figuration through which the literate body expresses itself. Capitalizing on the pun buried in her repetitive use of the word "figure," figure as both a rhetorical pattern and as a human outline, Woolf reconnects the broken lines of communication between mind and body, aesthetic and natural form. Thus the climax of her novel appropriately announces itself as a set of figurative relations. The "reunion" of the novel's characters at Hampton Court produces a moment in which, as Rhoda says, the structure is now visible. Bernard articulates that structure: "The flower, the red carnation that stood in the vase on the table of the restaurant when we dined together with Percival is become a six-sided flower; made of six lives" (p. 335).

Bernard's rhetorical turn on "flower" is probably the most condensed statement in Woolf's fiction on the nature of aesthetic transformation. The six lives of the speakers had always stood in a double relation to reality, one a naturalistic relation, in which their individual life provided the "realistic" subject matter of the novel, the other a figurative relation, in which their individual life provided symbolic projections of the mind's power to impose design and order. The two powers, as Woolf noted in "Phases of Fiction," are innately incompatible:

A power which is not the power of accuracy or of humour or of pathos is . . . used by the great novelists to shape their work. As the pages are turned, something is built up which is not the story itself. . . . For the most characteristic qualities of the novel—that it registers the slow growth and development of feeling, that it follows many lives and traces their unions and fortunes over a long stretch of time—are the very qualities that are most incompatible with design and order.[27]

In the climax of *The Waves,* this continual warfare between the naturalistic and the structural powers of the novel is momentarily transcended in a figure—the flower—that is doubly referential and triumphantly rhetorical. The real flower in the vase, whose presence signifies the body of reality to which Percival was attached, is transformed and *superseded* by a flower that signifies the reflexive and self-containing powers of language and of thought. The flower Bernard speaks of is the "flower" of rhetoric which is alone capable of uniting divergent styles and separate interpretations of reality into a complementary design. Moreover, the six-sided flower, with three female and three male sides, represents one of the finest "figures" of spiritual cooperation between masculine and feminine styles in all of Woolf's fiction:

> "Marriage, death, travel, friendship," said Bernard; "town, and country; children and all that; a many-sided substance cut out of this dark; a many-faceted flower. Let us stop for a moment; let us behold what we have made." [p. 335]

Marriage, death, travel, friendship—those threads that compose for narrative "the slow growth and development of feeling"—are woven into a fabric in which no single thread and no one determining vision takes priority or dictates direction. "We" is the important word in Bernard's summation; male and female combine creative efforts to produce a moment in which nothing

27. "The Phases of Fiction," *Collected Essays,* vol. 2, p. 101.

goes unassimilated. All that can be transformed into pattern and figure has been transformed into pattern and figure. "Very little," approves the normally dissatisfied and alienated Rhoda, "is left outside" (p. 335).

Once that figurative pattern composed of many and separate lives has completed itself, Bernard is ready for his summation. Yet it would be wrong to assume that Bernard's closing monologue exists beyond the design of complementarity that *The Waves* builds up. He does not comment upon, as much as complete, the continuous effort to lift the veil off the mystery of things. His ending complements and answers the novel's initial questioning of beginnings. Thus he returns at the conclusion of his monologue to the original impressions and the "first faces" (p. 352) of his childhood, and to his childhood's initial landscape—Elvedon, in which a woman sits writing. Coming to the end of his life when "the dusky veil was falling upon our endeavors" (p. 370), Bernard takes note that the orderly progression through time, the illusion of a consecutive life, is "a convenience, a lie" (p. 353): "There is always deep below it, even when we arrive punctually at the appointed time with our white waistcoats and polite formalities, a rushing stream of broken dreams, nursery rhymes, street cries, half-finished sentences and sights—elm trees, willow trees, gardeners sweeping, *women writing*—that rise and sink even as we hand a lady down to dinner" (pp. 353-54, emphasis mine). In that woman writing Bernard finds his ending as well as his beginning. Previously he had wondered, "But if there are no stories, what end can there be, or what beginning?" (p. 362).

But *The Waves* generates its own answers. As Bernard idly muses on how to describe the world seen without a self, a childhood memory supplies a start: "The old nurse who turns the pages of the picture-book had stopped and had said, 'Look. This is the truth' " (p. 376). Woolf's wry domestic wit subtly asserts itself in this image of the nanny communicating

to the succeeding generations the truth about life. It is finally
mother wit that emerges out of the "long ranks of magnificent
human beings behind" Bernard to unveil the mystery of
things. Bernard accepts his election without question: "I was
the inheritor; I, the continuer; I, the person miraculously appointed to carry it on" (p. 353). And carry it on he does, concluding the novel by "taking upon me the mystery of things":

> "Day rises; the girl lifts the watery fire-hearted jewels to
> her brow; the sun levels his beam straight at the sleeping
> house; the waves deepen their bars; they fling themselves
> on the shore. . . . The birds sing in chorus; deep tunnels
> run between the stalks of flowers; the house is whitened;
> the sleeper stretches; gradually all is astir. Light floods
> the room and drives shadow beyond shadow to where
> they hang in folds inscrutable. What does the central
> shadow hold? Something? Nothing? I do not know."
> [p. 379]

In Bernard's description of the mystery of things, *de rerum
natura, The Waves* makes its final and completing turn. His
description imitates, at times it echoes verbatim, the action
described in the lyrical prefaces of the novel, prefaces nar-
rated by an invisible and inscrutable narrator hidden in a central shadow. Bernard becomes a vehicle for Woolf's playful
ventriloquism, speaking the truth that she beholds. The
movements of the novel, like the motions of the earth, revolve
around a solar mystery:

> "Dawn is some sort of whitening of the sky; some sort of
> renewal. Another day; another Friday; another twentieth
> of March, January, or September. Another general
> awakening. The stars draw back and are extinguished."
> [pp. 382–83]

Bernard returns to the novel's initial image of creative activity
—light driving out the darkness. The "true order of things"
that Bernard, the story-teller obsessed with sequences, has

sought, reveals itself in the simplest miracle—"the majestic march of day across the sky" (p. 365). Dawn, the veiled goddess of the opening panel of the novel, now becomes identified with both Genesis and Apocalypse, a creation and an uncovering ("apocalypsis": to uncover or to disclose) of the real cycles in natural and human history. In that continuing miracle all the threads, "the thin, thick, the broken, the enduring of our long history, of our tumultuous and varied day" (p. 316) finally coalesce.

The world in *The Waves* is justified, as Louis reminds us, as an aesthetic phenomenon. "Let us suppose," speculates Louis, "that I make reason of it all—one poem on a page, and then die" (p. 316). The poem Louis cites, the *only* complete poem that actually enters into the novel as part of its texture, is a simple lyric expressing a complex sense of loss, of exile in the wilderness, of the longing for home; and it is written, tellingly enough, by a poet named Anon:

> O western wind, when wilt thou blow,
>   That the small rain down can rain?
> Christ! that my love were in my arms,
>   And I in my bed again!

[p. 317]

One poem is enough in *The Waves*. Sufficient, too, is the presence of an anonymous poet who makes a reason of it all. The narrative "She" of *The Waves* recalls Woolf's belief that "Anon" was a woman:

> Indeed, I would venture to guess that Anon, who wrote so many poems without signing them, was often a woman. It was a woman Edward Fitzgerald, I think, suggested who made the ballads and the folk-songs, crooning them to her children, beguiling her spinning with them, or the length of the winter's night. [*Room*, p. 51]

"Anon" is Woolf's most representative type of the female artist, the mother who croons, the artificer who spins her enchanted webs, the dreamer who beguiles the length of the winter's night, the poet who insists on her anonymity. The pseudonym appealed to Woolf, who thought of titling a novel that was to follow *The Waves, Anon.* Anon signifies, of course, the central paradox in Woolf's narrative technique—*on án,* meaning in one or together[28]--the voice that speaks in one fluid, idiosyncratic style, yet the voice that expresses the common thought, the common feeling.

The Waves, then, is centered in a figure of opposition—the figure of the anonymous artist embattled in a world of "disorder, sordidity and corruption" (p. 380). The final paragraph of the novel reaffirms the need for that figure in a scene that conflates Percival's wild charge in India, Bernard's mental challenge delivered to death, the enemy, and Quixote's mad contest with phantom windmills and illusory armies of the dead. The heroic note with which the novel concludes is quixotic, a reminder that the novel's origins and ends inevitably refer to the triumphs and limits of human illusion. Yet Bernard's comic charge against death, "unvanquished and unyielding," is both ironically suicidal and ironically self-renewing. The novel concludes with Bernard's euphoric apostrophe, "O Death!" His apostrophe is the last human utterance in *The Waves,* the last rhetorical figure of opposition. As a figure of thought, the apostrophe addresses an absent person or an abstract idea, the "central shadow" that suggests both absence and abstraction in *The Waves.* Puttenham's *Arte of English Poesie* designates apostrophe as "the turne tale." Bernard's climactic cry thus constitutes both the anagnorisis and peripeteia of the novel, the recognition and change of fortune that reinstates the literary figure as a formidable and tenacious presence in the "life" of the novel. Life against death, the vitalistic myth of the body against the everpresent "mystery of things"—at

---

28. This *OE* etymology for "Anon" is cited by Nancy Topping Bazin in her *Virginia Woolf and the Androgynous Vision* (New Brunswick: Rutgers University Press, 1973), p. 147.

last the two antagonists square off for a definitive confrontation. And with an ease seldom encountered in Woolf's fiction,
the narrator can concede, without apparent anxiety, the
inevitable outcome: *"The waves broke against the shore."*
Indeed, after "all this little affair of 'being' is over" (p. 376),
the anonymous narrator of *The Waves* restores to her creation the larger, disinterested, perhaps ruthless perspectives
of comic time. But then comedy is ruthless in subordinating
the fretful motions of "one" life to the larger temporal movements of the historical and natural order. And, as Woolf
reminds us in her essay "Reading," Shakespeare dismissed
Falstaff callously enough. The great comic writers, like Shakespeare and Cervantes, "have this large way with them, nature's
way."[29] The triumph of *The Waves,* Woolf's comic romance in
prose, is not, then, in its momentary victories over death,
mutability, and eternal silence. *The Waves* documents a more
important victory for the disciplined imagination—that comic
enlargement of reality by which art rivals nature in dismissing
the life it creates, and by which art often surpasses nature by
dismissing *its* life at the very moment when it is most distinctly articulated.

29. "Reading," *Collected Essays,* vol. 2, p. 31.

6

Between the Acts

THE PLAY OF WILL

Love's Allegory

The Waves anatomized in order to resurrect the literary "figure" in the modern novel, a quixotic enterprise perhaps, as Woolf herself hints in her ironic homage to Cervantes's crusading knight in the novel's concluding tableau: Bernard's charge against death, the enemy. The title of Woolf's next novel, originally designated *The Pargiters,* then *Here and Now,* and finally *The Years,*[1] suggests a still further erosion of the novel's human ground by the remorseless force of temporality and its indomitable figures—mutability, transience, all the meteorological and seasonal metaphors of irrevocable change that pervade Woolf's vision of time passing. But in *Between the Acts,* her last novel, Woolf returns, in the face of immense historical pressures, to the time-honored and time-resistent figures of her native tradition. The novel traces the historical evolution as well as the permanent configurations of "Britannia," a cultural symbol more comprehensive than Percival, the figure in *The Waves* who evokes the English genius embodied in Arthurian romance, and more representative of national destiny than the family chronicle charted in *The Years.*

---

1. See *WD,* p. 183, describing Woolf's plans for an "Essay-Novel" called *The Pargiters,* and p. 205, for the first indication that *The Pargiters* might be replaced by the title *Here and Now.*

The historical pageant at the center of the novel reenacts and experiences the history of the world as an island history.[2] The vast reaches of geological time that fascinate Lucy Swithin are aesthetically foreshortened to form a prologue memorializing that geomorphic, quasi-mythical event when England was "A child new born / Sprung from the sea."[3] And even this cosmic drama serves as a prelude to that more engrossing, if perplexing spectacle which is human history. The pageant begins by acknowledging that "vast vacancy" between prehistorical and historical existence, between the wild child and the singing villagers who "Dug [themselves] in to the hill top . . . Ground roots between stones . . . Ground corn . . . till [they] too . . . lay under g–r–o–u–n–d . . ." (p. 78). The ellipses are Woolf's, denoting the gaps in time and leaps in consciousness that constituted the gradual, unrecorded advance from a state of nature to a state of culture. The multiple pun on "ground" which concludes the prologue announces the pageant's obsessive theme: the problematic relation of cultural figures to their native ground. Beginning with the heroic lays of Anglo-Saxon warrior societies, the pageant proceeds to recreate the distinctive figurative identities of successive British cultures: Chaucer's "Merry England," Elizabethan majesty, Restoration and Augustan "Reason," Victorian marriage of messianic imperialism and the cult of Home. Only contemporary England is represented without its informing and presiding genius, its unifying spirit of the age. The playfully reconstructed myth of Britain's epic past and epic destiny, alternately celebrated and mocked in the refrain invoking "The valiant Rhoderick / Armed and valiant / Bold and

2. See Brenda Silver's excellent discussion of the native traditions of minstrelsy and stagecraft underlying Woolf's historical sense and concept of community in *Between the Acts,* in "Virginia Woolf and the Concept of Community," *Women's Studies* vol. 4, 2/3 (1977): 291–98. I am extremely indebted to Silver's work, particularly because it was Silver's article that introduced me to the "Anon" manuscripts which Woolf wrote contemporaneously with *Between the Acts.*

3. Virginia Woolf, *Between the Acts* (New York: Harcourt Brace Jovanovich, 1969), p. 77. All further citations are to this edition.

blatant / Firm elatant," disintegrates into orts, scraps, and fragments.

While Woolf's historical perception of "Present time" as an epoch of cultural and personal disintegration was undoubtedly influenced by T. S. Eliot's theoretical and poetical pronouncements on the modernist crisis of disassociation, another figure, political rather than literary, insinuated itself into her thought and art in that crucial decade between 1930, when *The Waves* was written, and 1939, the crisis year in which *Between the Acts* is set: Fascist man. As described in *Three Guineas,* Fascist man represents human nature corrupted and emboldened by the blind absolutes of patriarchal culture:

> It is the figure of a man; some say, others deny, that he is Man himself, the quintessence of virility, the perfect type of which all the others are imperfect adumbrations. He is a man certainly. His eyes are glazed; his eyes glare. His body, which is braced in an unnatural position, is tightly cased in a uniform. Upon the breast of that uniform are sewn several medals and other mystical symbols. His hand is upon a sword.[4]

The figure of Fascist man represents the quintessence of that sterile and aggressively destructive masculine will whose tyrannies, petty and titanic, Woolf had examined with ever finer precision since *Mrs. Dalloway* and *To the Lighthouse.* It confirms her intuition that "the public and the private worlds are inseparably connected; that the tyrannies and servilities of the one are the tyrannies and servilities of the other." Behind Fascist man, hand on sword, stands a long, and presently debased tradition of martial epic, with "as Herr Hitler puts it, the hero requiring recreation, or, as Signor Mussolini puts it, the wounded warrior requiring female dependents to bandage his wounds."[5] Woolf's opposition to the mythologies that

4. *Three Guineas,* p. 142.
5. Ibid., p. 111.

glorify martial virtues and legitimize the tyrannies and servilities of patriarchal states finds its rallying cry in the words of
Antigone "worth all the sermons of all the archbishops":
" 'Tis not my nature to join in hating, but in loving."[6] Woolf
repeatedly returns to the example of Antigone in *Three Guineas* and *The Years* to illustrate her moral and imaginative
stance toward the tyrannies, servilities, and barbarities endemic to Fascist cultures, a stance epigrammatically rendered
in the maxim—"Those also serve who remain outside."[7]

Woolf's disassociation from patriarchal culture is no mere
"experiment in passivity,"[8] as some critics suggest. Her act of
withdrawal from the official culture, like Antigone's, permits
her to exercise a natural and therefore superior right: to reenact the sanctified rituals that constitute the original ground
of all human and natural law and, in doing so, to fulfill her
own feminine nature to join in loving. The state of war, civil
or global, preempts or abrogates those rights in the name of
that martial law whose basis necessarily resides in hating. To
end war, Woolf argued, culture and intellectual liberty must be
protected against dictatorial wills and those totalitarian states
that express the final, one might venture, the terminal form of
their desires. Woolf defines this adversary, anterior culture as
"the disinterested pursuit of reading and writing the English
language,"[9] implying that for the modern Antigone the verbal
rites are the objects of her disinterested love. Woolf's love, as
intense as it is disinterested, perceives in British culture a rival
literary tradition and rival genius whose visible and presiding
spirit is Shakespeare: the English theater. In a world at war
where the word theater came to connote the arenas of embattled armies, Woolf remained the purist, the outsider who recalled and preserved the creative and controlled denotations of
an inherited vocabulary of form. And Woolf's own work,

6. Ibid., p. 82. Also see accompanying note on p. 170.
7. Ibid., p. 119.
8. Ibid., p. 117.
9. Ibid., p. 91.

always straining to approximate the intensities of dramatic form,[10] finally turns from the lyricism of *The Waves* and the essayistic, discursive, and episodic chronicle of *The Years,* to the perils and anxieties of public enactment—the play.

That the title of the novel is *Between the Acts* itself announces this ordering of priorities: time will be treated as an aesthetic occasion and the action of the drama to unfold will transpire in a self-insulated and self-enclosed aesthetic scene *outside* or *apart* from history's battlegrounds. Like Jane Austen writing during the Napoleonic Wars, Woolf rarely permits the chaos of history to perturb her own loving performances. Offstage, behind, not in the acts, yet inevitably shadowing Woolf's own performance, is the Nazi juggernaut, threatening to cross the channel, invade and occupy English ground.[11] Lucy Swithin, who does not believe in history, thinks about the time when no channel separated England from the European continent, a thought that must have filled the contemporary reader with horror. Distance and natural division, the creation of aesthetic space of which the stage is the primary symbol, is as essential to Woolf's intention as the forging of community and the celebration of the "one world, one life" all men and women share. The walls of the stage, like the walls of civilization invoked at the pageant's conclusion, exclude as much life as they contain.[12]

History in the making is never allowed onstage, for it would destroy the achieved sublimations in violence that distinguish the decorums of dramatic representation. The novel alludes and adheres to the "bienséances" of Racinian theater and the stylizations of Chinese drama in its historic reporting; an air-

10. The interdependence between narrative and dramatic form is the theme of many of Woolf's discussions of narrative art, but it is best expressed in "The Narrow Bridge of Art," where Woolf analyzes the relation between "poetic play" and poetic fiction. Cf. *Collected Essays,* vol. 2, pp. 218–29.

11. See the diary entry for September 13, 1940, for Woolf's reaction to the "strong feeling of invasion in the air." *WD,* pp. 335–36.

12. Cf. *WD,* p. 326, quoted in my conclusion.

plane flying overhead, like a dagger on the table, is sufficient
to symbolize a bloody battle (p. 142). History as "present-
time reality" proves too strong when allowed to flood the
mind without the necessary mediations of art. To be comprehended history must be transmuted into text, dialogue, and
symbolic gesture. What immediate historical reality is accom-
modated in the novel appears in its vivid presentness in the
form of newspaper reports, what Woolf termed in *Three
Guineas* "history in the raw."[13] To shield her audience from
the senseless, hideous, and stupefying chaos of contemporary
history serves Woolf's ideological and aesthetic purpose, a purpose necessarily undermined, however, by Woolf's own ironic
self-consciousness as an interpreter of history. *Between the
Acts* is a war book of the most compelling and searching kind,
a novel that makes history its subject matter in order to question the validity of art, the limits of the book, and the powers
of illusion in a world absorbed in the work of destruction.
Such self-questionings are the sign both of Woolf's "culture"
and its disinterestedness.

The anxiety of art is the central problem of the novel and it
is first posed by Isa, the aspiring poetess through whom all the
anxieties of her generation are voiced. Isa is thirty-nine, the
age of the century, an age book-shy and gun-shy, indicating
that the two phobias are not unrelated. Unlike the "foolish,
flattering lady" who naively held that "Books are the mirrors
of the soul" (p. 16), Isa anxiously surveys both the ground and
the figures of an art that foolishly flatters with its ennobling
and consoling representations:

In this case a tarnished, a spotted soul. For as the train
took over three hours to reach this remote village in the
very heart of England, no one ventured so long a journey
without staving off possible mind-hunger, without buying
a book on a bookstall. Thus the mirror that reflected

13. *Three Guineas,* p. 7.

the soul sublime, reflected also the soul bored. Nobody could pretend, as they looked at the shuffle of shilling shockers that week-enders had dropped, that the looking-glass always reflected the anguish of a Queen or the heroism of King Harry. [p. 16]

The sublime pretendings of romantic fiction are chastised by the ennui of a shell-shocked present. Woolf suggests that her own art will mirror "English" nature and the village life that, though remote in time and space from war-torn London, still remains at the "heart" of British culture. The contemporary ennui and despair afflicting the British "soul" is reflected in the audience which both attends and participates in the performance of a village pageant. Woolf's implied aesthetic focus echoes George Eliot's prescription for literary realism:

There are few prophets in the world; few sublimely beautiful women; few heroes. I can't afford to give my love and reverence to such rarities.[14]

But the dramatic year, 1939, is a world of extremes in which "to give the loving pains of a life to the faithful representing of commonplace things"[15] is but to produce shilling shockers and newspaper dispatches which compose "the book of reality" for Isa and her generation. In a newspaper account in the *Times,* Isa accidently discovers the narrative line that imitates the total action of the war:

"The troopers told her the horse had a green tail; but she found it was just an ordinary horse. And they dragged her up to the barrack room where she was thrown upon a bed. Then one of the troopers removed part of her clothing, and she screamed and hit him about the face. . . ."

That was real; so real that on the mahogany door panels she saw the Arch in Whitehall; through the Arch

14. George Eliot, "In Which the Story Pauses a Little," *Adam Bede* (New York: Holt, Rinehart & Winston, 1967), p. 182.
15. Ibid.

the barrack room; in the barrack room the bed, and on
the bed the girl was screaming and hitting him about the
face, when the door (for in fact it was a door) opened
and in came Mrs. Swithin carrying a hammer. [p. 20]

Isa's imagination, like the victim's, is lured on by the fantastic (the horse with a green tail), encouraged by the romantic
(the guard at Whitehall), only to be betrayed by the real.
Abandoning the romantic, Isa traces the evidences of the real
through the Arch in Whitehall, where councils of war convene,
through the barrack room to the bed where war culminates,
according to Woolf, where it begins, in sexual estrangement
and violation. That love and war share the same strategies of
deceit, dissimulation, disguise, but employ them toward different social and human ends is no mere feminist simplifica-
tion, but an expression of the proverbial wisdom emerging
from the collective experience of the race. Woolf's fearless
literalization of this figurative analogy becomes the principle
of her dramatic composition and yields her an authentic
psychological, historical, and aesthetic insight. The love battles
between men and women, the immemorial drama of love and
hate naturally and necessarily center in the "act" of love, an
act that may signal the fruition of that natural relation between the sexes out of which life issues or the violation of that
relation by which life is betrayed and degraded. Woolf's insight
into tragic form is essentially that of Georg Lukács when he
argues that "The formal laws of drama arise out of the material of actual life," and that "the same inner laws of form" are
"the laws of movement of life itself, of which the plays are
artistic images."[16] These dynamic images of historical and
natural life, formalized by the collisions, climaxes, reversals,
and resolutions that shape tragic action, are not "pure" or
idealized representations, but generalizations and intensi-
fications of what Lukács calls "a typical fact of life."[17] For

16. Georg Lukács, *The Historical Novel,* tr. Hannah and Stanley Mitchell (London: Merlin Press, 1965), p. 105.
    17. Ibid., p. 99.

Woolf, of course, the facts of life derive primarily from the natural, rather than historical movement of life; her tragedy remains essentially a sexual tragedy. Between the acts of the village pageant the narrative suggests the presence of this unfolding sexual tragedy, a tragedy whose commanding temporal metaphor has traditionally been the ironic fruition of the past in the image of an aborted future. This sexual tragedy in turn yields an image of the tragedy of the war writ large: time and life cut short, destroyed, deprived of a future. *Between the Acts* begins with a discussion about a cesspool and from then on the novel seems mired in the murky, material reality of human waste and death that Woolf's own art seeks to mirror and transform.

If the sexual tragedy mirrors the larger action of world war, that mirror is itself the visible sign of unnatural or perverted vital energies. The barbaric energy unleashed by the war is psychologically registered in the sadism that infects the emotions dramatized in the novel, especially the emotions of the young and still passionate, those still capable of producing new life. Mrs. Haines, for example, the wife of the mysterious gentleman farmer Isa admires, yearns to disrupt the charged, illicit emotion generated by their unspoken flirtation in a singularly sadistic image: "In the car going home to the red villa in the cornfields, she would destroy it, as a thrush pecks the wings off a butterfly" (p. 6). The pressure of undischarged emotion, of the pandemic aggressiveness unleashed by the war, is relieved in the novel's moment of real violence, the moment when Giles squashes the snake with a toad in its mouth, the only time blood is drawn in the novel. Giles's act dramatically discharges the irresistible desire to destroy, to inflict pain, to draw blood that infects all those whose future is shadowed by the war. Only Lucy Swithin seems free of this pandemic hatred, she who does not believe in history nor in the differences between the sexes, nations, or races that history makes evident. But she has not, as she herself intuits, yet touched earth: "Skimming the surface, she ignored the battle in the mud" (p. 203).

Ignoring the battle is not, however, synonymous with ignorance; keeping to the surface is a strategy, by custom become a habit, of the unifying imagination in Woolfian fiction. Mrs. Swithin, "Old Flimsy" or "Batty" as her maid prefers, is the incorrigible, perhaps anachronistic monist indigenous to Woolf's fictional world, a reminder of the effortless epiphanies —and certitudes—of the past. Through Lucy Swithin, whose first name recalls the translucent, innocent beings of romantic, Wordsworthian persuasions, Woolf comments on the visionary cadences of the style perfected in *To the Lighthouse* and *The Waves*. To Lucy she attributes the only panhistorical vision in the novel, a vision spanning from prehistoric man, half-human, half-ape, to modern man. Reading an Outline of History, thinking of the time "when the entire continent, not then she understood, divided by a channel, was all one." Lucy effortlessly envisions the evolutionary links connecting the iguanodon, the mammoth, and the mastodon with their human descendents:

> It took her five seconds in actual time, in mind time ever so much longer, to separate Grace herself, with blue china on a tray, from the leather-covered grunting monster who was about, as the door opened, to demolish a whole tree in the green steaming undergrowth of the primeval forest. Naturally, she jumped, as Grace put the tray down and said: "Good morning, Ma'am." "Batty," Grace called her, as she felt on her face the divided glance that was half meant for a beast in a swamp, half for a maid in a print frock and white apron. [p. 9]

Lucy's imaginative reconstruction of the past, directed by a supplied "outline" of evolutionary sequences, depends on her talent for "increasing the bounds of the moment" to accommodate the magnified images of the prehuman past within the homely, diminished confines of the present. Only the intercession of "Grace" recalls her to the disjunction between "actual" time, in all its remorseless chronicity, and "mind-time" with its synchronic fluidity. The shock of Lucy's recognition is comically rendered, thus deflating the potentially frightening distance separating the past from the present. "Batty," the mind-divided Lucy who could have been, Woolf reminds us at the end of the novel, "a tragic figure from another play" (p. 214), like the schizophrenic Septimus Smith, for example, is rescued by the comic rhythms and sanities of Woolf's play. Disruptions and deflations of Lucy's visionary moments never end with the terrifying alienations native to tragedy. With comic regularity, one thing succeeds, almost miraculously, in following another, just as Lucy quickly resituates herself in the present by venturing "How those birds sing!", which, certainly, the narrator comments, they were doing (p. 9).

For Woolf, the play of imagination, assisted, of course, by the timely entrance of "Grace," always yields a comic perception of resurgent life singing its own triumph, of nature obliging the mind with its own irrational intimations of continuity. War deranges the human perception of historical and natural time because it suggests more tragic images of the moment as occasions of apocalyptic or abortive finalities. To such images of the end, Woolf opposes the comic intuition of time as duration, a duration measured, as Locke taught and Sterne reminded us in *Tristram Shandy,* by the train or succession of ideas. Woolf relies on the associationalism endemic to British comic fiction as her authority in arguing for a form of succession that insures that one thing will follow another. The mechanical motions of Lucy's comically undisciplined mind in linking the iguanodon to the figure of intervening "Grace" may be a flimsy, yet still successful way to adjust to reality, to assimilate the discrete impressions, memories, and ideas confronting the mind. The random associations of Lucy's ideas, for example, never trail off into irrelevancy or inconsequentiality, but describe, through the circuitous digressions favored by comic imaginings, the circularity of thought and the essential integrity of all experience. Thus when Isa mentions her fears that the fish she had ordered would not be fresh, Lucy's mind moves effortlessly from the topic of fish, to the thought of the time when there was no sea between the continents, to Pharaohs, to dentists to false teeth to marriage between cousins to the Swithin and Oliver lineage and back, finally, to the problem at hand: "Oh yes, you were saying, Isa, you'd ordered fish; and you were afraid it wouldn't be fresh. And I said, 'That's the problem . . .' " (p. 31). Lucy's inability to fix her gaze on the problem at hand is precisely what permits the comic enlargement and comic assimilation of reality. Lucy's mind-time may be a breach in the unity, or rather the monotonous succession of actual time, but it is, as Sterne says, "the true scholastic pendulum."[18] Woolf joins Sterne's Tristram in "abjuring and detesting the jurisdiction of all other pendulums whatever."[19] Lucy's scholastic pendulum, which encompasses all the orts, scraps, and fragments of her arcane archaeological and geological musings, composes another kind of history, what Sterne, comically appropriating Locke, calls "a history of what transpires in a man's mind."[20] Lockean psychology, child of the British empirical spirit, colors Lucy's all-too-human understanding of history. Nor is the order articulated by "Batty's" meditative meanderings factitious. Her mind is engaged throughout the novel in a comic, if relentless pursuit of the originating "ground" for those very superstitions or irrational conjunctions of sensations which pass for ideas in her mind. It is she who proposes, for example, the mythopoeic source for the superstition "touch wood": "Antaeus, didn't he touch earth?" (p. 24).

18. *Tristram Shandy,* ed. James A. Work (New York: The Odyssey Press, 1940), vol. II, ch. 8.
19. Ibid.
20. Ibid.

If Lucy is the unifier who can never touch earth, but merely skims the surface of her own randomly associating, unifying mind, her brother Bartholomew is the separatist, her complementary opposite in the English stock of comic characters. He is the rationalist who honors all the discriminations both nature and history produce in their separate, sometimes overlapping cycles. In the sibling love of Lucy and Bartholomew, the unifier and the separatist, the mind-divided relations of the sexes finds a sublimated expression of comic tolerance and conciliation: "Nothing changed their affections; no argument; no fact; no truth. What she saw he didn't; what he saw she didn't—and so on, *ad infinitum*" (p. 26). The irreconcilable differences between the unifier who harbors a prayable being in her breast and the agnostic who stoutly believes in history and the acts of representative men are never resolved. They are only mediated by the affection through which sister and brother silently communicate. Between the lines of their dialogue persists a rhythm of mechanical repetition that for Woolf, as for Bergson, is a source of comic effects. The clash of their contrary natures is contained by the comic predictability of their exchanges and the comic regularity by which their differences are dissolved, like a mist, into less impervious attitudes. Like all comic "relations," they achieve that concord in discord and unity in dispersity by which society paradoxically renews itself—*ad infinitum.*

But for the modern poet, Isa, the rhythms of comic plotting and comic dialogue no longer repeat themselves in the same reassuring sequence and the same reassuring register. She becomes impatient with the comic litany of responses Mrs. Swithin rehearses and re-rehearses with her brother about whether the "forecast" will be fine or not:

> Every summer, for seven summers now, Isa had heard the same words; about the hammer and the nails; the pageant and the weather. Every year they said, would it be wet or fine; and every year it was—one or the other.

The same chime followed the same chime, only this year
beneath the chime she heard: "The girl screamed and hit
him about the face with a hammer." [p. 22]

Isa notices a break in the comic pattern of natural alternation
between male and female, summer and winter, wet or fine.
The dialogue in the human comedy remains the same, but a
note of urgency and brutality disturbs the chime—or harmony—such alternations produce in the person who overhears.
This is one of many instances in the novel in which the spectator or audience actively questions the set-piece played out
before them. Such moments form a subplot of the drama that
is played out between the acts. Spectators measure the artifices of order against the reality of disorder. Isa, too, has her
own associations, tragically, not comically linked to the figure
of Lucy and her hammer. Her thoughts do not follow each
other in swift, mechanical succession, but are arrested and
fixated on an image of traumatic and brutal violation. Isa
brings to the drama of Pointz Hall a tragic perception of life
despoiled, vanquished, and betrayed. Her vision of life at
enmity with itself is internalized in the alternations of her own
mind-divided glances between inner love and outer love, between love for her husband, the stockbroker, and love for the
silent, romantic gentlemen farmer. She awaits for a *deus ex
machina,* a miraculous intrusion of "Grace," to resolve the obscure and tangled emotions of her own erratic will: "O that
our human pain could here have ending!" murmurs Isa near
the conclusion of the pageant, hoping for deliverance.

Isa's sense of relation, then, is not one of comic contrast
and concord, but of tragic entanglement. In the play of Isa's
imagination, the dialogue between Lucy and Bartholomew
provides moments of comic relief in the larger tragedy which
seems to be her own life. Unlike Lucy, Isa can never keep to
the surface, but casts her lines into the depths where they
inevitably are entangled with the object of her love and her
hate—Giles Oliver. Her love for Giles dates to their first meet-

ing when "her line had got tangled" (p. 48), and the memory of that entanglement informs and qualifies her adulterous fantasies about herself and Haines as "swans floating downstream": "His snow-white breast was circled with a tangle of dirty duckweed; and she too, in her webbed feet was entangled, by her husband, the stockbroker" (p. 5).

The motif of entangled and obscure desire implies that Isa's potential tragedy does not proceed, as with classical tragic heroines, from an irrepressible will, an inalienable individuality. Isa is the modern tragicomic heroine in the tradition of Ibsen and Chekhov, a heroine whose will is incommensurate to her desire, whose actions are never complete expressions of her intention: " 'Abortive,' was the word that expressed her. She never came out of a shop, for example, with the clothes she admired; nor did her figure, seen against the dark roll of trousering in a shop window, please her" (pp. 15–16). The "figure" Isa cuts is an object not of tragic awe, but of satiric observation, a figure Woolf consistently illuminates against a "novelistic" background of material and social facts: "She looked what she was: Sir Richard's daughter; and niece of the two old ladies at Wimbledon who were so proud, being O'Neils, of their descent from the Kings of Ireland" (p. 16). Woolf's careful characterization of Isa depends, finally, on the detailed circumstantial evidence of clothes, family lineage, and social surroundings—all those "ghosts of convention" by which the novel traditionally claimed to penetrate the being and explain the peculiar existence of its characters. Far from investigating the psychological depths of Isa's unhappy marriage, Woolf prefers to minimize and record her suffering in the rhetoric of novelistic cliché: "Their relations . . . were as people say in novels 'strained' " (p. 106).

Woolf's blend of satire and tragedy, in its larger generic configurations, culminates in another moment of abortive action and figurative illumination—Giles's killing of the snake with a toad in its mouth. The tragedies of Giles's life do not, like Isa's, slip "into the cliché conveniently provided by fiction" (p. 14). Rather they are displaced in another kind of imaginative play—a child's game, a game that allegorically expresses the moral typology by which human nature was once represented. Giles's is a game of controlled aggression in which a stone must be kicked to a goal in ten tries:

> The first kick was Manresa (lust). The second, Dodge (perversion). The third, himself (coward). And the fourth and the fifth and all the others were the same. [p. 99]

Giles's child's game is the vehicle for his own Dantesque allegorization of evil, for which his own experience provides both the text and the gloss. His allegory of selfhood traces the inevitable and, for him, eternally recurring declension from incontinence (excessive desire) to perversion (misdirected desire) to cowardice (shadow of desire). On reaching his goal, the allegorical figures of play are unexpectedly confirmed and replaced by a real image: "There, couched in the grass, curled in an olive green ring, was a snake. Dead? No, choked with a toad in its mouth. The snake was unable to swallow; the toad was unable to die" (p. 99). This figure of "monstrous inversion," with which nature mocks the despairing, incapacitated will, echoes Dante's portrait of Satan, the demonic agent whose own will is paralyzed, radiating evil from his frozen heart, held and bound in the frozen cesspool of the world. "There"—in the center of life, the heart of darkness, the bottom of the abyss—the tragedy of a soul that turns away from its spiritual sources combines with the satirical trope of inversion (*mundus inversus*) to produce a "mirror" of reality, but never the Love that animates it. Woolf's image of pure negation, an image provided by nature, of birth the wrong way round, of a deathless death, also combines satiric inversion with the tragic incapacity of the moral imagination, the moral will. Dante's paradoxical notion of freedom is imported into Woolf's fiction as a psychological truism: the will that acts out of hate, against the Love that moves the sun and the other stars, only secures its own self-bondage.

Woolf's own allegorization of figure, her reduction and compression of character into moral "types," and her identification of personalities through epithets (old Flimsy, Bossy) assimilates Giles's self-allegorizing play within the larger perspectives of her own human, historical, if not divine comedy. It is particularly through the artifice of the play within the novel that Woolf displays that analogical imagination which is alone capable of establishing a network of meanings and correspondences upon the unstable, chaotic materials of the self and its history. Through the pageant's allegorical presentation of history, in which various characters impersonate the ruling ideas of successive ages, the moral identity of Britannia is recovered and her present instability rationalized. At the center of the pageant within the novel, *there* is presented a Restoration play in which "Reason" is finally allowed to speak out against Unreason. The words of "Reason," which serve as an epilogue to a parodic treatment of Congreve's comedies, summarize the moral and imaginative vision of the pageant:

> *And so to end the play, the moral is,*
> *The God of love is full of tricks;*
> *Into the foot his dart he sticks,*
> *But the way of the will is plain to see;*
> *Let holy virgins hymn perpetually:*
> *"Where there's a will there's a way."*
> *Good people all, farewell.*

[p. 148]

" 'God's truth!' cries Bartholomew, catching the inflection of the language, 'There's a moral for you!' " The inflection of language caught by Bartholomew's exclamation, like the infectious parodic rhetoric that informs Woolf's representation of scenes from British history, is double-edged: such playful mimicry chronicles the inevitable degeneration of figurative language into cliché, while simultaneously revitalizing and restoring cliché, the petrified expression of hereditary wisdom, to its pristine signification. "God's Truth" is precisely "Where there's a will there's a way." For Woolf, the will to life is allied to the will to comedy and conciliation, not the will to power and domination. The homely nature of her moral does not diminish the depth of her social and historical vision. As Freud argued, Eros, the God of Love, *is* full of tricks, but Eros is still War and Death's mighty antagonist. In "Why War" Freud proposes the same indirect methods of combatting war and hatred that Woolf suggested in *Three Guineas*—to join in loving:

> If willingness to engage in war is an effect of the destructive instinct, the most obvious plan will be to bring Eros, its antagonist, into play against it. Anything that encourages the growth of emotional ties between men must operate against war.[21]

If, as Isa speculates, the basic plot of life is love and hate, it is the God of love who emerges triumphant—as long as there is a will to seek its own way. This is the moral of the Restoration comedy presented in the middle of pageant, a moral observed from the marriage of Reason and Love. As Avrom Fleishman has observed, at the center of the pageant is a moment of silence in which lovers embrace, signalling the renewal of nature's and society's creative cycles.[22] "All that fuss for nothing!" (p. 138) a cynical, skeptical, but probably good-humored voice exclaims as Valentine and Flavinda rapturously embrace. But, of course, all the fuss is for something, and Woolf's insight is to see in the "fuss" of courtship and mating, the much ado about nothing, the very "something" which knits men and women, nature and culture together: the exchange of vows, the faithfulness of lovers to each other and to the life which will proceed from their union. The Restoration tableau concludes with a procession of lovers singing, often inaudibly, the strains of a comic song:

21. Sigmund Freud, "Why War," *Standard Edition,* vol. 22, p. 212.
22. Fleishman, *Virginia Woolf: A Critical Reading,* p. 213.

> *. . . Summer and winter, autumn and spring return . . . All*
> *passes but we, all changes . . . but we remain forever the*
> *same.* [p. 139]

The triumph of Eros is also the triumph of time the preserver and continuer over time the destroyer. As the proces-
sional song resumes, the lovers call out the catalogue of those
ruins of time recorded in the book of life: *"Babylon, Nineveh,*
Troy . . . And Caesar's great house . . . all fallen they lie. . . ."
Only a few great names—Babylon, Nineveh, Clytemnestra,
Agamemnon, Troy—survive time, haunting the present with
their stories of passing civilizations, of family ties betrayed, of
estranged lovers, of the falls of great houses. The ancestral
memory of strife is never far from Woolf's consciousness in the
tale of Pointz Hall, her own symbolic center for a civilization
that is threatened by the enemy without and dissension within.
It is this perception of the destructive passage of time that
paralyzes La Trobe's imagination and imperils the comic
rhythms of her play: "Illusion had failed. 'This is death,' she
murmured, 'death' " (p. 140).

La Trobe's potentially fatal silence, her imaginative impotence in the presence of untransfigured historical time, is redeemed by one of the most daring comic reversals in Woolf's
fiction. "In the very nick of time"—testimony to the comic
faith in providential timing—Nature rescues Art with her own
deus ex machina. The imagination's inability to resist the urge
to death and destruction is rescued by the primeval voice of an
outraged maternal nature. The herd instinct of dumb, yearning
cows bellows its protest "as if Eros had planted his dart in
their flanks and goaded them to fury." Nature brings Eros into
play against death, annihilating the gap between past and
present time, bridging the distance between illusion and the
reality it denominates, filling the emptiness momentarily
afflicting the mind, and continuing the emotion generated by
the spectacles of the past.

Woolf's romantic appeal to Nature and its furious Eros to
reinspirit the flagging, moribund energies of her imaginative
play is both dramatically effective and historically reductive.
Her vision of history is intentionally antipositivistic, anti-
historicist, ignoring those complex and complicating conver-
gences of accident, contingency, circumstance, human decision, and cultural change by which history is "made." History
for Woolf *is* a process, but a process that primarily engages her
imagination for its underlying generative rhythms, not for
those surface discriminations of manners, dress, speech, class
and economic organizations, cultural and philosophical beliefs
that constitute the idiosyncratic, local and inalienable "style"
of any given historical period. Woolf's project in her pageant is
to de-idealize history by minimizing the importance of its
plots, by underplaying the role of particular social, economic,
or cultural determinants, and by denying to historical process
any teleological or rational principle except the love and hate
by which it, like Nature,[23] is goaded and impelled to manifest itself:

Did the plot matter? . . . The plot was only there to
beget emotion. There were only two emotions: love; and
hate. There was no need to puzzle out the plot. Perhaps
Miss La Trobe meant that when she cut this knot in the
centre? [pp. 90-91]

Woolf may be consciously playing on the word "denouement," that dramatic untying of the knot, that unravelling of

23. Cf. the following fragment from Empedocles that comprehends the cosmic
process in the everlasting dialectic between Love and Hate:

For even as Love and Hate were strong of yore,
They shall have their hereafter; nor I think
Shall endless Age be emptied of these Twain.

[Fragment 16]

The Fragments of Empedocles, ed. and tr. William Ellery Leonard (Chicago: Open
Court Publishing Co., 1908), p. 20.

"life's tangled skein" by which dramatic form imitates and comprehends the riddling complexities of life. The knot of reality, the puzzling "fuss" of life, is cut out of the pageant and displaced onto the intervals between the acts. The play within the novel dispenses with the complications and resolutions of an intricate plot, preferring to cut through the tense knot of dramatic exposition to expose its generating rhythms. The pageant reduces, through allegorical impersonation and symbolic condensation, all human history to an elemental conflict between love and hate. The primordial war between these two emotions, Woolf proposes, animates history and determines its emplotted forms—tragedy and comedy. Tragic form generates and is generated by the emotion of what Isa calls "hate." That Isa and Giles are the only central characters to feel this hate, and to feel it as a necessary component of their love, suggests that tragic hatred does not spring from a Satanic spirit of denial and negation, but from the aggrieved spirit of thwarted individuality, from the mistimed conjunctions of will and desire, from the intolerable passivity that is compensated by real or imagined acts of sadistic aggression. Comic form, on the other hand, is rooted in the vicissitudes of love, in the opportune and timely conjunctions of will and desire, in the final coincidence of love and its objects. The competition and interdependency of these two plots, traceable throughout all of Woolf's fiction, is sufficient to explain the vagaries and direction of human life and human history: " 'It was enough. Enough. Enough,' " Isa observes during the performance. "All else was verbiage, repetition" (p. 91).

What J. Hillis Miller has termed the skeletal "Ur-Drama"[24] of *Between the Acts* is sufficient as a principle of historical explanation and aesthetic form because its resolution—or

24. I refer to Miller's "Interpolation and Extrapolation in *Between the Acts,*" in his forthcoming book on repetition. For a theoretical introduction to the problem of repetition and rhythm in Woolf's novels, see Allen McLaurin's *Virginia Woolf: The Echoes Enslaved* (London: Cambridge University Press, 1973), part 2.

denouement—is classically and economically timed to coincide with a moment of recognition. As Isa is formulating her own theories about the meaning of the play presented by Miss La Trobe, she is nevertheless caught up in the immediacy of the climactic recognition scene that concludes the first major parodic tableau in the pageant. Theoretically committed to the notion that "the plot's nothing," Isa cannot forbear wondering "But what was happening?" (p. 91). On stage, what happens is a complex series of recognitions in which a withered beldame recognizes a young Prince thought lost and now found: "My child! My child!" she shrieks. This triumphant image of the rescued child prepares for the second major recognition, this time between lovers: "My love! My lord!" This double image of rescued child, whose birthmark links him to nature's cycles of generation, and of reunited lovers, whose pledge links them to society's rituals of regeneration, constitute a symbol, as Isa rightly interprets, of "Love embodied." The fruition of love through time marks Woolf's most persistent symbol of human and natural creativity. All else pales to verbiage and repetition in the presence of that initial act of creation in which the midwife is Time.

The allegorical meaning of Woolf's historical vision can best be seen in the Restoration parody. That tableau also concludes with a complex recognition scene in which Valentine, the resourceful hero of "Where there's a Will there's a Way," is literally trapped in the entrails of a timepiece until the auspicious and inevitable moment of his deliverance. The allegorical significance of Valentine's—or Eros's—confinement within time is doubly referential. It refers to Valentine's own status within the play as a hero awaiting his love and his rightful inheritance, and it comments on the temporal mode of the allegorical situation in which he is placed. As Paul de Man has observed of allegory's temporality: "Allegory exists entirely within an ideal time that is never here and now, but always a past or an endless future. It appears as a successive mode capable of engendering the illusion of continuity it knows to be illusionary."[25] The allegorical experience of time as duration, of meaning suspended in its own process of engenderment and articulation, is Woolf's aesthetic defense against the demoralizing chronicity of contemporary history. The collective mind represented by the novel can never, in its despair, see beyond the here and now. Even those content with the here and now, like Lucy and her brother Bart, are representatives of a cycle coming to conclusion, not of a cycle continuing or about to begin again. It is Isa who represents the anxiety of contemporary history, for whom the present is not enough, not sufficient, "No, not for us, who've the future . . . the future disturbing our present" (p. 82). It is to assuage anxiety about the future that Woolf implements her allegory of love in which Eros, full of tricks, conspires *with* time to create a sustaining vision of love embodied *in* time. Woolf's comic vision of a love rescued in time is illusionary, a creation of the imagination's play, but, as Huizinga has noted, to maintain illusion is, etymologically speaking, to keep reality within the confines of the playing, active imagination. If the failure of illusion is, as Miss La Trobe says, Death, the triumph of illusion is, as Huizinga says, "in play."[26]

Playing Out the Play

The problem of *Between the Acts,* then, is to devise ways of "playing out the play." Miss La Trobe, who has a passion for getting life up into art, realizes that even her pageant is incompletely played out, for the resources of life, unlike the resources of art, are illimitable. Although her play concludes and incorporates the reality of "Present time," its ending consti-

---

25. Paul de Man, "The Rhetoric of Temporality," in *Interpretation: Theory and Practice,* ed. Charles Singleton (Baltimore: The Johns Hopkins Press, 1969), p. 207.
26. Johan Huizinga, *Homo Ludens: A Study of the Play Element in Culture* (Boston: Beacon Press, 1950), p. 11. Huizinga emphasizes the etymological root of illusion in "ludere," to play.

tutes only a point, not a conclusion in that continuing sequence of particulate "times" or moments which is history. How to continue the emotion generated by her play haunts her as she tries to forget her own incipient sense of failure in a local pub. As she seeks to drown herself in drink, to lose herself in that heart of darkness, that fertile mud that for Woolf, as for Conrad, is the essential *materia* of all life and all art, she hears the first words of a new play arising from the depths of her mind:

> There was the high ground at midnight; there the rock; and two scarcely perceptible figures. Suddenly the tree was pelted with starlings. She set down her glass. She heard the first words. [p. 212]

At midnight, the witching hour, imagination conjures up the "first scene" of which all succeeding times are mere repetitions: the mythic high ground and its first informing human figures. Animating this timeless landscape of myth is La Trobe's specific memory of a "bird-buzzing, bird-vibrant, bird-blackened tree," a rhapsody of birds "syllabling discordantly life, life, life, without measure" (p. 209). And if life's discordant syllabling energizes and activates the potential for myth, so La Trobe's mythic imaginings can actuate the potential for new life. The perfect translatability of the visions of art and the actions of life apprehended in La Trobe's midnight imaginations provides the novel with its closing, if not terminating scene. The two mythic figures, barely perceptible in La Trobe's vision, are appropriated into Woolf's narrative terrain, there to undergo one final metamorphosis. Isa and Giles, left alone for the first time in the novel, face each other in their drawing room, there to reenact the primal drama of love and hate which it is their destiny to play out:

> Alone, enmity was bared; also love. Before they slept, they must fight; after they had fought, they would embrace. From that embrace another life might be born. But first they must fight, as the dog fox fights with the

vixen, in the heart of darkness, in the fields of night.
[p. 219]

What Lukács has enumerated as those historically determined
and verifiable "facts of life"—the day of reckoning, the parting
of the ways, the calling to account[27]—are all potentially
present in the mythic "now" of Isa's and Giles's encounter.
And primarily it is a sexual reckoning and a sexual calling to
account that Woolf dramatizes, the immemorial battle of the
sexes, in animal and human life, that provides the mythos of
her dramatic fable.

The novel's closing mythic tableau portends an auspicious
renewal of an enduring natural cycle, but not unqualifiedly so.
Woolf's rhetoric elides from the imperative (and mythic)
"must," to the future (and dramatically portentous) "would,"
to the conditional (and novelistic) "might" in narrating Isa's
and Giles's confrontation. The rhetorical declension from the
imperative to the conditional mood as the curtain rises on
their drama of love and hate suggests that a new life embodying
the Olivers' love may, not necessarily will, proceed from their
love-battles. The climactic and terminal moment of dramatic
transfiguration contains within itself its own negation, recalling the reader to the problem of abortive drama, abortive
poetry that does not possess the power to recreate a world out
of the dark cesspool of human and natural history. If art is the
mirror of the soul sublime that perceives the world and itself
through the magnifying lens of myth, it is also the mirror of
the soul bored that fails to bring a common meaning to birth.
Much of the elemental plot of love and hate the novel continually reenacts issues in dissension, in disrupted pattern, in
missed communication. The mirror Woolf turns on life reveals,
through a double or superimposed image, the untranslatable,
unassimilable details of existence that resist, often defy,
incorporation into the ordered world of imagination. If one

27. Lukács, *The Historical Novel,* pp. 100–01.

purpose of Woolf's "game" in the novel is to project and affirm the playing imagination by which the soul "in Love" embraces all the generative emotions of the mind and of nature, the other is to preserve, with almost scholarly fidelity to her scholastic pendulum, the stubborn particularities of the present historical moment, to keep faith with the canons of realism in representing, without evasion or subterfuge, the discriminations and distinctions separating the real and the imaginary, the literal and the figurative, the historical and the mythic fields of her play.

One way in which Woolf's artifice isolates even as it relates the literal objects of her imaginative play is through rhyme. As one of the most instantly recognizable and pleasurable instances of verbal play, rhyme satisfies the mind's need for relation between sound and sense, the sensory and the ideational. The power of rhyme is, as W. K. Wimsatt has observed, the power of binding the unbound, and "the greater the difference in meaning between the rhyme words the more marked and the more appropriate will be the binding effect."[28] Wimsatt's argument that the need for binding is predicated on the difference or separation between things to be bound is well taken, although his further claim that if things are "already close together, it is superogatory to emphasize this by the maneuver of rhyme"[29] is not—at least not in Woolf's fiction. It is precisely such superogatory rhymes that prove difficult to establish, especially for the soul "in love." For example, early in the novel, Isa sits before her own looking-glass, meditating on the condition of her soul in love. Groping "in the depths of the looking-glass for a word to fit the infinitely quick vibrations" of her emotions for Haines, she retrieves an image of an airplane propeller she had once seen at dawn at Croydon:

28. W. K. Wimsatt, *The Verbal Icon* (New York: Third Noonday Edition, 1962), p. 153.

29. Ibid.

> Faster, faster, faster, it whizzed, whirred, buzzed, till all
> the flails became one flail and up soared the plane away
> and away. . . .
>
> "Where we know not, where we go not, neither know
> nor care," she hummed. "Flying, rushing through the
> ambient, incandescent, summer silent . . ."
>
> The rhyme was "air." She put down her brush. She
> took up the telephone.
>
> "Three, four, eight, Pyecombe," she said. [p. 15]

Isa's search for the unifying word appropriate to the infinitely quick vibrations of her emotion concludes with the
superogatory rhyme "care-air." The rhyme itself is never
spoken, but replaced by the arbitrary sequence of numbers
three, four, eight, which, oddly enough, do connect one line
to another. Isa's soulful rhapsody is abruptly cut short by the
clearly factitious nature of her image and the superogatory
nature of her rhyme. Woolf's gentle satire juxtaposes two
modes of communication, one the self-communications of
lyric, the other the practical communications of the telephone,
to suggest the essential arbitrariness of all orderings and connections created by the resourceful intellect. Isa nevertheless
continues her singsong reverie to suggest still a third rhyme for
air and care: "There to lose what binds us here," she murmurs.
Here—the world of care from which one longs for the "there"
of sublime imaginings—both the subject and the problem of
Isa's poetry are one and the same. To get from "here" to the
lyrical "there" Isa must unloose what binds her here, thus her
impatience with those superogatory or necessary rhymes
which "ground" her existence and prevent her from "taking
flight." Isa's entanglement with the world of care is a permanent condition, for even the "air" out there is patrolled by real
airplanes, not ones that through memory have faded into
insubstantiality. Analogies and the rhymes that establish them
must be founded in Nature, in the Baconian sense, or in
history. Isa's poetry is abortive essentially because she is
enthralled by the idols of her own mind, which is why her

rhymes fail at the moment when the fundamental connections or contradictions at the very heart of her emotional and historical existence are about to be articulated.

Thus later on in the day, Isa's lyrical reveries are again aborted when she silently reproaches Giles for his summary judgment of William Dodge: "Isa guessed the word that Giles had not spoken." Isa's obsession with yet another unspoken word is displaced into another trinity of rhymes:

> Well, was it wrong if he was that word? Why judge each other? Do we know each other? Not here, not now. But somewhere, this cloud, this crust, this doubt, this dust——
> She waited for a rhyme, it failed her; but somewhere surely one sun would shine and all, without a doubt, would be clear. [p. 61]

Isa's inability or refusal to speak the unspoken word, a failure of imaginative nerve, results in an aborted rhyme. The issue is not, as Isa wrongly interprets, judgment of others here and now, but responsibility for the words by which the here and now of reality are denominated. Isa's rhyme fails because she cannot make the obvious, superogatory connection between "crust" and "dust" and the implied "must" rhymes in which the contradictions of her own identity are succinctly formulated. The crust or mask of the physical body, the dust to which that body is destined to return, and the "must" by which the will can assert its own way against the threatening, extinguishing spectres of death—these are the binding and recurring motifs in Woolf's own investigation into the powers of imagination. If Giles unfairly condemns Dodge for the "dodges," real or imagined, of his impotence or perversion, such impotence is often manifested in the poetry Isa vainly tries to create, creations that often evade those basic rhyme words which, like the facts of life they often represent, are unavoidable.

Perhaps the most obvious symbol of the double power of artifice to bind and to loose, to join and to unjoin, to order and to disorganize, to unify and to disrupt is the mad music that blares at the conclusion of the pageant:

> What a cackle, a cacophony! Nothing ended. So abrupt. And corrupt. Such an outrage; such an insult; And not plain. Very up to date, all the same. What is her game? To disrupt? Jog and trot? Jerk and smirk? [p. 183]

The smirk and jerk, the cacophonies and disharmonies are part of the underlying rhythm of *Between the Acts,* a music that reminds its audience of the unassimilable orts, scraps, and fragments that defy incorporation into order, of the hatred and the stubborn differences between man and man that fly in the face of the artist's one-making. What is, as an anonymous voice asks, her game? The rhythmic disruption is, admittedly, "very up to date, all the same," acknowledgment perhaps of the irreverent young who can't make, but only break, smash into atoms what was whole: "What a cackle, what a rattle, what a yaffle—as they call the woodpecker, the laughing bird that flits from tree to tree" (p. 183).

The final reference to the laughing bird, Woolf's favorite emblem of irrepressible, unconfinable life, links the very modern note of dissonance to "the strangled difficult music of the prelude"[30] of some new creation struggling to be born:

> The tune began; the first note meant a second; the second a third. Then down beneath a force was born in opposition; then another. [p. 189]

The discordant syllablings of life represent a force born in opposition to the endless ongoing medley of comic form. The comic rhythm of continuity, in which one note implies a second, and the second a third, is counterpointed by the more chaotic rhythms of the abyss, of the dehumanized will which the idea of order must ultimately accommodate:

---

30. Virginia Woolf, "American Fiction," *Collected Essays,* vol. 2, p. 121.

On different levels they diverged. On different levels ourselves went forward; flower gathering some on the surface; others descending to wrestle with the meaning; but
all comprehending; all enlisted. The whole population of
the mind's immeasurable profundity came flocking; . . .
from chaos and cacophony measure; but not the melody
of surface sound alone controlled it; but also the warring
battle-plumed warriors straining asunder: To part? No.
Compelled from the ends of the horizon; recalled from
the edge of appalling crevasses; they crashed; solved;
united. [p. 189]

Woolf's all-comprehending double rhythm, one confined to
the surface where flowers bloom and measure prevails, the
other committed to the embattled depths where the really epic
work of spiritual warfare transpires, informs the difficult
music of Woolf's multitudinous play. The necessarily antithetical relation between the unifying cadences of her surface
melodies, attuned to beauty, and the separatist tune of war,
wrestling in the depths for meaning, underlies Woolf's reformulation of the postromantic questioning of the consonance of
beauty and truth. Beauty demands organic relatedness; truth
asserts the irreducible and inviolate separateness of material
and human life. It is in the name of this truth, culled from the
depths where the mind descends for its meanings, that Woolf
disassembles, jars, reduces, and decreates the visions and orders
of the past. But it is in the name of beauty that Woolf's art
compels the warring spirits of truth from the edge of the abyss
back to the measured spaces of aesthetic form.

The Creative Mind

The gramophone's affirming voice, then, is neither simple
nor effortless. At its nether limits, La Trobe's pageant is held
together by the senseless gibberish of singsong: "A.B.C.,
A.B.C., A.B.C.—someone was practising scales. C.A.T. C.A.T.

C.A.T. . . ." (p. 114). Out of this stupefying reduction of musi-
cal and literary language into its semiotic components, words
gradually do form. The introduction of music to announce each
new act of creation is often accompanied by such primitive
stutterings. La Trobe employs the inherent rhythms of language to build up from the irreducible alphabet of thought the
first words of each new scene. A.B.C. becomes, by a quantum
leap of metaphoric transformation, associated with that
dogged "practice" by which the collective consciousness embodied in her audience attempts, like a child rehearsing its
scales, to master its speechifying legacy. La Trobe builds up
the first words of her play, cat, then dog, constructing an
abecedarian naturae. And in the repeated use of the homely
nursery rhyme

> The King is in his counting house
> Counting out his money,
> The Queen is in her parlour
> Eating bread and honey

[p. 115]

La Trobe suggests the process by which consciousness theoretically might have freed itself from its bondage to nature
and perceived the world in terms of its romantic imaginings.
From such childish, even humble beginnings, and through such
simple romantic outlines, the world may have been rearticu-
lated by the collective intelligence of the group mind.

Woolf's representations of the group mind echoes and
addresses Freud's *Group Psychology and the Analysis of the
Ego,* a work she read while writing *Between the Acts.*[31] Like
Freud, she localizes the creative genius of the group in its use
of language, particularly in the collective productions of folk-
song and folklore.[32] La Trobe's pageant, whose diction is composed primarily of idiomatic phrases, clichés, commonplaces,

---

31. See *WD,* p. 310.
32. Sigmund Freud, *Group Psychology and the Analysis of the Ego, Standard
Edition,* vol. 18, p. 83.

celebrates this shared language as the true, if unrecorded history of English culture. Like the nursery rhymes and folksongs counterpointing the more sophisticated parodies of individual works of genius, such popular expressions as "a flea in her ear," "the whole hog," or the recurrent "touch wood," represent the linguistic resources available to the artist who assimilates the collective speech of her audience into her own representational style. Perhaps this is what Woolf meant when she noted in her diary that her last novel was to substitute "We" for the implied narrative "I," the group for the individual mind as the controlling intelligence of her work (*WD*, p. 279). The narrative "we" implied in the novel certainly is in keeping with the "philosophy of anonymity" which Woolf had been formulating ever since *Mrs. Dalloway* as her own solution to what she feared was the egocentric and therefore exclusionary point of view which the modern novel had adopted in its attempt to deal with the postromantic legacy of subjectivity. In her bid to return to a more inclusive, impersonal narrative mode, Woolf rightfully saw the play, with its dramatic displacement of the imaginer into the imagined, the single speaker into many voices, as the generic model best suited to her needs and best understood by her audience. In Woolf's primary substitution of the communal "we," with its vast stores of racial memory and folk wisdom, Woolf simultaneously recovers and enlists the creative genius of her audience. Especially in the *abecedarian* stutterings of the child who recreates in its linguistic play—A.B.C., cat, dog—the first speech of the world, the miracle of linguistic consciousness, the source of all thought, is reenacted as the originating, enduring, and recurring rite of art.

The most magnificent example of the creative "folk-mind" which is rediscovered and celebrated in the pageant is Mrs. Manresa. Her very presence in the novel argues how seriously Woolf regarded the morality of accommodation and inclusion. Like the idiot who must be accepted as part of the tradition, Mrs. Manresa is the socially clichéd character who must not

only be included, but listened to. Paradoxically, Mrs. Manresa
is one of the most naturally spontaneous characters in the
novel essentially because she accepts the necessary artifices
of her existence and her social role. Like a child, Mrs. Manresa
disrupts the customary rituals and decorums of society, but
unlike a child, she does so by self-consciously acting according to the impulses of the jolly human heart. Mrs. Manresa is
a cliché, a cliché in terms of her social status as the pushy
parvenue, a cliché in terms of her vulgar Rousseauistic gambols
as the wild child whose innocence is superior to any cultured
sophistication, a cliché in her very role as the flirtatious
temptress who invades a staid country society.

But in the play between the acts, clichés work. Precisely
because of her theatrical demeanor, Mrs. Manresa succeeds, to
use a favorite Woolfian image, in making waves, drawing,
inevitably and irresistibly, all life in her wake. Appropriately,
she is honored as the "Queen of the Festival" (p. 79), a personification, for all her ludicrous artificiality, of the jolly
human heart. Her comic regality is confirmed in that climactic
and privileged moment when Mrs. Manresa, alone of all the
spectators of the pageant, can bear to have her image reflected
in the shattered mirror of the present. Other spectators protest
in being imaged forth as scraps and fragments by mirror-
bearers who are "malicious; observant; expectant; expository"
(p. 186). Mrs. Manresa welcomes the fragmented reflections of
the broken glass: "Alone she preserved unashamed her identity, and faced without blinking herself. Calmly she reddened
her lips" (p. 186). Her bold gesture substantiates and upholds
the metaphoric connection between identity and role, the self
and its masks, that constitutes the most persistent analogy in
literary psychology. She, of all the characters in the novel,
defies the expository and mind-divided glance that seeks to
separate the soul from its social mask, the self from its social
disguises, the painted from the hidden faces. When the looking-
glass of art turns on the audience to reveal and expose each

member separate, isolate, alone, or to expose a world of social and political cruelty—a world of liars, thieves, gun slayers, bomb droppers (they do openly what we do slyly, maintains the gramophone voice), murderers, tyrants—Mrs. Manresa remains unabashed, unashamed, unimplicated, serenely powdering her nose. She resists the injunction of the "megaphonic, anonymous, loud-speaking" voice: "Let's break the rhythm and forget the rhyme" (p. 187). A creature of pretense, she nevertheless possesses the "valuable, at least desirable quality" of challenging the unadulterated truth with her own adulterations. Mrs. Manresa is that rarity in Woolfian fiction—the woman who never loses face.

But the other spectators of the pageant react guiltily and nervously to the penetrating satire of the mirror's "inquisitive insulting eye" (p. 186). For them the dramatic unveiling of the Nietzschean truth "without larding, stuffing or cant" occasions mass panic. That the group mind celebrated throughout the pageant disintegrates under the pressure of the present crisis does not negate the actuality and the power of its historical existence. As Freud observed in *Group Psychology and the Analysis of the Ego,* the group mind paradoxically does away with itself in one of its most striking manifestations—panic.

> The typical occasion of the outbreak of a panic is very much as it is represented in Nestroy's parody of Hebbel's play about Judith and Holofernes. A soldier cries out: "The general has lost his head!" and thereupon all the Assyrians take to flight. The loss of the leader in some sense or other, the birth of misgivings about him, brings on the outbreak of panic, though the danger remains the same; the mutual ties between the members of the group disappear, as a rule, at the same time as the tie with their leader. The group vanishes in dust, like a Prince Rupert's drop when its tail is broken off.[33]

33. Freud, *Group Psychology,* p. 97.

Woolf, it may be argued, intentionally provokes this crisis of authority by substituting the neutral, demystifying reflections of mirrors for the substantiating, unifying figures of group identity represented by the succession of English sovereigns. She instills the seeds of panic in her audience by playing on that typically British political anxiety—the fear of the mob, of anarchy, of the "headless" body politic. But she does so, it may be further argued, to create the space necessary for the emergence of what Freud called "the secondary leader," the leader whose authority derives, not from his charismatic presence, but from his relation to an idea or abstraction that he more or less embodies. Woolf considers seriously Freud's speculation about whether "an idea, an abstraction, may not take the place of the leader (a state of things to which religious groups, with their invisible head, form a transitional stage), and whether a common tendency, a wish in which a number of people can have a share, may not in the same way serve as a substitute."[34]

Woolf's search for substitutes leads her to propose the Reverend Streatfield as the transitional, interpretative, and "representative spokesman" for her audience, "a butt, a clod, laughed at by looking-glasses, . . . an irrelevant forked stake in the flow and majesty of the summer silent world" (pp. 190–91). He is the most Shakespearean figure in the novel, an image of the fool laughed at by looking-glasses and an image of authority abdicated, the kingly majesty of man unmasked and reduced to a poor naked forked animal. He is both Lear's fool and the diminished reflection of the King himself translated out of the stormy territories of tragedy into the eerie landscapes of the summer silent world. The allusive traces of Shakespearean authority support Streatfield's epilogue and invest it with unanticipated interpretative power. Thus despite the audience's universal expectation that Streatfield, "in the livery of his servitude" to the invisible head he obeys and

34. Freud, *Group Psychology*, p. 100.

represents, will reduce to simplified absurdity the meanings of the play, Streatfield does articulate, with admirable if humble certainty, the recurring ideas of the pageant:

"We act different parts; but are the same. That I leave to you. Then again, as the play or pageant proceeded, my attention was distracted. Perhaps that too was part of the producer's intention? I thought I perceived that nature takes her part. Dare we, I asked myself, limit life to ourselves? May we not hold that there is a spirit that inspires, pervades. . ." [p. 192]

Streatfield's hesitant interpretative questionings are not reductive, but expansive and primary, addressing as they do the most unanswerable of mysteries—the mystery of divine or artistic intention. To hold that there is a spirit that inspires and pervades life is a rhetorical question in Woolfian fiction. The legitimate, ever-to-be-answered question is to decide the role and extent that power plays in human history, human life, human imagining. Streatfield can question, but can never supply an answer because he is a transitional figure between the disinterested and interested cultures portrayed in the novel. He soon becomes an advocate of "interested" culture, soliciting donations for the illumination of the dear old country church. His authoritative voice must bow to the disinterested figure of the "gifted lady" whose spirit inspires and pervades the pageant, an invisible head of the visible community. La Trobe, like all prime movers, withdraws from her creation, refusing to come out of the wings, a "hidden god" who controls and abides in the collective mind of her audience but never appears *in propria persona* to embody and articulate the meaning of the destiny she both represents and directs.

Yet it is precisely towards the apotheosis, however anonymous and unremarked, of the artist as leader, as the exponent of "disinterested" culture, that the novel finally tends. It is the artist who completes the transition from those "primitive and complete" communities of belief centered around histori-

cal personages,[35] through those religious communities dedicated to an invisible head, to the community united in the
service of a "leading idea"—for Woolf the idea that "we are
members one of another." The artist is that invisible head who
reveals to her audience those ties of filiation and identification
that have united them throughout the chaotic mutations of
history. Her play provides her attendant audience with the
opportunity (a recurring word in Streatfield's peroration) for
those multiple identifications on which, Freud argued, groups
necessarily depend.[36]

The marginality of the pageant, located between historical
reality and imaginative play, is crucial to its aesthetic and
social success. As Geoffrey Hartman has remarked in an essay
dealing with the problem of history as answerable style, art
provides its spectators with a chaos of roles unavailable to it in
reality but necessary to its understanding of social identity and
social structure. Art functions, suggests Hartman, much like
an aggregation ritual, a *rite de passage,* in which the spectator-
participant discovers "both his individuality and his isolation,
both selfhood and the meaning of society":

> The artist is surely the liminal or threshold person par
> excellence, while art provides society with a "chaos of
> roles" strengthening the individual's sense of unstruc-
> tured community yet offering him ideal parts to try.
> Only the concept of liminality, moreover, as developed
> by Turner from Van Gennep explains why art is statusless
> despite its civilizing role. Art is not reality; the relation of
> the one to the other is essentially liminal; between art
> and its translation into immediate relevance a threshold
> intervenes which cannot be crossed without destroying
> art's very place in society.[37]

35. Freud, *Group Psychology,* p. 100.
36. See Freud's chapter on "Identification" in *Group Psychology,* pp. 105-10.
37. Geoffrey Hartman, *The Fate of Reading* (Chicago: Chicago University Press,
1975), p. 109.

The artist, then, is more than that "twitcher of individual strings" whose glory it is to stir in her audience their unacted part, a glory desperately communicated by Lucy Swithin when she attempts to thank La Trobe: "What a small part I've had to play! But you've made me feel I could have played . . . Cleopatra!" (p. 153). The artist is also the Prospero-like magician "who seethes wandering bodies and floating voices in a cauldron, and makes rise up from its amorphous mass a re-created world." As the threshold person par excellence, the artist provides her audience with a chaos of possible roles out of which is reembodied and recreated an organized and sustaining vision of the world.

The artist's glory survives for only a moment, however. The unity and harmony promoted by art as an answerable and liminal style is affirmed, inevitably as Hartman makes clear, in triumphant yet valedictory tones: "Dispersed are we; who have come together" (p. 196). At the pageant's conclusion, La Trobe, like Prospero, releases her audience from the enthrallments of her art; bodies are again set wandering, voices again set floating. La Trobe's vision of the world one and entire, like Prospero's, must acknowledge itself as a "baseless fabric" and yield itself, gracefully, generously, to the necessary deformations, fragmentations, interpretations of multitudinous historical life. The aggregating, assimilating and unitary fullness of La Trobe's dramatic representations thus disintegrates as her audience is "set free," questioning, in their bodiless voices, the partial meanings apprehended in the spectacle played out before them, reacting, some irritably, some sympathetically, even intelligently, to the emotions generated by its art.

The most haunting question put to the artist and her play is the question the dreamed ones always ask their dreamer when they are awakened: "He [Streatfield] said she meant we all act. Yes, but whose play? Ah, that's the question!" (pp. 199-200). The question *is* a serious one, but, interestingly, it does not seem to be seriously asked. The comic inflections of the question, may, of course, betray the depth of the metaphysical and aesthetic anxiety expressed. If the world is a stage, if existence is acting and assuming a role in a play whose form and meaning eludes us, if art is the play within the larger play of time, and if the creative mind, like Miss La Trobe, refuses to come out of the wings and reveal its intentions, knowledge can only come in playing out the play unto the last syllables of recorded time. Until the universal revels are ended, the creator can only be known through his creation. And like that divine creative mind whose power the artist simultaneously usurps and expresses, La Trobe's mind can only be known by those displacements, projections, dissimulations of self which compose and constitute the baseless fabric of her vision.

Anon and the Motherly Heart

For Freud, of course, the first and necessary role adopted by the self-expressive, self-assertive mind is the role of epic poet who "disguised the truth with lies in accordance with his longing" and invented the heroic myth.[38] It is this individual who initiated the reign of freedom through the imaginative advancements of myth-making, constructing a self-legitimizing play in which he projected himself as the hero who "by himself had slain the father—the father who still appeared in the myth as a totemic monster."[39] But Woolf's monsters are not totemic beasts who remind the community of the envied and usurped power of the primal father. The monsters recalled in *Between the Acts* are mastodons, naturalized figures in the primeval landscapes of Darwinian history, not totemic idols haunting the dreamscapes of Freudian anthropological myths. Nor is her creative leader a dragon-slayer who usurps the role of the father, that "primary leader" in Freud's primitive and naturally "complete" communities. Woolf posits no originating act of rebellion, usurpation, and ritual murder in which the

38. Freud, *Group Psychology*, p. 136.
39. Ibid., p. 136.

"king must die" in order for the creative individual to emerge
from its servitude to the pieties of the group mind awed by its
sacred totems. For Woolf the course of social and historical
progress is determined by the fluid and natural, and therefore
untraceable operations of "the motherly heart" (p. 169). Unlike Freud, Woolf sees Eros as a maternal life-force, and the
longings which disguise the truth with lies the longings of the
mother's "dumb yearning" for her lost, imperilled child.
Woolf's novel celebrates the mastery, universality, and beguile-
ments of the motherly heart that simultaneously occupies and
bridges the distance between the child's saving play of illusion
and the fatal estrangements of undisguised reality. Woolf's
tribute to this threshold presence, this mediating and transformative power, is the feminized personification of "Reason"
whose extended, sheltering arms foster the advances of art:

> *Beneath the shelter of my flowing robe . . . the arts arise.*
> *Music for me unfolds her heavenly harmony. At my*
> *behest the miser leaves his hoard untouched; at peace the*
> *mother sees her children play. . . . Her children play . . .*
> she repeated, and waving her sceptre, figures advanced
> from the bushes.
>   *Let swains and nymphs lead on the play, while Zephyr*
> *sleeps, and the unruly tribes of Heaven confess my sway.*
> [p. 124, ellipses Woolf's]

Under the scepter of feminized reason, the pastoral and idyllic
potential represented by the novel's country setting is actual-
ized in play. The triumph of feminine rule is signalled by the
"peace" of children's play, the subjection of Freud's unruly
tribes and primal hordes, a peace whose pastoral resonances
are especially powerful given the war-torn present in which
such maternal representations are made.

The mother's images are peaceful because they predate and
challenge the self-assertions of heroic myths of individuation.
Where Freud's epic poet displaces his longing onto the figure

of the dragon-slaying hero, the motherly heart articulates
the longings for and the longings of her children. She does
not sing of arms and the man, of war and wandering. Hers is
the song of "Anon," the one who is the voice of the many.
The song of Anon, the "call to our primitive instincts," is
a choral song, its origins, Woolf speculated in a late, as yet unpublished essay entitled "Anon," traceable to the common
movements of rhythmic labor out of which came dance, folk-
song, the first poetic utterance:

> Thus the singer had his audience, but the audience was as
> little interested in his name that he never thought to give
> it. The audience was itself the singer; 'Terly, terlow,' they
> sang; and By by / lullaby / , filling in the pauses, helping
> out with a chorus. Everybody shared in the emotion of
> Anon's song, and supplied the story. . . . Anon is some-
> times man; sometimes woman. He is the common voice
> singing out of doors.[40]

In *A Room of One's Own* Woolf seriously entertained Fitz-
gerald's speculation that Anon was often a woman. Later her
growing philosophy of anonymity, which sought for "story" in
the rich reservoir of the group mind, abandoned the premise of
a sex-determined art, perhaps in the service of the more
inclusive and integrating myth of androgyny. But traces of
her feminine bias remain in Woolf's proposition that the song
"filling in the pauses" between acts of labor and continuing
the emotion produced and experienced by the common voice
is a lullaby. Woolf repeatedly returns to the lullaby as the pristine form of song, the original artful utterance by which the
primitive, mythic mind beguiled the time of lengthening

40. "Anon" and "The Reader" were the first draft chapters of Woolf's "idea for
a Common History book" (*WD*, p. 335). The manuscript and typescript drafts are
kept in the Henry W. and Albert A. Berg Collection, The New York Public Library,
Astor, Lenox, and Tilden Foundations in "Articles, Essays, Fiction and Reviews,"
vol. 8, 1938–39, hereafter cited as AEFR; and in a set of folders filed under "Anon"
and "The Reader," hereafter cited by title, followed by folder and page number.
"Anon," 6, 1–2.

winter nights. It is the lullaby that completes and fulfills the drama of day, where love and hate are the emotions that reign, with its soothing benediction enjoining sleep, rest, peace: "Peace was the third emotion. Love. Hate. Peace," muses Isa. "Three emotions made the ply of human life. Now the priest, whose cotton wool moustache confused his utterance, stepped forward and pronounced benediction" (p. 92). Peace is the emotion generated by the "first" lullaby the mother sings to the child, by the lullaby Anon supplies to the mature and fruitful song of labor, and by what George Eliot called the "last" lullaby—the dirge.[41] Peace is thus the emotion generated by the antidramatic, lyrical content of *Between the Acts,* the emotion that transports the mind of child, laborer, even of the dead, beyond the spectacle of its own history into the darker regions of another, inhuman world ("Dare we limit the universe to ourselves," as Streatfield rightly asks), a world represented by the lily pool where the lady Ermyntrude drowned herself. The lily pool is that feminine heart of darkness where dreaming, existing, and playing are all one. It is the original ground of all our being, the impacted center which exists before and is destined to survive the fretful motions of human life and human history. It is the dark center to which the old crone in the pageant play is permitted to pass, "She to whom all's one now, summer or winter" (p. 92). La Trobe must descend to that heart of darkness and make its mud fertile when her audience disperses. Isa, the potential lyrical poet, must drop her wishes into that deep well: "Let me turn away," she murmurs during an interval, "from the array," adding, as if suddenly understanding the implicit symbolism in her own murky drama of entangled and confused desire: "That the waters should cover me of the wishing well" (p. 103).

It was Nietzsche who suggested, even before Freud, that the will to truth might well be hostile to life, "if life aimed at semblance, meaning error, deception, simulation, delusion,

---

41. George Eliot, *Middlemarch,* p. 309.

self-delusion." It was Nietzsche who argued that the great sweep of life "has always shown itself to be on the side of the most unscrupulous *polytropoi.*"[42] As Anon, the myriad-minded common voice, or as the Shakespearean dramatist who delights his audience with impersonations, projections, simulations of their own unacted parts, the Woolfian artist can only affirm the world of nature, history, and life by concealing the presence of another world where all is one. The Woolfian artist understands the double dissimulation Nietzsche perceived in those who will the truth, a will that in unmasking all, still conceals its own identity as a will to death.[43] The difference is that the Woolfian seekers after truth drown themselves, not for truth, but in the name of that love that truth betrays, fulfilling, ironically, their own feminine nature to join in loving.

The novel's icon for this feminine nature is the nameless "lady" who was "a picture bought by Oliver because he liked the picture" (p. 36). Her portrait hangs opposite to an open window next to a portrait of a family ancestor who has a name: "He was a talk producer, that ancestor. But the lady was a picture." While the masculine presence produces talk, the feminine presence produces nothing. She is the pure representational icon "holding the still, distilled essence of emptiness, silence" (p. 37). As a speechless presence, an empty sign, she appeals to a vision beyond words:

> In her yellow robe, leaning, with a pillar to support her, a silver arrow in her hand, and a feather in her hair, she led the eye up, down, from the curve to the straight, through glades of greenery and shades of silver, dun and rose into silence. [p. 36]

Without a name, without a history, existing only as an enigmatic collection of barely realized signs, suggestive emblematic

---

42. Friedrich Nietzsche, *The Gay Science,* tr. Walter Kauffman (New York: Vintage, 1974), p. 282.
43. Ibid., p. 282.

gestures, she invites the eye to explore the static rather than the kinetic perfections of art, art "singing of what was before time was." In "real life," the narrator coyly informs us, "they had never met, the long lady and the man holding his horse by the rein." But they do meet in the material artifact of the book itself, in the written text that occupies the liminal, potentially dangerous ground between "real life" and the silence of pure, unadulterated vision. The text itself has its talk and its speechless moments that suggest the presence of "thoughts without words" (p. 55), a possibility that even the separatist Bartholomew seriously considers. The ancestor and the long lady thus speak to and incarnate the two rival traditions warring in the text, one male, one female, one tracing his semblance, imposing his likeness, speaking his name, producing talk to drown out that roar, as George Eliot heard, that lies on the other side of silence; the other speaking from the heart of that emptiness and silence that underlies and surrounds the illusory materiality of the world.

So if the lady and the ancestor never meet, it is sufficient that Isa and Giles do. They take upon themselves that primeval war between man and woman that for Woolf, as for Lawrence, accounts for our civilization and all its discontents. In whose play? Ah, that's the question. Perhaps in the play of no-one, an Anon, a nameless presence whom Nietzsche identifies as "the continually creative person, a 'mother' type in the grand sense, one who knows and hears nothing any more except about the pregnancies and deliveries of his spirit," or the artist "who no longer has any desire to assert his taste and simply forgets it."[44] Such Nietzschean self-forgetfulness, a version of Keatsean negative capability, is briefly experienced in La Trobe's "passion for getting things up" (p. 58), her anxiety to insure that the curtain will rise one final time and the first words again be spoken. But Woolf's artist, finally,

44. Nietzsche, *The Gay Science*, p. 326.

is neither the Nietzschean "mother-type" rapt in the pregnancies and deliveries of her own spirit, nor the "mother-type" of Freudian thought, an all-encompassing, all-engendering womb that symbolizes the first and last principle of pleasure. La Trobe is society's outcast, but it is not to her own spirit that she listens. She is the final avatar of the Woolfian artist who is the slave of her audience, set apart from her kind in order to hear more distinctly "the unheard rhythms of their own wild hearts" (p. 65). And she is also Nature's outcast, rivalling even in relying on Nature's generative energy to pervade and inspire her art. Between Nature's acts of generation, the artist produces acts of alternate creation. But "O to write a play without an audience—*the* play" (p. 180), the perfect play envisioned in the lily pool of La Trobe's mind but never played out in the novel itself. For perfection, as Nietzsche reminded us, "brooks no witnesses." That movement toward perfection is persistent in Woolfian fiction, as the culminating silent encounter between Giles and Isa testifies, but it is a longing wisely resisted. "It was in the giving that the triumph was," La Trobe thinks in assessing her play. The triumph fades, the gift means nothing, may, in fact, be a failure: "Now it had gone to join the others" (p. 209). Woolf's unitive vision always triumphs, ironically, in its own susceptibility to dispersity. Her art becomes through this ironic triumph the prime symbol of that disinterested culture she advocated, art as gift, mere gift, free gift. Unlike that of Shakespeare's visionary Gonzalo, the latter end of Woolf's commonwealth never forgets its beginning: Not sovereignty, but mutual exchange, not hateful tyranny, but loving peace, not ideology but art, art that, like the spontaneous operations of "Grace," is gratuitous, fragile, and free.

7

Conclusion

Sunday, June 9, 1940, Virginia Woolf writes in her diary:

> I will continue—but can I? The pressure of this battle
> wipes out London pretty quick. A gritting day. As sample
> of my present mood, I reflect: capitulation will mean All
> Jews to be given up. Concentration camps. So to our
> garage. That's behind correcting *Roger,* playing bowls.
> One taps any source of comfort—Leigh Ashton at Charles-
> ton yesterday for instance. But today the line is bulging.
> Last night aeroplanes (G.?) over: shafts of light follow-
> ing. I papered my windows. Another reflection: I don't
> want to go to bed at midday: This refers to the garage.
> What we dread (it's no exaggeration) is the news that the
> French Government have left Paris. A kind of growl be-
> hind the cuckoos and t'other birds. A furnace behind the
> sky. It struck me that one curious feeling is, that the writing
> "I" has vanished. No audience. No echo. That's part of
> one's death. Not altogether serious, for I correct *Roger,*
> send finally I hope tomorrow: and could finish *P.H.* But
> it is a fact—this disparition of an echo. [*WD,* p. 323]

The novelist who began her career desiring to write a novel
about silence, about things people don't say,[1] approaches the
end of her career serenely contemplating—as if it were not
serious—the vanishing of the writing "I," the "disparition" of

---

1. *The Voyage Out,* p. 262.

an echo to her comic intonations, her lyrical soliloquies, her strange but urgent communications.

Publicly Woolf would ignore or at least minimize the immense pressure of the war, insisting, for example, to a meeting of the Worker's Educational Association that the writer still retains an identity both substantive and tenacious: "A writer is a person who sits at a desk and keeps his eyes fixed, as intently as he can, on a certain object . . . ," the object being, of course, no less than "human life."[2] And she would continue to repeat, again and again, the peroration to all her critical pronouncements on fiction, feminism, the politics of war and peace—the ideal of literature as disinterested culture: "Literature is no one's private ground; literature is common ground. It is not cut up into nations; there are no wars there. Let us trespass freely and fearlessly and find our own way for ourselves. It is thus that English literature will survive this war and cross the gulf—if commoners and outsiders like ourselves make that country our own country, if we teach ourselves how to read and to write, how to preserve, and how to create."[3]

But the realities of the war continue to make their own illegal forays into the common and neutral territories of art, trespassing and challenging Woolf's belief in the primacy and absolute sovereignty of literary over historical ground. Beyond and behind the literary horizon lurks the machinery of annihilation, aeroplanes patrolling the night, the furnace behind the sky. And the menacing growl of Unreason begins to disturb the song of Woolf's "cuckoos and t'other birds," whose irrepressible syllablings of "Life, Life, Life" could always lift the despondent mind with portents of a renascent visionary power. "I will continue—but can I?" becomes, for once, no mere rhetorical question in Woolf's self-communications:

All the walls, the protecting and reflecting walls, wear so terribly thin in this war. There's no standard to write

2. "The Leaning Tower," *Collected Essays,* vol. 1, p. 162.
3. "The Leaning Tower," p. 181.

for: no public to echo back; even the "tradition" has become transparent. Hence a certain energy and recklessness
—part good part bad I dare say. But it's the only line to
take. And perhaps the walls, if violently beaten against,
will finally contain me. [*WD,* p. 326]

The protecting and reflecting walls of tradition wear thin,
assuming transparent shapes in a spectral architecture no
longer capable of enclosing, merging, and reverberating the
single voice in the voice of the many, of validating the fragile
communications between the writing "I" and that common
reader who remained the ideal audience for Woolf from the
beginning to end of her literary career. English history, English
culture, English character had provided Woolf both the subject
and the medium of her narrative consciousness, a tradition, she
proposed in *Mrs. Dalloway,* capable of transmitting her voice
as "the walls of a whispering gallery return a single voice expanded and made sonorous by the might of a whole cathedral"
(p. 26). But in 1940 the walls grew porous, the might of the
cathedral less formidable.

With the vanishing of those answering echoes that could
expand and make sonorous the single voice of the writing "I,"
Woolf was forced to reformulate and reexamine her models of
literary identity and the mimetic assumptions of her own art.
Such self-searching into the powers of the writing "I" is the
subject of a late short story entitled "The Lady in the Looking-
Glass: A Reflection." The object of and for reflection is
Isabella, another avatar of that elusive "Mrs. Brown" Woolf
sought to transfix and thus make permanent in the looking-
glass of her art. As a figure of "human life," Isabella challenges
both the descriptive and analytic powers of the narrator: "One
verified her by degrees—fitted the qualities one had discovered
onto this visible body."[4] The narrator's attribution or "fitting"
of her own perceptions, observations, imaginative penetrations

4. "The Lady in the Looking-Glass: A Reflection," *A Haunted House and
Other Short Stories,* p. 93.

onto the visible body reflected in the looking-glass seems to be paradigmatic of that process by which the mind endows the "indeterminate outline" of reality with determinate shape and determinate meaning. By degrees, some "logical process" seems to set to work on the qualities discovered in the blurred, unrecognizable, and irrational form looming in the looking-glass, "ordering and arranging them, and bringing them into the common fold of experience" (p. 90). But the paradigm is broken, the process of discovery and interpretation falters when "Truth" is finally disclosed to the rapt spectator-narrator:

> the looking glass began to pour over her a light that seemed to fix her; that seemed like some acid to bite off the unessential and superficial and to leave only the truth. It was an enthralling spectacle. . . . Here was the woman herself. She stood naked in that pitiless light. And there was nothing. Isabella was perfectly empty. [p. 93]

The corrosive action of the mind's illuminating power transforms an opaque figure into a transparent reflection. But this transparency of figure, like the transparency of that literary ground called tradition, only discloses nakedness, emptiness, an echoless nothing. Imaginative desire and its necessary dissimulations—its "seems" and "seems" and "seems"—can no longer be sustained. Woolf concludes her reflection with a typically wry, if uncharacteristically sardonic moral: "People should not leave looking-glasses hanging in their rooms."

"The Lady in the Looking-Glass" contains a reflection shadowing Woolf's later fiction, a reflection that helps explain why Woolf modified her view of human life as a "luminous halo surrounding us from the beginning of consciousness to the end" and began increasingly to explore "the world beneath our consciousness; the anonymous world to which we can still return."[5] To return to this anonymous world, unreflecting yet rich as a "reservoir of common belief," is, as Woolf says in her

5. "Anon," 6, 5–6. See my note on p. 230.

diary, "the only line to take." It is a line that led her back to the roots of English literature in oral poetry, in the communal art of Anon, a voice issuing out of the common heritage of the race that "could express, embody, give voice to the hidden instincts."[6] In her privately formulated philosophy of anonymity and in her identification with the figurative identity of Anon, Woolf sought to reconstruct and renovate the spectral architecture of the house of fiction and make it once again resonant with song.

In a fragment from her late essay on Anon, Woolf argues that at the heart of the "vast proliferation of printed pages is the song":

> The song has the same power over the reader in the twentieth century as over the hearer in the eleventh. To enjoy singing, to enjoy hearing the song, must be the most deep-rooted and toughest of human instincts. It is an instinct of self-preservation, for only when we put two and two together do we overcome dissolution. Two lines, two words, two bricks make way against oblivion; and the passion with which we seek for these creations, and attempt to make them, is of a piece with the instinct that sets us preserving our bodies from wet, or cold.[7]

The power of the song bridges the gap between the written and the spoken, the reader and the hearer, and thus unites us to the past and to each other through the submerged, yet still recuperable voice of deep-rooted instinct. To enjoy singing and hearing the song is the surest sign that we have, as Wordsworth sang, one human heart. Song is the passion of the heart, at once its natural language and its soundest instinct, the instinct of self-preservation. Never are the monistic urges in Woolf's aesthetics more in evidence than in her refusal to discriminate between the instinct to shield our bodies from the material

6. AEFR, v. 8, 64. See my note on p. 230.
7. "Anon," 8, 3.

forces of dissolution—the wet, or cold—and the heart's desire to make way against oblivion. To put two and two together, to make necessity a pleasure, is the first economy of the distinctly human passion to preserve and to create.

Historically, Woolf realized, the pleasures of a necessarily anonymous and communal art of song began to vanish with the printing press: "with the printing press, came into existence forces that cover over the original song."[8] It was Caxton, she surmised, who destroyed Anon by separating the singer from his audience, Caxton who raised the mirror of self-consciousness and so helped to create the figure of the writing "I." It was not, at first, a completely transparent mirror. Malory, she concedes, is not distinct from his book. His is "still the voice of anon, speaking to the voice of anon. The dream is still dreamt."[9] But with Malory, the artist begins to awaken from a long communal dream and the hearer of song necessarily begins to develop into a reader of words.

In describing this great awakening into self-consciousness, Woolf sees the difference between Malory and Spenser, the sleeping and the waking dreamer of those romances that project the hopes and ideals of a society in the heroic quest for cultural fertility and individual fulfillment, as part of a larger material and cultural change that eventually made possible the birth of Elizabethan drama and the consummate, universal art of Shakespeare. The drama, which both conceals and reveals the distinction between the spoken and the written word, preserves, as part of its historical heritage, both the voice and the audience of Anon. Anon, the lyric poet who "repeats over and over again that flowers fade; that death is the end," survives in the semi-anonymous playwrights whose plays "no one has troubled to set a name to." The semianonymous playwrights who preceded and made way for Shakespearean art shared

8. Ibid.
9. "Anon," 7, 7.

with Anon a "nameless vitality, something drawn from the crowd in the penny seats and not yet dead in ourselves."[10]

But at some point, Woolf goes on to speculate, "there comes a break when anonymity withdraws": "It comes presumably when the playwright has absorbed the contribution of the audience; and returns it to them in a single figure." It is not a complete break; Woolf's historical consciousness never gladly entertains the prospect of abrupt discontinuities. Anonymity withdraws, but the playwright is not yet in control of his own voice. The audience, if no longer the exclusive source of his stories nor master of his emotions, is not yet separate from him:

A common life still unites them, but the playwright becomes increasingly dominant. This separation comes fitfully. Now we say He is speaking our own thoughts. Now we note the beauty of the words. But often it is a suspended, derelict beauty. Chaos intervenes. The relation of part to part is outraged. The balance is imperfect. Here is profusion; there bareness. The anonymous playwright is irresponsible. He cares nothing, has no conscience about truth; he cares only for the plot. We are left in the end without an end. The emotion is wasted.[11]

The nascent disassociation of the playwright from his audience can be discerned in the first semiarticulated, often wasted emotions roused by the independent, if derelict beauty of words that bear little resemblance to the speech of common thoughts. The value of these words, their "beauty," does not reside, Woolf suggests, primarily in their communicative or expository function, but in their aesthetic appeal. Their very presence implies that the relation of importance is becoming less the common life uniting playwright and audience and

10. "The Reader," 2, 29.
11. "The Reader," 2, 30.

more the relation, within the work of art, of part to part. Now it is the aesthetic emotion, emancipated from the material instinct of self-preservation, that must not be dissipated in the profusion, nor enfeebled by the bareness, of its expression. Chaos is now perceived to exist within the work of art as well as outside it, with this difference: this new chaos is the vital chaos of a new language as yet uncontrolled by the grammar of form.

Gradually, Woolf concludes, truth inheres in beauty, freedom finds its responsible expression in the perfectly balanced art of Shakespeare. As the curtain rises again and again, "it rises finally upon the completely embodied; and upon the completely controlled. It rises upon Hamlet and Cleopatra and Falstaff and MacBeth. Finally it rises upon the *Tempest.*" Anon, the common voice singing out of doors, is replaced and succeeded by Shakespeare, the playwright of the Globe, the "theatre of the brain." Such replacements and consolidations are attended, in Woolf's mind, by a sense of loss: "Anon is replaced by a man who writes a book. The audience is replaced by the reader." And then, as if it were an afterthought, perhaps commemorative, perhaps wistful, perhaps merely clarifying, Woolf appends to her typescript the hand-written remark, "Anon is dead."[12]

In *The Tempest* Woolf sees the end of an evolutionary line of development from Anon, the common voice singing out of doors, to Shakespeare's Prospero, working his magic in that enchanted isle that is both the natural "stage" of his art and the place of his exile. *The Tempest* is the play whose presence is most immediately felt in Woolf's last novel, *Between the Acts,* and Prospero is the most important model for Woolf's last portrait of the artist, the playwright, Miss La Trobe. La Trobe is the waking dreamer who refuses to appear on stage and take credit for the play, the "dreamed" life of our common history redreamed—and redeemed—in the creative

12. Ibid.

mind. She adopts the self-effacing mask of an "Anon" as a conscious disguise, a necessary dissembling of self, for she is aware, as Anon was not, that she is society's and nature's outcast. Should she speak, out of her own passion, anger, or fear, as Prospero does at the conclusion of his pastoral masque, her dream, too, might be disturbed, her harmonies modulate into the discordant music of confusion. Such repression is not easy, nor always complete. Even within the dream, La Trobe dreams the last dream of romance, the desire of the play *without* an audience, the definitive play in which the writing "I" has no need for a public, yet does not vanish. Such a dream would, if realized, signal the complete emancipation of the imagined world and the imagining mind from its servitude to the audience in the penny seats from whom Prospero, in his epilogue, begs his freedom to return to reality.

Woolf would never appear, like Prospero, fully revealed in his distinct humanity, her charms overthrown, her strength her own. Like a dreamer intent on having her dream, she persists in her willful illusionism. She writes in her diary: "I insubstantiate, willfully to some extent, distrusting reality—its cheapness" (*WD,* p. 56). The "cheapness" of reality is transvalued through the willful insubstantiations of the Woolfian dreamer defiantly at work in distorting, condensing, displacing, and symbolizing the innumerable impressions of the Real into those immutable forms by which imagination gratifies the heart's mutable desires. To accredit the mutability of human desire—now for community, now for solitude, now for identity, now for anonymity and mystic completion in the One, now for the Truth that ennobles and invigorates, now for the Beauty that appeases and consoles, now to remember, now to forget—this, too, is a work Woolf performs in her psychic and narrative economies.

Of all these economies, the balance between remembrance and forgetfulness, memory and oblivion, is the most difficult and the most painful to establish. Woolf's great theme, like Proust's, is spiritual recuperation through a rescued image of the past recaptured. Perhaps this is why Woolf suggested that her novels, as poetic structures elaborated in prose, constituted a prosaic form of elegy. It certainly explains why the figure of the dreamer in Woolf's fiction always finds his shadow, his complement, or his double in the figure of the mourner. Abiding in the heart, the empty center of Woolf's representations is the mourner who continually observes and records from "within" his life the fragility of identity, of community, of love and its objects—people, places, freedom, civilization. It is this "giant mourner" who conducts the most perilous and delicate transactions with the forces of death and unreason, transactions that compose the work of elegy—the reparation of the broken, the compensation, where reality does not admit of restoration, of what has been irretrievably lost. The elegist makes peace with the reign of Death, what Freud called "the verdict of reality," by restoring confidence in the laws of life, the life of the present and the future.

Both the dream work and the work of mourning conclude their transvaluations of the distrusted, discredited, dehumanized Real, in the production of the same image of regeneration —the dawn. Like Joyce and Proust, those epic redreamers of the past, like Milton, the elegiac poet of *Lycidas* who heralds the dawn of his poetic vocation, Woolf found in the advent of a new day and in the miracle of day following day, a portent of the mind's general wakening into transfigured reality. As Bernard says in *The Waves:*

> "Dawn is some sort of whitening of the sky; some sort of renewal. Another day; . . . Another general awakening. The stars draw back and are extinguished. . . . Yes, this is the eternal renewal, the incessant rise and fall and fall and rise again." [*Waves*, pp. 382-83]

The will of the comic imagination is to provide stationary traces of this continuing natural miracle—eternal renewal. Through the double power of dream and dissimulation, the creative mind imagines that eternal dawn that is both Genesis and Apocalypse, a creation and an uncovering of what Bernard calls "the true order of things"—the "majestic march of day across the sky" (*Waves,* p. 365). And this renewed discovery of the comic mythos that underlies the British tradition from Chaucer and Shakespeare to Sterne, Austen, Dickens, and Meredith yields Woolf her own identity as the inheritor, the continuer, the person, as Bernard confesses in amazement, "miraculously appointed to carry it on" (*Waves,* p. 352). The recognition that she, too, was an inheritor of a great tradition was an essential part of Woolf's comic peripeties, her narrative designs. For literary history, like natural history, observes the eternal rhythm of rise and fall and rise again. In her youth there was the failure of the Edwardians, "comparative yet disastrous": "How the year 1860 was a year of empty cradles; how the reign of Edward the Seventh was barren of poet, novelist, and critic."[13] And in her last years came the eclipse of her own reputation, and the attack of Wyndham Lewis.[14]

But the power of dreaming remained, the dreaming of "books I intend to write" (*WD,* p. 325). Despite the vicissitudes of literary fame and the presence of public and private demons that haunted Woolf's historical life—Fascism, the threatening spectre of social and political Unreason, madness, childlessness, the seemingly unending part death played in her life—she never abdicated her artistic will, the will to futurity, nor did she ever abandon her comic dream of inaugurating a reign of freedom, of imagining a fuller humanity. "The real novelist," speculates Bernard, "the perfectly simple human being, could go on indefinitely imagining." That extended license with reality, that perfect simplicity of being, that indefinite and therefore ever-renewable power to preserve and to create was the dream of Virginia Woolf. It was also a dream from which she continually awoke to the loud, startling insistent clammerings of a hostile, as yet unhumanized reality.

13. "On Re-Reading Novels," *Collected Essays,* vol. 2, p. 122.
14. Lewis's attack was the most vicious, but in a diary entry for November 22, 1938, Woolf, assessing her position as a writer, concludes that his was one of many voices contributing to the decline of her literary reputation. See *WD,* pp. 296–97.

Index

Meredith, George: and comic tradition, 6-8, 13, 15, 18-19, 20, 103, 245; *Egoist, The,* 103
Mill, John Stuart: "On Liberty," 46; *Subjection of Women, The,* 117
Miller, J. Hillis, 52n, 210
Milton, John, 16, 65, 66; "Lycidas," 68, 244
Montaigne, Michel de, 9
Moore, George, 4n
mourning. *See* elegy (mourning), and narrative form
Murry, John Middleton, 66
Muse (muses): and artistic inspiration, 7, 8, 65-66, 128, 129, 130, 134, 153, 171. *See also* women writers (feminine imagination); Woolf, and narrative voices
Mussolini, Benito, 192

Napoleon Bonaparte, 81, 177, 194
narrative: and biography, 11, 117-20, 121, 127-28, 131, 136, 140-41; and dissimulation, 139-40, 149-53, 158-59, 171, 183, 197, 228, 232, 238, 244; and history, x, 14, 23, 24-26, 28, 29-30, 42-44, 98-99, 101, 111, 113, 118, 119, 125, 136-38, 140, 177, 190-99 *passim,* 201-02, 206-15 *passim,* 225-26, 227, 229, 232, 241; and Nature (nature), 36, 37-38, 59, 62, 75, 81, 85, 90, 91, 93, 95-100, 128, 131-32, 133, 138, 149, 161, 171, 205, 208-09, 211, 214-16, 220, 234; and space, 33-38 *passim,* 41, 60, 173; and succession, ix, x, 2, 7, 64-66, 110, 112, 116, 156, 170, 186, 204, 224, 245; and time, 27, 30-33, 35, 63, 70, 93-96, 99-100, 125, 142, 174-75, 178, 181, 185, 191, 194-95, 199-200, 201, 208, 211-13, 228. *See also* allegory, and narrative form; dreams, and narrative art; elegy (mourning), and narrative form; fantasy, and narrative; satire (parody), and narrative; Woolf, and narrative theory; Woolf, and narrative voices
Nature (nature). *See* narrative, and Nature (nature)
Neumann, Erich, 75

Nicolson, Nigel, 12n, 111n
Neitzsche, Friedrich, 25, 26n, 52, 223, 231-32, 233, 234
Nohrnberg, James, 124n

Odyssey, The, 148-49
Oedipal structure, 65, 69, 71-74, 88, 104-08 *passim*

parody. *See* satire (parody), and narrative
Pater, Walter, 15, 126
patriarchal fiction. *See* authoritarian orders, and patriarchal fiction
Penelope, 148
Percival: Knight of the Grail, 152-53
Persephone, 76
Philipson, Morris, 61n
Piaget, Jean, 114
Plato, 17-18, 177
play: theory of, 62, 114-15, 143-44, 205, 212, 228, 229. *See also* comedy, nature of; Woolf, and comic vision
Poole, Roger, 56n
Pope, Alexander, 1, 133, 134-35, 137; "Epistle to a Lady," 121-22; *"Rape of the Lock, The,"* 126
Potts, Abbie Finlay, 69
Pound, Ezra, 65n
Prospero, 227, 242-43
Proust, Marcel, 145, 243, 244
Puttenham, George: *Arte of English Poesie, The,* 188

Racine, Jean, 194
Rahv, Philip, 55-56
Richardson, Henry, 14n
Richter, Harvena, 4n, 72n
Roll-Hanson, Diderik, 29n
Rose, Phyllis, 63n
Rosenbaum, S. P., 4n
Rousseau, Jean-Jacques, 222

Sackville-West, Vita, 111, 126, 127
Saint Paul, 151-52, 159
Sand, George, 17
Satan, 205, 210
satire (parody): and narrative, 21, 117, 120, 124-25, 126, 130, 136, 137, 140, 142, 144, 152, 158, 204, 211,